ABOUT THE AUTHOR

Charles Parkinson is a son of the late Professor C Northcote Parkinson, the naval historian and author of 'Parkinson's Law'. He was born in Singapore in 1954, but the family moved to Alderney in the Channel Islands for a few months in 1959, before settling in Guernsey in 1960. During their time in Alderney, Charles was introduced to T H White, the author of the Arthurian classics, 'The Sword in the Stone' and 'The Once and Future King'. White wanted to adopt the young Charles, on the grounds that "parents always do a lousy job of raising children", but the offer was politely refused.

Charles was educated in England, and read Law at Emmanuel College, Cambridge. After university, he qualified as a Chartered Accountant in London, and was called to the Bar, although he has never practised as a Barrister. During a successful career in the financial services industry, principally in Guernsey, he wrote a book called 'Taxation in France', his first foray into literature. In 2004 he was elected a Deputy in the island's parliament, and he served as Guernsey's Minister of Treasury & Resources from 2008 until he stood down at the 2012 general election. He speaks good French, and a smattering of several other European languages, knowledge that has assisted him in the research for this book.

In 2012 he published 'Lisia; Vortigern's Island', a book about the ancient and early medieval history of Guernsey (revised 2013).

THE DUKE AND THE DECOY
the story of Arthur

Charles Parkinson

Armoricana Books
PO Box 552
St Peter Port
Guernsey
GY1 6HX

First published by Armoricana Books 2013

ISBN: 978-0-9574732-1-8

Copyright 2013 © Charles Parkinson

Charles Parkinson has asserted his right under the Copyright, Designs and Patents Act 1988 to be identified as the author of this work.

All Rights Reserved. No part of this publication may be reproduced in any form or by any means without the written permission of the publishers.

Cover Artwork and Typeset by Shore Books, Blackborough End, Norfolk.

Printed and bound in the United Kingdom.

Introduction

For nearly 900 years the western world has been fascinated by the medieval legends of 'King Arthur', which are as much alive today as they have ever been. He has been a hero of recent television, film and theatrical productions, including the 2008 – 2012 BBC series 'Merlin', the 2004 film 'King Arthur', starring Keira Knightley, and the musical 'Camelot'. The list of books about Arthur and his associates is a long one, and the reader may well ask whether there is room on the shelves for yet another contribution. But the story of the real Arthur has not been properly told, and it is a fascinating one. And just as interesting is the story of how the legends reached us, so this book sets out to shed new light on both of these subjects.

The real Arthur lived in the late 5th and early 6th centuries, and he made his name leading the indigenous population of southern Britain in a war against the 'Anglo-Saxons', a mixed group of tribes from northern Germany and Denmark. However, according to the authors of the 12th and 13th century Arthurian histories and romances, Arthur subsequently fought a campaign on the Continent. This aspect of the legends receives far less attention in Britain, but the people of Brittany in France have long held that part (or even all) of the story of Arthur was set in their country. This conviction stems in part from the fact that the 12th century literature on Arthur was written by authors with Norman-French backgrounds, but it is reinforced by the fact that the underlying source material for their works appears to have come from Brittany, or via Brittany from Wales.

The first and most important of those authors was Geoffrey of Monmouth, who despite his name probably came from a Breton family, and it is clear that Geoffrey's work was politically motivated. The story of Arthur was intended to legitimise the Norman Conquest, and was given as much exposure as possible in the 12th century, as Geoffrey and his followers expanded the limited knowledge of Arthur that was in existence out of all proportion. But later, in the 15th century, political considerations had quite the opposite effect. The first Tudor monarch had learned a key fact about Arthur while he was living in Brittany as a youth, so politically sensitive that he and his associates felt obliged to keep the information confidential. The result of these convolutions is that the task of trying to get back to the underlying truth is not an easy one. So even some of those who believe that there was a real British commander called Arthur have been forced to rely on the argument that "there is no smoke without fire". I firmly believe that there is an underlying substance to the legends, and that there is enough historical evidence available to enable us to see the outline of Arthur's military career.

The fact that the name of Arthur still resonates down the ages is partly explained by the context of his life. In the early 5th century, the island of Britain descended to possibly the lowest point that it has ever reached in its long, and sometimes illustrious, history. The economy and social order collapsed completely, the population was devastated by famines and plagues and the south of the island was ravaged by foreign barbarians. The historical figure of Arthur shines so brightly in the history of this region precisely because the world into which he was born was so dark, and because of the brilliant role that he played as Britain began to recover from the wreckage.

Brittany was also affected by the calamity, although possibly not to the same extent as insular Britain. The underlying cause of the disaster was the collapse of the Western Roman Empire, and the chaos which followed before the establishment of a new European order. And I believe that there is substance to Geoffrey of Monmouth's assertion that Arthur fought on the Continent, because Arthur went to the assistance of the British in the peninsula in a war against the Franks. The Arthurian legends were not merely preserved in Breton folklore, some of them were created in Brittany.

Southern Britain and Brittany had sprung from the provinces that had formed the basis of civil government in the Roman Empire, and the constitutional history is important background information. But the areas under the control of Arthur's people did not exactly correspond with any of those provinces; they were ill-defined and amorphous territories, held together by little more than tradition, their tribal origins and the languages that they shared. So we need also to have an understanding of the pre-Roman tribal affiliations in

Introduction

these parts of northern Europe. These were the primitive building blocks of what became nations, they defined the 'them' and the 'us', the people that Arthur stood for and their enemies. So, counter-intuitive as it may be, we need to take some steps back in time before the story can move forwards, and I begin with an explanation of the background to the Britain of the 5th century. However, before any of that, I need to describe the source material, to which I make reference throughout the remainder of the book.

The Sources

The most contemporary source for the period of Arthur's life was a Welsh monk called Gildas, who probably wrote in c. 540, probably from a monastery in Wales but just possibly from one in southern Brittany. Gildas does not mention Arthur by name, an omission which may be explained by his own remark that his purpose was to decry the sins of the British leaders of his day, rather than to celebrate British heroes. The only British military leader that he mentioned was a commander called Ambrosius Aurelianus, who appears to have been a generation older than Arthur.

Arthur is mentioned in several other early, but non-contemporaneous, Welsh sources, principally a compilation of histories attributed to a monk called Nennius, and probably assembled in c. 830. Further references followed in another chronicle called the 'Annales Cambriae', which is an assemblage of material probably dating from the 10th or 11th centuries and there are a handful of references to Arthur in various poems which reflect the Welsh folklore of the first millennium. All of the 'British' source material that has survived comes from Wales, which has given the story a pronounced Welsh accent that may be misleading.

Unsurprisingly, given that Arthur fought against the Anglo-Saxons, he is not mentioned in the Anglo-Saxon sources, which are principally the 'Anglo-Saxon Chronicle' (maintained from the late 9th century onwards until at least 1154), and the work of the Anglo-Saxon monk Bede (c.672 – 735). The dates in the Anglo-Saxon Chronicle' for events of the 5th and 6th century are unreliable, but Bede ("The Father of English History") was a serious historian to whom accurate dates were very important. Bede does not name Arthur, but, like Gildas (on which his work is partly based) he does name Ambrosius Aurelianus and a battle in which the British defeated the Anglo-Saxons at a place called Mount Badon. Tantalisingly, he wrote *"But more of this hereafter",* and then never returned to the subject.

The Sources

And that is a summary of all of the literature specifically devoted to the history of Britain in the 5th and 6th centuries, written before the year 1100. The Anglo-Saxons became literate in the 7th century, and wrote material on Christian themes or about their own folklore, such as the epic poem Beowulf, but of course they were almost entirely ignorant of the history of Britain before their arrival. And they took little interest in the indigenous people of the island, after their arrival, regarding them as inferior. The result is that the Anglo-Saxon sources contain relatively little information useful to my purposes. As Winston Churchill remarked, history is written by the victors, and in the end, Arthur was on the losing side.

Rather more contemporary literature is available from Continental sources, even if references to Britain are scarce. The Greeks and Romans produced a mass of writing, although the supply inevitably tailed off as the Western Roman Empire came to an end. Most of the material of the 5th and 6th centuries was written by churchmen on religious subjects, but some of this is relevant to Britain. Unfortunately, it seems that very few people were interested in recording current events, and very few authors in the centuries which followed wrote histories. Indeed, history was regarded with disdain by some – in c. 477 Sidonius Apollinaris wrote *"Historical writing begins in spite, proceeds in weariness and ends in ill-repute"*!

Gildas explains the lack of early literary sources by saying that any British records that may once have existed had been destroyed by the Anglo-Saxons: *"I shall not follow the writings and records of my own country, which (if there ever were any of them) have been consumed in the fires of the enemy,* or have *accompanied my exiled countrymen into distant lands".* Nennius, in contrast, blames the British rather than the Anglo-Saxons: *"I...have endeavoured to write some extracts which the dullness of the British nation had cast away, because teachers had no knowledge, nor gave any information in their books about this island of Britain."*

Although the surviving early histories of Britain are mostly Welsh, in some cases they have come to us via Brittany, to where some of the population of Wales emigrated in the 6th century. For example, the oldest manuscript of Nennius that is known to us (the manuscript Z of Chartres) was a Breton copy, dated to about 900, which was unfortunately destroyed by allied bombing in the Second

World War. But the former existence of this manuscript is sufficient proof that there were chroniclers of the Arthurian period working in Brittany in the late 9th or early 10th centuries, and this in itself sheds some light on the later sources as we shall see.

As noted in the Introduction, interest in British history was revived by a tutor in Oxford, called Geoffrey of Monmouth, who wrote a book called the 'Historia Regum Britanniae' (History of the British Kings) in about 1136. This book is the foundation stone of most of the Arthurian legends as we know them, and it led to the production of a plethora of medieval poetry and romances on the Arthurian theme. However the book was not solely about Arthur, and it purported to be a history of Britain from its origins, based largely on the account of Nennius for the early material. It has been generally dismissed as a 'pseudo-history', of little or no evidential value, but as will become apparent, I believe that it contains a few grains of truth, which are immensely helpful to our understanding of the Early Medieval world of north-western Europe.

Geoffrey, despite his Welsh sounding name, was probably from a Breton family that had been granted land in Britain by William the Conqueror, in return for their support of his campaign of conquest. And he was followed by many others from a similar Norman French background, for example the late 12th century Chrétien de Troyes, who introduced us to Lancelot and the Quest for the Holy Grail. One contributor to the legends was Wace (c.1110 – 1175), who was born in Jersey and ordained in Normandy (most literate people of the period were churchmen, and therefore many of the authors of the legends were clerics). But there were so many contributors to the legends, telling such fanciful stories, that Wace was moved to complain about the Arthurian industry, in his 'Roman de Brut':

"The marvels were proved and the adventures performed which are so much told about Arthur that they have been turned into fables. Not all of them are false and not all true; not all foolishness and not all sense; but the story-tellers have told so much and the writers of fables have fabled so much to embellish their tales, that they have made the whole seem fables."

His cynicism about the 'fables' did not however prevent him from further embellishing the legends by adding the element of the Round Table and altering the name of Arthur's sword from Caliburn (per

Geoffrey of Monmouth) to Excalibur. He was also the first author to record the Breton legend that Arthur is still alive *"He is still there; the Bretons await him; they say he will come back and live again."* The legend of the Arthur who would return to lead the Bretons was one factor which made his memory so dangerous to the later rulers of the province.

Other than these sources, I have relied extensively on general histories and records, as referenced in my text. In particular, this book builds on theories that I developed in 'Lisia; Vortigern's Island' (revised 2013).

Contents

Chapter			Page
1	Setting the Scene		1
	1.1	The Peoples of Britain	1
	1.2	The Arrival of the Romans	4
	1.3	The Celtic Tribes of Brittany	5
	1.4	Life Under Rome	9
	1.5	Decline and Fall	10
	1.6	The First Wave of Emigration to Armorica	17
	1.7	The Roman Army in Britain After Maximus	20
	1.8	The Beginning of the End	22
	1.9	The Departure of the Roman Officials	23
2	The Age of Despair		27
	2.1	Britain After Rome	27
	2.2	The Groans of the Britons	29
	2.3	Climate Change	32
	2.4	Life After Rome in Brittany	33
	2.5	The Intervention of the Huns	38
	2.6	The Restoration of Roman Rule in Brittany	40
	2.7	The Early Anglo-Saxon Settlers	41
	2.8	Vortigern	46
	2.9	The Raid of 441/442 and the Second Wave of Emigration	51
	2.10	Vortigern's End	53
3	The Anglo-Saxon War		56
	3.1	The Arrival of the 'Anglo-Saxon' Mercenaries	56
	3.2	The War of c.455 – 457	59
	3.3	The Succession	64
	3.4	Ambrosius Aurelianus	65

		3.5	The Family of Ambrosius	69
		3.6	Ambrosius in the Legends	70
4	Northern Gaul; 450 – 475			71
		4.1	The Invasion of Gaul by the Franks	71
		4.2	Merovech	72
		4.3	Childeric	73
		4.4	Riothamus	76
		4.5	The Saxons in Gaul	80
		4.6	Ælle	85
		4.7	Description of the Franks	86
		4.8	Clovis	88
		4.9	The Bretons Franks and the Bretons	91
		4.10	Archaeology in Brittany	97
	5	Arthur		103
		51	Introduction	103
		5.2	Name	106
		5.3	Ethnic Origin and Family	108
		5.4	Arthur the Soldier	110
		5.5	Arthur in Brittany?	112
		5.6	Arthur's Personality	112
	6	Arthur's Campaigns		115
		6.1	Battles Identified by Nennius	115
		6.2	Mount Badon	119
		6.3	The Breton Campaign	124
		6.4	Toponymy of a Breton Campaign	129
		6.5	Arthur's Last Battle	130
		6.6	The Third Wave	133
		6.7	Footnote on Warfare in Arthur's Day	136
	7	The Aftermath		137
		7.1	The Conquests of ' the Britains'	137
		7.2	The Fourth Wave	142
	8	The Making of the Legends		146

9	The Grail Quest		160
10	Arthurian Britain and Brittany		169
	10.1	Introduction	169
	10.2	The Kingdom of Ambrosius	170
	10.3	The Kingdom of Audren	173
	10.4	Toponymy of Arthur	176
	10.5	Where Would we Expect to Find Places Associated with Arthur?	181
11	The Cult of St Armel		183
	11.1	Introduction	183
	11.2	St Armel	184
	11.3	Is it Likely that St Armel des Boschaux was the Real Inspiration?	187
	11.4	The End of Breton Independence	189
	11.5	King Henry VII and St Armel	190
12	So What Really Happened?		198

Appendix 1	The Arthurs of Brittany	201
Appendix 2	Dramatis Personnae	204
Appendix 3	The Land of Cal	217
Appendix 4	The Language of Arthur	222

Selected Bibliography	239
Index of Place Names	243
Index of People	248

ILLUSTRATIONS

Front Cover: Foreground: statue of St Armel in the Henry VII Lady Chapel at Westminster Abbey (copyright Dean and Chapter of Westminster), showing the Saint's arms and hands in full plate armour. Background: Model in Roman armour.

Central section: The Megalithic Alignments at St Just, with the fertile agricultural land of the Morbihan in the background.

Quiot Brooch Style Brooch, 5th century, found in Kent (courtesy of British Museum).

The Chapel at Lomarec (1606), home to the sarcophagus of a 6th century British King.

The Cathedral at Dôl, 13th to 15th centuries.

Arbury Hill, looking west, scarred by a motocross track.

Arbury Hill, looking north-east towards the valley below.

The remains of part of the east wall and a tower of the Camp de César, at Binic

The Jesse Tree window at Ploërmel church. The Virgin Mary and Jesus are shown top centre, but below that King Jesse, seated under a canopy, is surrounded by his Biblical descendants. The figures are all in medieval costume, and the scene could equally well depict King Arthur surrounded by his courtiers.

Back Cover   The author at the Camp de César, with the town of Binic in the background.

Chapter 1
Setting the Scene

1.1 The Peoples of Britain

Nennius wrote that Britain was founded by Brutus, a Roman consul (after whom he said the island was named). Brutus was allegedly descended partly from the Romans and partly from the Greeks, and he came to Britain after having conquered Spain. Not surprisingly, this account has been dismissed as utter nonsense for most of the last 1,300 years, but recent genetic research has highlighted a strong link between the people of North Wales and the population of Albania and Greece, a link which goes back 4,500 years.[1] The migration highlighted by this genetic link seems to have been connected with copper mining, and specifically with the pre-historic copper mine at Great Ormes Head, in Llandudno.

Be that as it may, the majority of the British population is descended from the people who first colonised the region after the last Ice Age, about 10,000 years ago, at a time when Britain and Ireland were still joined to Europe by a land bridge across the North Sea.[2] This basic substratum was affected very little by subsequent periods of immigration, with two exceptions. There is an influence which appears to have arrived in Britain by a process of migration of peoples up the Atlantic seaboard from the Pyrenees. And there is a marked Germanic influence, particularly in the eastern parts of England, associated primarily with the arrival of the Anglo-Saxons. However some of this Germanic influence may predate the Anglo-Saxons, because there was an earlier immigration of people called

---
1 Stephen Oppenheimer, 'A Reanalysis of the Multiple Prehistoric Immigrations to Britain and Ireland aimed at Identifying the Celtic Contributions' in 'Celtic from the West' (edited by Barry Cunliffe and John T Koch (2009)).
2 *"Nearly three quarters (73%) overall of British and Irish ancestors arrived before the first farmers"* (ie before c.5000 – 4500 BC)" - Stephen Oppenheim op.cit

the Belgae, who came from the parts of the Continent immediately opposite the south-east of Britain.

The people who arrived in the British Isles from the Pyrenees are often referred to as Celts, although that term might more appropriately be used to describe all the peoples who shared a Celtic culture or language. The culture that we associate with the Celts seems to have originated in Central Europe, and their languages were members of the family of Indo-European languages, which appear to have arisen in the area north of the Black Sea. By this definition, all of the pre-Anglo-Saxon population of the British Isles was Celtic, although the dialect of the south-east of England was, in my opinion, influenced by the originally Germanic language of the Belgae.

The Celts came to occupy most of what is now France, Spain and south-western Germany, and for a time they held lands in the north of Italy. The Romans called the Celts 'Gauls', and thus France and Belgium were known to them as Gaul. Indeed the Roman provinces of 'Gaul' included Britain, Spain and even western North Africa, so the concept of Gaul was far wider than the modern association of that word with France. But what is now called France was a land famously described by Julius Caesar as divided into three parts. The south-west was Aquitaine, a region populated by people closely related to their neighbours in Spain, the central part, stretching diagonally from Brittany down to the south-east was called Gallia Lugdunensis (the Gaul of the city of Lyon) and the north-eastern part was Gallia Belgica, the land of the Germanic Belgae. The boundary between the Gauls of the central region and the Belgae had been fixed at the River Seine ever since the early 3rd century BC, when the Belgae had won a decisive battle against their Celtic neighbours at what is now Ribemont-sur-Ancre. The area to the west of the Seine and to the north of the Loire was called Armorica, from the Gaulish words 'are-mori', meaning 'at the sea'.

Shortly after they gained uncontested control over the lands east of the Seine, the Belgae started to migrate into south-eastern Britain, and thereafter gradually expanded their territory on the island. By the first century BC, they had besieged and sacked the hillfort at Solsbury Hill in Somerset, and they possessed most of lowlands England from the Cotswolds eastwards.

Caesar observed that the Celts and the Belgae spoke different languages, although it appears that the two languages were slowly merging. The language of the Celts, which we call Gaulish, was the ancestor of the Insular Celtic languages spoken in Britain and Ireland. And while the order of the process of evolution is the subject of much academic debate, the Insular Celtic languages had split into two groups. Gaelic (or Goidelic) languages were spoken in the highlands of Scotland, Ireland and the Isle of Man, while the languages of southern Scotland, Wales and much of northern and western England are called Brythonic. In Wales it is possible that the people of the north-west spoke a language which was more Gaelic, but this is a discussion beyond the scope of this book. The peoples of lowlands England (the midlands and the south) spoke dialects which, while generally retaining a Brythonic substratum, had been influenced by the language of the Belgae.

The west of Britain, and particularly the south-west, had long been culturally and commercially linked to the Gauls of France and Spain, and was part of an Atlantic trading system, the origins of which are lost in the mists of time. Exports of metals from Britain, particularly tin, had started early in the second millennium BC, and there had been corresponding imports of manufactured goods from central and western parts of the Continent since that time.[3]

The Belgae of the south-east of what is now England were mainly engaged in a separate, and less active, trading system centred on the Straits of Dover. While the value of commodities exchanged was probably lower at the eastern end of the English Channel, the trading system was somewhat more sophisticated, because the Belgae introduced to the island the concept of using coins as a medium of exchange (ie 'money'). The coins of the Belgae are found all over the south-east of Britain and date from their arrival in the early 3rd century BC onwards.

The extent of the area of Britain which spoke the dialect influenced by the language of the Belgae can be estimated by observation of the use of the word 'cal' in place names. This word appears to me to have been a Belgic word for a standing stone, including milestones, in contrast to the Celtic word for the same objects, which was 'men'. In Appendix 3, I use this distinction to illustrate the approximate area of the island under Belgic control, but I do not want to exaggerate

---

[3] See 'Lisia; Vortigern's Island' for a full discussion.

the differences between the two languages. I suspect that the people on either side of the linguistic divide could probably understand each other. In comparing the languages of the tribes in Britain and in northern Gaul, Tacitus, writing in AD 100, tells us that *"The two languages differ but little"*, and I suspect that the same applied to the dialects of the Belgae and the western British.

1.2   The Arrival of the Romans

In 58 – 55 BC, Julius Caesar conquered Gaul, and southern Britain fell under the influence of Rome. Britain was not actually conquered until AD 43, but the tribes of the island had agreed to pay tribute to the Romans on a scale which effectively gave the Romans dominion over the population. The last resistance of the tribes of the south-east was a revolt led by Boudicca, the Queen of the Iceni in what is now Norfolk, which took place in AD 60 or 61. This revolt was eventually crushed in a battle near Watling Street, the road which ran from Uttoxeter, in the West Midlands, to London, and then onwards from London to the ports of Richborough and Dover in Kent.

In political terms, the conquest merely consolidated the dominion of the Romans over southern Britain. But it also gave the island the economic benefits of expanded trade: British farmers grew wealthy growing grain to supply the Roman legions in Britain and in Gaul, and the country benefited from a stream of subsidies from Rome to finance the large standing army in Britain. However, having given up their political independence, the tribes of southern Britain became over time wholly dependent on Rome for their defence.

The Roman era also gave additional impetus to the expansion of the Belgae on the island, because the tribes of the south-east soon became close allies of the Romans. Shortly after their arrival, the Romans built a road and line of defences stretching from Exeter in the south-west to Lincoln in the north-east, to defend the territory that came immediately under their control. The tribes of the north and west continued to be troublesome to the invaders for a long time, and although the whole of England and Wales were eventually subdued, the tribes of what are now Scotland and Ireland successfully resisted Roman occupation and much of their territory was never incorporated into the Empire.

One particular Belgic tribe which deserves a mention was the Catuvellauni, who inhabited the area north of the Thames and east of the Cherwell River in Oxfordshire, as far north as Northamptonshire and as far east as western Cambridgeshire. They were notable warriors, who had put up a fierce resistance to the invaders, and they continued to play a leading role in the province as Roman allies after the conquest.

It was the Belgic tribes like the Catuvellauni which were 'first in the firing line' when the Anglo-Saxons invaded Britain in the 5th century. And, among the tribes of the island, it was these tribes that had enjoyed the closest alliances with the Romans during their period of rule. They were the most militant of the tribes of what is now England, and accordingly the tribes that are most likely to have provided troops to the Roman army. Taking all of this into consideration, it is very likely that the British forces of the 5th century were drawn from the areas historically occupied by the Belgae, and it is a reasonable deduction that Arthur was a member of one of these tribes.

1.3 The Celtic Tribes of Brittany

According to the Romans, there were five tribes in Brittany, the Osismes in the far west, the Veneti around Vannes in the south, the Coriosolites around Corseul (near St Malo) in the north, the Redones around Rennes and the Namnetae around Nantes. However, when the Romans crushed the Veneti and their allies (including some British Celts) in 56 BC, they executed the elders and enslaved the rest of the tribe, so the Veneti effectively disappeared. While the resulting vacuum was no doubt partially filled by five centuries of migration during the Roman era, it may not be a coincidence that the 5th century British migration to the province was focused on their former lands, in the area around the city of Vannes.

The population of the peninsula, then as now, was concentrated in towns around the coast, and the central massif was almost a desert. In the central areas of Brittany, a vast forest extended from St Brieuc down to Auray, and here again the interior was sparsely populated.

The Duke and the Decoy

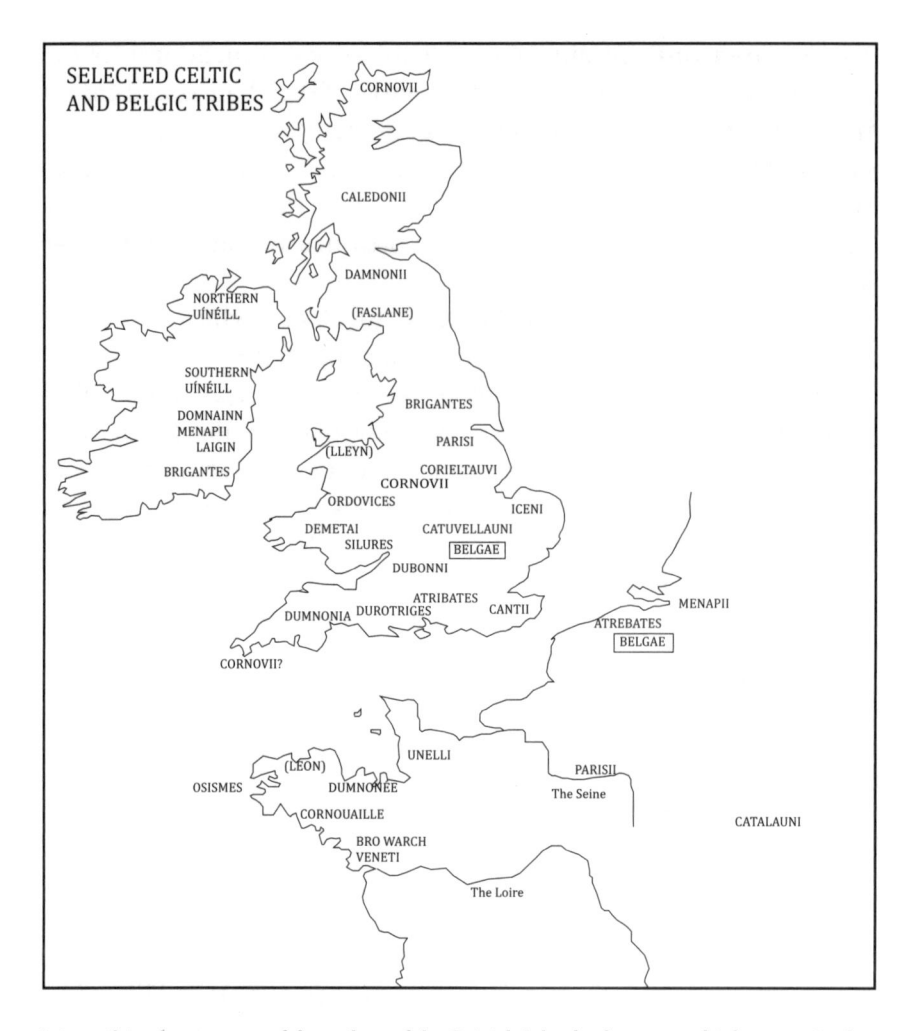

SELECTED CELTIC AND BELGIC TRIBES

It is striking how many of the tribes of the British Isles had names which were similar to those of Continental tribes. In eastern England, the Parisii, the Catuvellauni and the Atribates all had counterparts in Belgic Gaul, while the Menapii of Flanders also appear in south-east Ireland. The Celtic tribes of the Cornovii, Dumnonii, Brigantes and Laigin appear to have been distributed along the Atlantic sea routes, while the Uí Néills of Ireland may have been related to the Unelli of Normandy. The division of southern Britain into an eastern Belgic region and a western Celtic one brings to mind the description of 'Brittia', by Procopius, writing in the 540s, of an island divided in two by a fence running north-south, separating the world of the living from the world of the dead!

The Coriosolites of the northern coast, between St Brieuc and Le Mont St Michel, were particularly important to the tribes of Britain, because they controlled the port of Alet (which is now St Servan, just to the west of St Malo) and another port at Hillion, on the eastern side of the Bay of St Brieuc. Alet was particularly significant, because it appears to have been the port at which most of the British tin exports arrived. It seems that the Coriosolites also possessed Jersey, but not the other Channel Islands, because vast hoards of Coriosolite coins have been found on the island.

There is a mass of archaeological evidence which proves that the Coriosolites engaged in an extensive trade with the Durotriges of what is now Dorset, and through them with the Atrebates of Hampshire, probably via the Channel Islands. Coins minted by the Coriosolites are found in Dorset and Hampshire, while the coins of the Durotriges are occasionally found in Brittany.[4]

The Osismes was the name that the Romans gave to the peoples of the sparsely populated west of the peninsula, who would also have been known to the British through their control of the ports of Le Yaudet and L'Aberwrac'h. It appears that their principal town was Carhaix, which was known to the Romans as Vorgium. The Veneti on the south coast were, until the Roman conquest, the most powerful of the tribes of Brittany and the strongest maritime power in the region, possessing a formidable navy. They were also known to the British, because Caesar remarked that the ships of the Veneti were capable of sailing to the island, and indeed that the fleet which fought against the Romans included ships of their British allies.

It is convenient, although chronologically illogical, to deal with the topic of the subsequent names of the 'counties' of Brittany here, for reasons which will become apparent.[5] During the middle of the first millennium, a British 'county' of Dumnonée was established in northern Brittany. This was certainly related to the Dumnonia of England, the province in the south-western peninsula which was ruled, under the Romans, from Exeter. Indeed it is probable that for periods of time the two areas were ruled by common 'kings'.

4 The coins of the Durotriges and the Coriosolites were decorated with images, but not inscriptions, which suggests that neither tribe could write.
5 I use the word 'counties' in this section, although the rulers of these areas would no doubt have called themselves kings.

Dumnonée spanned the area which under the Romans had been administered as the territory of the Osismes and the Coriosolites.[6]

At a similar time, another British 'county' was established in the former territory of the Veneti in what is now the Morbihan. This eventually became known as the Bro Waroch, after a 6th century 'count' of the region called Waroch (or Erec), but the polity had certainly existed long before his time.[7]

Rather more debatable is the status of the south-western part of the peninsula, which came to be known as Cornouaille. On the face of it, this was part of another 'kingdom' that spanned the Channel, like Dumnonia, and it was ruled by nobles from Cornwall. But the matter is controversial, because the earliest surviving reference to Cornwall (as Cornubia) dates from the late 7th or early 8th centuries, long after Cornouaille is supposed to have been in existence.[8] It is also possible to make the case that the tribes of the peninsula identified by the Romans were not the only tribes present there. The Romans divided their Empire into territorial units that were convenient to their administration, sometimes with little regard for the pre-existing tribal relationships, and there are parts of the peninsula that have names which appear to connect them to tribal areas in the British Isles. For example the Breton district known today as the Léon may be associated with the Laigin of south-east Ireland, who may also have colonised the Lleyn Peninsula in North Wales, but this discussion is outside the scope of this book.

---

[6] It is interesting to note however that the language of the Bretons really only took hold in the former territories of the Osismes and the Veneti, so there is a linguistic boundary where the lands of the Osismes met the lands of the Coriosolites. This boundary runs right through the middle of Dumnonée. To the east of St Brieuc, the population of the Middle Ages spoke Gallo, the vulgar Latin of the north of France, while to the west the population spoke Breton.

[7] 'Bro' meant something like 'county', and it seems to me that the personal name Waroch may have been derived from Warwick in Britain. This is a moot point, because Warwick is thought by most to have Anglo-Saxon origins.

[8] For an interesting discussion see Magali Coumert, 'Le Peuplement de l'Armorique: Cornouaille et Dumnonée de part et d'autre de la Manche aux premiers siècles du Moyen Age' in 'Histoires de Bretagne' (2010) pp. 15 – 42.

1.4   Life Under Rome

Until about 250 AD, the Roman Empire was prosperous and mostly peaceful. In Britain, tensions between the Romans and the Picts of Scotland persisted, and resulted in occasional outbreaks of violence, but a modus vivendi was eventually reached when the Romans constructed Hadrian's Wall, starting in 122. Twenty years later, the Romans tried to move the border northwards to the neck of Scotland formed by the Firth of Forth and the Firth of Clyde, where they constructed the Antonine Wall, but this advance proved unsustainable.

One particular Roman commander of the late 2nd and/or early 3rd century deserves special attention because his name was Lucius Artorius Castus. He was a centurion of various legions during his career, including at one time the Legio VI Victrix, which was based in York. What we know of his life derives from two (or possibly three) inscriptions, which show that he was a career soldier, serving as an officer first in the Middle East, later in Britain and finally commanding a Roman army in a campaign, probably in Armenia, after which he retired to a governorship in Croatia. On the relevant inscription, only the letters 'Arm' remain, so some have speculated that Castus fought in Armorica. However this seems unlikely, because it is not obvious who, in Armorica, he would have been fighting against, whereas it is known that the Romans were engaged in confrontations in Armenia. His name has excited the interest of some scholars, who have suggested that he may have been the historical Arthur, or that his memory may have been merged with that of other historical figures to produce a later legendary Arthur. There is no evidence for this, other than the similarity of the names, and clearly Lucius Artorius Castus cannot have been fighting Anglo-Saxons in the 5th century. Moreover, his position as third in command of the Legio VI Victrix does not suggest that he was particularly important. Nevertheless, his existence and his connection with the Legio VI Victrix do prove that the Roman family-name 'Artorius' would have been recognised in Britain from at least the 3rd century.

Castus probably fought under a Roman Emperor called Septimius Severus, who died in 211. Severus was succeeded by his son, Marcus Aurelius Severus Antonius Augustus, who was better known as

Caracalla, after the Gallic style of cloak that he wore. On inheriting his throne, Caracalla found the Empire short of resources, both of money and of Roman citizens, who were the only people entitled to hold high office. Accordingly, in 212 he issued an edict making all free men throughout the Empire 'citizens', which also meant they had to pay taxes. The people thus enfranchised were sometimes known as 'Aurelian', which is a point of some importance to the history of the Arthurian period, as we shall see. He further decided that the structure of government needed to be more decentralised, and, in Britain, he split the country into two provinces. 'Britannia Superior' was the name given to the southern province, governed from London, and 'Britannia Inferior' was the northern province, governed from York.

Within the provinces, government was largely conducted by local Roman citizens, the 'cives', as members of the local 'civitas', or by the members of the senates of the more important towns. Roman Emperors did issue edicts, and they gave instructions to the governors of the provinces on important matters, but much of the law and the administration of justice in a province like Britain was of local origin.

As an example of a civitas, the town of Winchester, which the Romans called 'Venta Belgarum' (the market of the Belgae), was the centre of government for the surrounding area of eastern Dorset and western Hampshire. North of what is now Basingstoke was another town called Calleva Atrebatum (now Silchester), which was the county town for a Belgic tribe called the Atrebates. But military towns had a higher status, and were called 'colonia'. Examples in Britain were Colchester (Colonia Claudia Victricensis), Caerleon (Isca Augusta), Chester (Deva Victrix), Exeter (Isca Dumnoniorum), Lincoln (Lindum Colonia) and York (Eboracum).

1.5 Decline and Fall

From about 250 AD, the colossus which was the Roman Empire began to collapse, mainly under its own weight but with a helping hand from its neighbours. German tribes had crossed the Rhine and devastated the eastern regions of Gaul in 233, leading to the murder of the last aristocratic Severan Emperor, Severus Alexander, in 235.

And over the next half century there were 25 to 30 claimants to the Imperial throne. The resulting civil wars and chaos are reflected in the fact that more than one hundred caches of coins have been found in Brittany, dating from 240 to 285, in one case containing 16,000 coins and in another 5,000. Clearly, the owners of these hoards never returned to find them, and we can only suppose that they became victims of the troubles. Outlaws called the Bagaudae (or Bacaudae) roamed the countryside in Gaul, and walls were built around the towns, which shrank in size. The result was that the authority of the Roman officials in their civitates extended little further than their city walls.

Against a growing threat from Saxon pirates, the Romans constructed a system of coastal forts, called the Saxon Shore, which stretched from Norfolk right round to Devon. And two similar systems of defences were constructed along the northern and western coasts of Gaul, the chain of forts protecting Armorica being known as the Armorican Tract. They also created two naval forces in the English Channel, the Classis Britannica being based at Richborough, Dover and Boulogne, and the Classis Armorica operating at the western end of the Channel. Like all warships of the period, the vessels employed were powered primarily by oars, although auxiliary sails could be rigged on a single mast. This development really marks the beginning of Britain's history as a sea power, and helps to explain why Britain and Armorica were closely linked, both during and after the time of the Empire.

With a succession of pretenders trying to usurp the Imperial power, it was not long before the British became involved in the civil wars. Throughout the Roman occupation of England, the country was the base for three or four Roman legions, perhaps 60,000 men in total, which was a significant portion of the whole Roman army.[9] And the commanders of this large standing army all too frequently found it impossible to resist the temptation to make their own bids for power. Repeatedly, during the late Empire, rebel British generals embarked their legions for campaigns on the Continent with the aim of overthrowing an incumbent Emperor, and in the course of these campaigns the British must have accumulated extensive experience of coordinating their land and sea forces.

---

9 The army grew in size from 250,000 men in Octavian's time to 600,000 men under Constantine.

The fundamental reasons for the increasing weakness of the Empire were internal. The Emperors faced the administrative problems of extended lines of communication, and also the economic problems of inflation, trade imbalances and an overweight government. When Diocletian became Emperor in the East in 284, he found himself in command of a Roman army that had grown to more than 600,000, which was simply unaffordable. The civil administration of the Empire had also expanded enormously, and the government's demands for tax revenue was correspondingly great. Diocletian reformed the tax system, reintroducing a land tax on property owners and maintaining a poll tax on all Roman citizens, but the senatorial class was exempted from both. The result was that the burden of tax on farmers and artisans was excessive, and the provincial middle class was financially ruined.

To make the Empire more governable, and to rid it of the threat of over-mighty military commanders, Diocletian and his successors (especially Constantine) further subdivided the civil administration and split it from the military command. To begin with, in 285 the Empire was divided into two, an Eastern Empire and a Western Empire, so that Britain and Gaul became subject to the authority of a Western Emperor based at Trier (now in Germany). And as we shall see, the provinces were later subdivided into more manageable units. The resulting multiplication of the imperial courts and civil administrations simply added to the burden of an already unwieldy public sector. The Emperors and their advisers had no precedents to inform their policies, and they responded to their financial difficulties with the time-honoured practice of debasing the currency. This was achieved by reducing the gold or silver content in the coinage, which did not go unnoticed by the public.

Soon, there was simply not enough credible coinage in circulation to support the economy, and the public reverted to barter as a basis of commercial life. The debasing of the coinage was compounded by the fact that wealthy senatorial families, who did not have to pay taxes, were hoarding much of the real gold in existence. The public knew that the base metal content of the coinage was increasing and that they were being cheated by their government. This led directly to several of the revolts in the west, as usurpers gained power by promising to restore the value of the money in circulation. And just as inevitably, those usurpers were overthrown in their turn, when they failed to achieve a lasting resolution to the problem.

The result was a downward economic spiral. As the economy declined and tax receipts fell, the Emperors further corrupted the money supply to pay their legions and civil servants, and the result was rampant inflation. The rulers simply did not know how to get out of this bind, and attempted to legislate the problem away. Diocletian issued a law to statutorily freeze prices at year 301 levels, fixing the value of a pound of gold at 50,000 denarii. This was utterly futile, and by 337, the year in which Constantine died, a pound of gold was worth 20,000,000 denarii. The Empire was entering the economic territory later explored by the Weimar Republic.

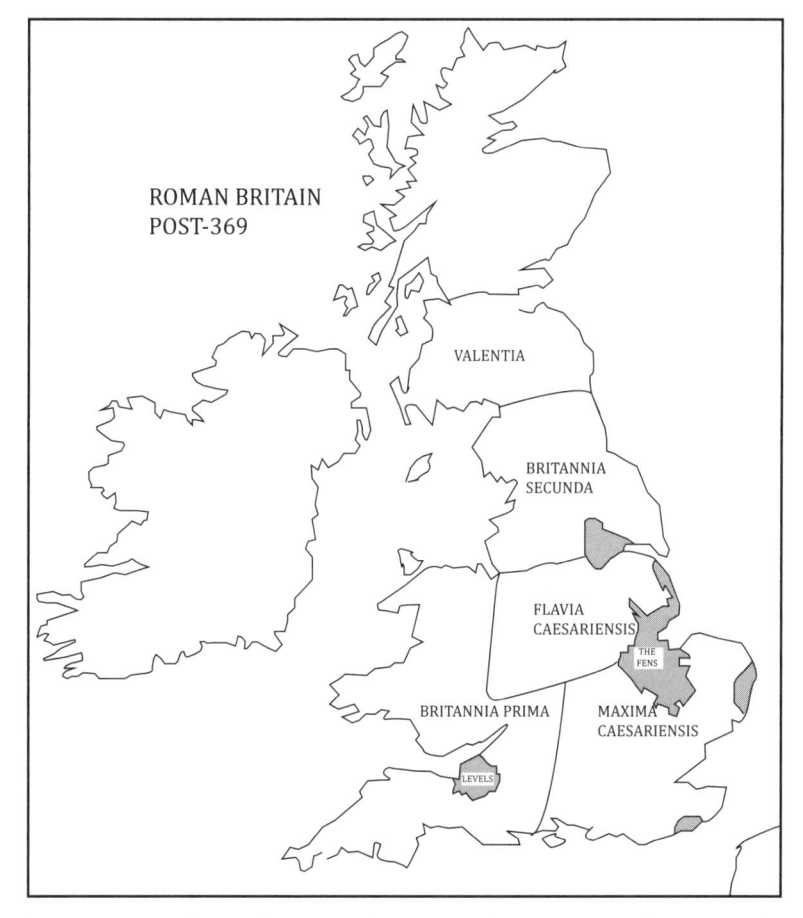

After Count Theodosius drove out the Picts and Scots in 369, he re-established a fifth Roman province north of Hadrian's Wall, which was called Valentia after the Emperors Valens and Valentinian. The prior provinces of Britannia Superior (the south) and Britannia Inferior (the north) had been split into four provinces in the early 4th century.

13

The Duke and the Decoy

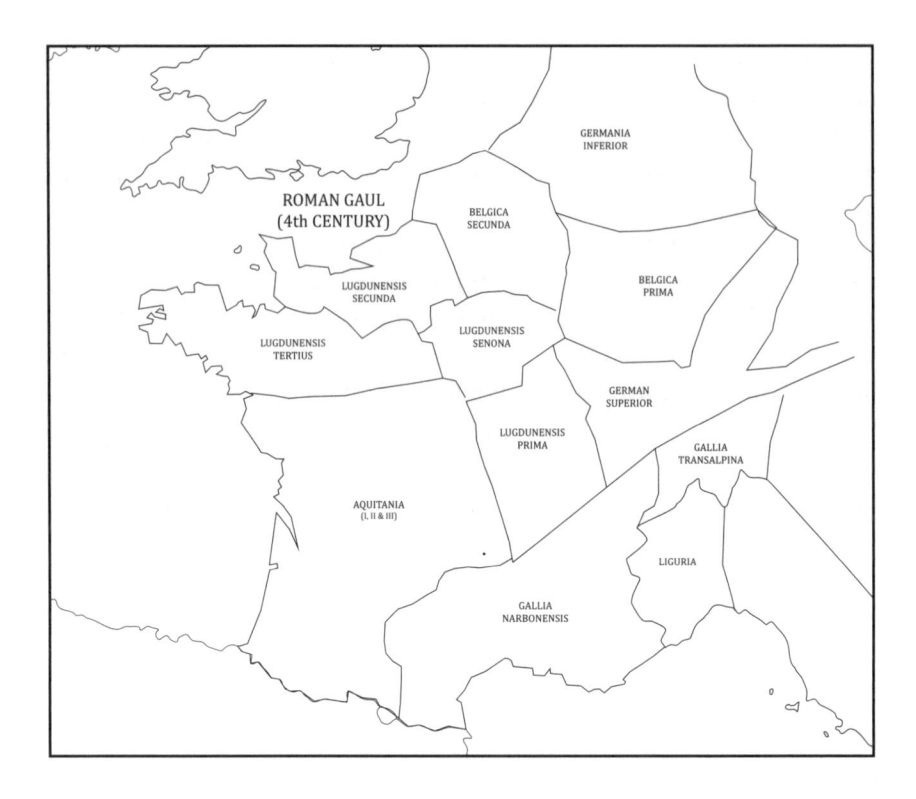

Map showing Roman Gaul (4th Century) with provinces labeled: Germania Inferior, Belgica Secunda, Belgica Prima, Lugdunensis Secunda, Lugdunensis Senona, Lugdunensis Tertius, Lugdunensis Prima, German Superior, Gallia Transalpina, Aquitania (I, II & III), Liguria, Gallia Narbonensis.

Like Britain, Roman Gaul was subdivided into smaller provinces for administrative convenience in the early 4th century. The province which formerly comprised modern Normandy and Brittany, was split into two, and Brittany formed the western half of Lugdunensis III (Tertius) (or the Third Lyonnais in English).

To add to the economic woes, there was an endemic trade imbalance between the Eastern Empire, which was a net exporter, and the Western Empire, which was a net importer, and this could not be solved without fiscal transfers or separate monetary systems. So the economy of the Western Empire simply started to collapse, leaving many unemployed workers to join the gangs of the Bagaudae.

A succession of usurpers took power in Britain, so the island several times found itself part of break-away 'empires', although they never lasted very long. The country had to be reinvaded in 296, and the leaders of the rebels were executed in London. Geoffrey of Monmouth tells us that their heads were thrown into the river 'Galobroc', and curiously over 100 skulls have been found in the bed of the Walbrook, the river which flowed through the centre of Roman

London. Since Geoffrey was writing more than 800 years after the event, it seems clear that he had access to more contemporary sources.

The Roman provinces were further subdivided in the early 4th century, so that the southern half of Britain, which was previously called Britannia Superior, was split into a western half called 'Britannia Prima', governed from Cirencester, and an eastern half called 'Maxima Caesariensis', governed from London. The northern 'Britannia Inferior' was split into northern and southern halves, to form 'Britannia Secunda', governed from York and 'Flavia Caesariensis', governed from Lincoln.

Similar reforms took place in Gaul, where the large central province of Gallia Lugdunensis was eventually split into four. The area now known as Brittany became part of Lugdunensis Tertius (the Third Lyonnais), a district comprising most of the Loire Valley west of Orléans. At the time, the peninsula had no particular connections with Britain, and its population comprised Gallo-Romans, but the vaguely understood geographical extent of the province is relevant to the Arthurian period. The capital of the Third Lyonnais was located at Tours, which also became the religious centre of the north-west of Gaul after St Martin of Tours became the Bishop of the city and established a monastery on the south bank of the River Loire in the 330s.

In overall command of Britain and Gaul was an official called the Praetorian Prefect of Gaul (whose realm also included Spain and western North Africa). The civilian governor of Britain was called the Vicar of Britain (or, to avoid confusion with the modern usage of 'vicar', the Viceroy of Britain). The Vicar was responsible for the whole 'diocese' of Britain, with its 4 provinces, each of which was governed by a Consular or President. Similarly, the governor of Gaul was called the Vicar of the Seven Provinces, and each of the provinces was governed by a President or Consular (in the case of the Third Lyonnais, a President).

The military structure in the whole of the region was headed by a Magister Militum, who we might refer to as a commander-in-chief. Below the Magister were Counts ('Comes'), separately appointed by the Emperors, who therefore owed their loyalty directly to their Emperor. They were appointed to specific commands, so for example there was a Count of Britain, and a separate Count of the Saxon Shore. Below the Counts were Dukes (each called a 'Dux'), who were the highest ranking officers in an individual province, typically commanding one or two legions. In Armorica a separate post was created called the Duke of the Armorican Tract ('Dux Tractus Armoricanus et Nervicanus'), who was the Continental equivalent of the Count of the Saxon Shore.

The reorganisations of the Empire continued, even as the security situation and economy gradually deteriorated. In Britain, attacks by the Picts of Scotland and the Saxons worsened and in 368 Count Theodosius came to save the country from a co-ordinated Pictish and Saxon invasion. Theodosius conquered Strathclyde, and established a fifth province north of Hadrian's Wall, which he called Valentia, but this expansion was short-lived. On the Continent, too, the Romans were exhausting their resources in a Canute-like struggle to hold back the Germanic tide, and in 376 a migration occurred which was to shape the remainder of the history of the Western Empire.

The Visigoths had been settled north of the Danube, but, finding themselves under attack from the Huns, arriving from the east, they asked the Emperor Valens for permission to migrate to the south bank of the river (and hence into Roman territory). Thinking that they might be useful as Roman allies, Valens assented and made various promises to provide the Goths with food and land. The Visigoths duly crossed the river, but soon found that the Romans were unable or unwilling to fulfil their promises. As a result the Visigoths suffered severe hardship and revolted against Roman rule, marching south towards Byzantium.

Valens confronted them at Adrianople, on the western shore of the Sea of Marmara, and, underestimating their numbers, brought them to battle in 378 before the Western Emperor Gratian could arrive to reinforce him. In consequence, the Eastern Roman army was crushed, and Valens was killed. Gratian briefly reunited the Empire, but later the same year promoted Theodosius I to be Eastern Emperor and returned to his own power base in northern Gaul. Over time Gratian became indolent and pretentious, and he lost the respect of his army, so in 381 the commander of the Roman army in Britain, Magnus Maximus (a Dux or Comes), decided to take advantage of his unpopularity. Having defeated an incursion of Picts and Scots and secured his power base at home, he invaded Gaul in 383. This operation must have involved the transportation of many thousands of men and horses across the Channel, a logistical exercise comparable, in terms of the resources of the day, to the D-Day landings. The forces of Maximus pursued Gratian to Lyon, where he was killed.

Magnus Maximus then declared himself 'Emperor' of the area known to the Romans collectively as 'the Gauls', being Britain, Gaul, Hispania and western North Africa. His reign was recognised by the Eastern Emperor, but when he tried to annexe Italy, the Eastern Empire sent an army to frustrate his expansion. Maximus was defeated and executed in 388. No subsequent Roman Emperor ever visited Britain, but his short reign had a lasting impact in Brittany, where he created the foundations for the British migrations.

1.6 The First Wave of Emigration to Armorica

According to British and Breton legend, one of Maximus's commanders was a Briton called Conan Meriadoc, and, after the defeat of Gratian, Maximus rewarded Meriadoc with the 'kingship' of Armorica. This seems to me doubtful, because the term 'Armorica' comprised at least two Roman provinces (the Second and Third Lyonnais), each of which would have had its own government structure. I therefore think it more likely, if Conan existed at all, that he was appointed the Dux of the Third Lyonnais, comprising Brittany, Anjou and the Touraine.

Academics have devoted much energy to debating whether this 'Conan Meriadoc' actually existed, but this seems to me pointless. Maximus was an historical character, and it is known that he took a British army onto the Continent in 383 in furtherance of his claim to the Gallic Empire. Maximus appointed his own men to positions in his Empire, an example being Andragathius, a soldier of Spanish origin, who became his Magister Militum. By this time, the civil administration of the provinces of the Empire had been divorced from the military commands, so someone was the President of the Third Lyonnais, and military commanders (probably Dukes) would have been appointed in the regions. It frankly does not matter whether the commanders in the Third Lyonnais were called Conan Meriadoc or any other name – what is important is that it is almost certain that the office holders between 383 and 388 were appointed by Maximus, a former general of the army in Britain, and that it is entirely possible that his appointees were of British origin. Indeed, the subsequent pattern of immigration from insular Britain into north-western Gaul suggests that the British felt particularly welcome in this region, and therefore suggests that the regional governors may have been British in origin.

Brittany was probably thinly populated prior to the arrival of the British, and the settlers may therefore have encountered little resistance from an indigenous population. To Paulinus of Nola, born in Bordeaux in c.352, and a resident of Bordeaux during the reign of Maximus, 'the north' was a wasteland peopled only by heathen bandits. As we have seen, the newcomers may well have been ethnically related to the locals, and probably spoke a similar language, so it is likely that the British migration was relatively peaceful. But the essential point about this first, military migration to Brittany is that the emigrants were soldiers in the Roman army. They had almost certainly been stationed at Chester or York, and they were probably ethnically Belgic Britons (although no doubt there were many foreigners serving in the British legions too).

How many British soldiers migrated to Brittany? The British force taken to the Continent may have numbered 10,000 or even 20,000 men, but some of them will have been killed in action and others will have returned to Britain (despite the words of Gildas – see below). Those that remained in Gaul will have been widely dispersed, many serving on the frontier of the Rhine. The only hard evidence for the scale of the deployments in Brittany that we have comes from the Notitia Dignitatum,[10] which tells us that about 4,000 troops (of all nationalities) were stationed in Brittany in c.420. And even allowing for the fact that many units from Britain would have been redeployed elsewhere between 383 and 420, it is hard to imagine that this first, military, settlement in Brittany comprised more than a few thousand men. During that interval, many of the first settlers must have taken local wives, and the 4,000 troops stationed in the peninsula in 420 could well have included descendants of the first British emigrants. Indeed few of them can have served under Maximus.

---

[10] The Notitia Dignitatum was a record of all of the official posts and deployments in the Roman Empire, which was accurate for the Western Empire for the period 400 – 420.

In conclusion, all we can say is that those soldiers who retired from the army of Maximus and settled in Brittany would not have been a vast horde, and would easily have been able to find agricultural land in the sparsely populated peninsula. They would have made little cultural or genetic difference to the local population, but may have constituted something of a ruling elite.

Where were they posted? The soldiers stationed in Brittany would have been based at the forts of the Armorican Tract, so essentially in coastal towns like Alet, Le Yaudet, Cherbourg and Vannes, though no doubt as they reached retirement the soldiers may have moved inland to find agricultural properties.

The result of these events is likely to have been that a British governor, probably based at Tours, commanded in the Third Lyonnais, which included Brittany and much of the Loire valley. And both Gildas and Nennius tell us that Magnus Maximus did not return the legions to Britain – that they were redeployed in Gaul to secure his borders with Germany. As we will see in the next section, it seems improbable that none of the expeditionary force returned, but the disposition of the Roman forces in Britain was certainly radically altered as a result of Maximus's campaign. There is no archaeological evidence of any Roman presence in Wales or Chester after 383, the Second Legion having been redeployed to Richborough by the end of the century. This may have coloured the view of Gildas, possibly writing from Wales, and it may explain why he thought that none of the legions ever returned home.

The deployment of British soldiers in Armorica was probably generally peaceful (they were there, after all, to protect the locals), but it certainly resulted in the dispossession of many Gallo-Roman landowners. Some of these were reduced to living in the woods and eating what they could kill – becoming what the Bretons called 'birgi'. In Redon in south-east Brittany, even citizens from senatorial families were reduced to the status of hunter-gatherers.[11] But whether the British caused more widespread destruction is hard to tell.

The Welsh legends relating to Magnus Maximus (who is called Maxen Wledic in Welsh tradition) describe a gruesome campaign of ethnic cleansing, when the British took the peninsula by force. One variant manuscript of Nennius tells us that: *"Now, the Armorican*

---
11 Chronicle of the Deeds of the Counts of Anjou, 'On Tertullus' (c.1100).

Britons, who lived beyond the sea, went out there on an expedition with the tyrant Maximus. As they were unwilling to return, they laid waste the western parts of Gaul and left alive not one who 'pisseth against the wall'.[12] *Taking their wives and daughters in marriage, they cut out their tongues, so that none of their descent should pick up their maternal language. For this reason, in our language, we also call them Lledewigion, that is half-silent, since they speak confusingly."*

However this account is not mirrored in any other source. While no doubt atrocities were committed in what was, after all, a brutal age, the general thrust of this story seems implausible. The legionaries and the Armorican Bretons probably spoke very similar languages. But there is a distinct probability that the British troops took Armorican wives, and that they may have obtained them by force.

1.7 The Roman Army in Britain After Maximus

As we have seen, the Welsh sources maintain that the legions taken to the Continent by Maximus in 383 never returned to Britain. However it is quite clear that there was a substantial Roman army in Britain in c.400, whether this was composed of troops that had returned from Gaul or of fresh recruits. The Roman army in Britain had, however, been significantly reduced, and it is entirely possible that many of its units were under-strength.[13]

Meanwhile, the effective power in Gaul, a general called Arbogast, died in 394, and when the Eastern Emperor Theodosius died the following year, his young sons Honorius and Arcadius became the Emperors of the Western and Eastern Empires respectively. As the boys were minors, Theodosius had appointed a Roman general called Stilicho (who was married to his niece) to be the guardian of Honorius. Another general called Rufinus served in a similar capacity in relation to Arcadius, and, since the boys turned out to be ineffective Emperors, the two generals became the de facto powers in the West and the East respectively (at least until Rufinus was hacked to death by his own troops).

---

12 a biblical phrase.
13 By the late Empire, only the primary legions remained at their full nominal strength of 5,500 men. A large number of secondary 'legions' comprised no more than 1,000 soldiers.

Setting the Scene

Stilicho was, according to Edward Gibbon, *"the last of the Roman generals"*, and he was certainly the last to fight in Britain. Having fought a partially successful campaign against the Goths, he arrived in Britain in c.398 to deal with a further incursion of the Picts and Scots. We know little of this campaign but it is clear that it did not succeed in eliminating the threats from the north and the west, because further attacks from those areas were recorded in the next decade. And after the campaign, it appears that the 20th Legion, which had been moved from Chester to defend the new province of Valentia, was withdrawn from Britain (and indeed that Valentia may have been abandoned). This unit does not figure in the list of Roman forces in Britain recorded in the Notitia Dignitatum.

According to the Notitia, the 2nd Legion, which had formerly been based at Caerleon, was now deployed at Richborough under the command of the Count of the Saxon Shore, and the 6th, under the command of the 'Duke of the Britons', was left defending the north, scattered across Yorkshire and Lancashire. The Duke also had a separate command comprising 18 cohorts of infantry and 6 squadrons of cavalry defending Hadrian's Wall. A further 12 squadrons of cavalry were based in Britain: 3 in the north (in addition to the 6 guarding the Wall); 3 along the Saxon Shore[14] and 6 under the direct command of the Count of Britain, who had overall command of all of the Roman forces in the island. The latter units were probably a 'rapid reaction force', which could be quickly deployed to reinforce the defences of the north and the east coast as necessary. In total, the standing army in Britain probably comprised some 18,000 men – small compared to the 60,000 troops that may once have been based on the island, but not insignificant.

The redeployments clearly demonstrate that the external threats now came from the north and the North Sea, not from Wales. And they help to explain the defence policies of the British authorities in the following century, in particular their employment of mercenaries in Kent

---

14 In 2013, Channel 4's 'Time Team' excavated a Roman cavalry base at Brancaster in Norfolk, which was probably part of the Saxon Shore defences.

1.8   The Beginning of the End

The regime of Arbogast had been based at Trier, and depended heavily on the military capabilities of the Franks, as Roman allies. But Stilicho was originally a general in the service of the Eastern Empire. His father was half Roman and half Vandal, and his mother was Roman, so he had no ethnic connections with the Franks. When he moved the western imperial court to the relative safety of Ravenna, in north-eastern Italy, and appointed colleagues from the Eastern army to key positions, the Franks were left out of power, and with little motive to defend any territory but their own. This was disastrous, because the Romans had withdrawn many of their own troops from the Rhine, and were increasingly dependent on their Frankish allies for the security of the border - in Gibbon's words, a frontier defended by *"only the faith of the Germans and the ancient terror of the Roman name"*.

Whether or not the Romans had taken a conscious decision to abandon Gaul, they certainly decided that they could no longer defend Britain. In 401, Stilicho withdrew some of the troops in Britain to fight against the Visigoths who were threatening north-east Italy, and, since no coins minted in Rome after 402 are found on the island, we can presume that any remaining Roman forces on the island were not being paid from the Capitol thereafter.

In 406, a vast army of Germanic tribes (possibly 500,000 men) under a leader called Radagaisus invaded northern Italy, and Stilicho recalled the Roman garrisons from the Scheldt, the Meuse and the Lower Rhine to defend their homelands, leaving the Franks alone guarding the Rhine frontier. Although Stilicho was able to defeat the invasion, the reduction in the defences along the Rhine was to prove disastrous when the river froze over that winter. On 31 December 406, a large group of Germans (including Alans, Vandals, Sueves and possibly Burgundians) walked across the river near Mainz. The Dux Mogontiacensis, with a Frankish force guarding the west bank, was on the verge of defeating the Vandals, when a force of Alans joined the battle in support of the invaders, and the Franks were routed. St Jerome wrote that Reims, Arras, Amiens and Tournai were entirely overrun by Germans.[15] Another group of Alans crossed the river at about the same time, but immediately allied themselves with the Romans (who still held a fragile control over Gallia Lugdunensis). The Germanic tribes were not a homogenous bloc, and just as there were Alans fighting on both sides, there were Franks among the invading forces.[16] In consequence, Gaul was for a time awash with Germans fighting for one side or the other. But the invading armies were financed by plunder, and like all such armies, had to move on to fresh territory, once they had despoiled an area. So the Vandals marched into Spain in 409, and the Visigoths moved on to invade Italy, and sack Rome, in 410.

In an attempt to stablilise the situation, Stilicho opened negotiations with the Visigoth King Alaric, to try to bring him into an alliance with Rome, but this manoeuvre greatly offended many Romans, and before his diplomatic efforts could bear fruit, he was executed. When Alaric himself died shortly afterwards, his army decided to abandon Italy, and in 412 they invaded Gaul, where the Visigoths made themselves at home in the south-west (Aquitaine). The Suevi and some Alans who had arrived in the first wave of raiders then joined the Vandals in Spain, and the three nations divided Iberia up between themselves. The Suevi took the north-west, the Alans the central band and the Vandals took the south, from where they eventually moved on to North Africa.

1.9 The Departure of the Roman Officials

The Vicar of Britain from 395 to 406 was Victorinus, who was regarded by his Roman contemporaries as a model governor.[17] But coins minted in Rome stopped arriving in Britain in 402, and the regime probably became very unpopular as a consequence. Victorinus inevitably became the focus of unrest, and whether of his

---

15 The Alans were mounted warriors from a group of Sarmation tribes, who spoke an Eastern Iranian language and who had migrated west, fleeing before the Huns. They were to play a pivotal role in several episodes in Western Europe in the 5th century.
16 Between 409 and 415, Trier was four times captured, sacked and burnt in further raids by Frankish armies, while at the same time Gaiso, also a Frank, was the Count of the Largesses and Master of the Forces at Rome.
17 Rutilius Namatianus, 'De Reditu Suo' (417).

own volition or at the command of the British authorities, he retired to Gaul (and subsequently, in view of the instability of that province, to Tuscany).

Following the departure of Victorinus, the Roman forces in Britain proclaimed Marcus, a soldier from among their ranks, as Emperor, but he was soon killed by his own troops and replaced by Gratian, apparently a civilian magistrate and a native of Britain. However, when the Vandals, Alans and Suevi crossed the frozen Rhine, in 406, the British army wanted to cross over to Gaul to confront the Germans, and Gratian refused. As a result, he was assassinated after a reign of only four months, and replaced in 407 by Constantine III, a common soldier, but a man of some ability with an auspicious name. Constantine was willing to lead a campaign in Gaul, and he took the army across the Channel to Boulogne in 409, another example of the ability of the British to mount a sea-borne invasion of the Continent.

Constantine eventually secured the Rhine frontier, but not without difficulty, and probably mainly because the invaders had departed for warmer climes in the south. He was therefore able to claim a victory, and he made his imperial capital at Arles, in the south of Gaul. There he appointed Apollinaris (possibly the grandfather of Sidonius Apollinaris, who we will come to in due course) as Praetorian Prefect of Gaul, and he extracted his own son Constans from a monastery to become a junior Emperor (a Caesar). Constantine then sent Constans, with his British Magister Militum, Gerontius, to Spain, where they had little difficulty in defeating several cousins of the Emperor Honorius. Honorius, who had been abandoned by his army in Ravenna, was forced to recognise Constantine III as co-Emperor in 409, and a few coins minted by the usurper made it back to Britain.

Just as had happened after the campaign of Maximus in Gaul a quarter of a century earlier, it is likely that many of the troops redeployed by Constantine in Gaul remained there, only this time in the eastern parts of the province. There are numerous places in France and western Germany with names that testify to the former presence of British troops, eg Bretteville (Normandy), Bretoneux (Picardy), Breteuil (Picardy) and Bretzenheim (in the Rhineland, formerly the Vicus Britannicus), and some of these may have acquired their names at this time. It is very unlikely that any of the troops were stationed in Brittany, but these events demonstrate that the

Setting the Scene

British were capable of intervening decisively in a Continental war in the early 5th century.

However, for their homelands, this expedition was a disaster. This time, Britain really was left totally defenceless, and the Picts and Saxons soon took advantage of the situation. The Chronica Gallica of 452 tells us that, in the year 409 or 410, *"The Britains were devastated by a Saxon invasion."*[18] If, as seems likely, the raid was conducted by Saxon pirates, with the objective of theft rather than settlement, the target would have been one or more 'high-value' locations, quite possibly including London.

Constantine was unable to respond expeditiously to this Saxon incursion, and the outraged British expelled his officials. Repenting of their allegiance to him, they apparently appealed to Honorius for help against the invaders, because Zosimus, a 6th century Byzantine scholar, refers to letters that he says were written by the Emperor in 410 – letters which no longer exist but which are now referred to as the 'Rescript of Honorius'. Zosimus tells us that *"Honorius wrote letters to the cities of Britain, bidding them to take precautions on their own behalf".* The end of Roman rule in Britain is usually dated to this correspondence, but some academics have questioned whether the reported instruction referred to Britain at all. The sentence appears in a passage of text concerning southern Italy, and it has been suggested that the correspondence from Honorius may really have been addressed to the civitates of the province of Britti in Italy.

Be that as it may, the British were certainly left to their own devices, and Constantine had lost his domestic power base. With his political power draining from him, he decided to take a big gamble, and marched into Italy with a view to overthrowing Honorius. But the army of Honorius, under the command of a general who went on to become Constantius III, defeated Constantine, who then retreated to Arles. Constantius followed, overcoming Gerontius outside the city, and putting it under siege. Constantine eventually surrendered and was executed in 411.

An account of these events is given by Zosimus, which explains

---

18 The Chronica Gallica was an annal maintained in Gaul, probably in the Rhône Valley or in the south of Gaul, by anonymous authors. Two editions survive, that of 452, and that of 511, the latter of which incorporates and extends forward the material in the earlier edition.

that Britain and Armorica became independent of the Roman Empire: *"Constans was afterwards a second time sent into Spain, and took with him Justus as his general. Gerontius being dissatisfied at this, and having conciliated the favour of the soldiers in that quarter, incited the barbarians who were in Gallia Celtica to revolt against Constantine. Constantine being unable to withstand these, the greater part of his army being in Spain, the barbarians beyond the Rhine made such unbounded incursions over every province, as to reduce not only the Britons, but some of the Celtic nations also to the necessity of revolting from the empire, and living no longer under the Roman laws but as they themselves pleased. The Britons therefore took up arms, and incurred many dangerous enterprises for their own protection, until they had freed their cities from the barbarians who besieged them. In a similar manner, the whole of Armorica, with other provinces of Gaul, delivered themselves by the same means; expelling the Roman magistrates or officers, and erecting a government, such as they pleased, of their own. Thus happened this revolt or defection of Britain and the Celtic nations, when Constantine usurped the empire, by whose negligent government the barbarians were emboldened to commit such devastations."*

Gildas, who habitually takes the Roman side in any issue between the Romans and the people of his own country, describes the departure of the Romans in these terms: *"The Romans, therefore, left the country, giving notice that they could no longer be harassed by such laborious expeditions, nor suffer the Roman standards, with so large and brave an army, to be worn out by sea and land by fighting against these unwarlike, plundering vagabonds; but that the islanders, inuring themselves to warlike weapons, and bravely fighting, should valiantly protect their country, their property, wives and children, and, what is dearer than these, their liberty and lives."*

Effectively, the people of the island of Britain, and the Bretons in Armorica, seem to have declared themselves independent, because neither remained willing to pay increasingly heavy Roman taxes for the now ephemeral Roman security. In the case of insular Britain, the divorce occurred by mutual consent, because the Romans needed their troops back to defend their motherland, and could no longer defend one of their remotest provinces. But as we shall see, the Romans took a different view of the events in Brittany.

Chapter 2
The Age of Despair

2.1 Britain After Rome

The end of Roman rule in Britain is traditionally dated to 410, as a result of the events described in the previous chapter. But it is likely that Roman civic organisation continued in the towns of parts of the province for some years after the departure of the last Vicar. This is particularly likely to have been the case in Britannia Prima (ie western Britain including Wales), with its capital at Gloucester or Cirencester. Here, Roman life in the towns continued into the early 5th century; streets in Bath were recobbled and the walls of Cirencester were repaired. However, even in Britannia Prima, the countryside was abandoned to lawless peasants or foreign raiders, and the many villas fell to rack and ruin.

The reasons for this are not hard to see, because the new rulers of Britain faced extraordinarily intractable problems. Firstly, they had to cope with the ongoing security issue on several borders, and secondly, Roman Britain was now plunged into an economic depression. As noted above, the economy of the Empire had been chaotic since the 3rd century, but Britain had at least benefited from subsidies paid to the legions in Britain. These now ceased, and the Romans also stopped procuring grain for their Continental armies from the island. The farming economy went into freefall, so landowners no longer needed a large workforce to manage their fields. The serfs were simply freed, and landowners reduced the scale of their activities to subsistence farming. Nearly all manufacturing industry came to a halt.

The consequences must have been mass unemployment, and, with the military absent, outbreaks of lawlessness on a scale comparable to the uprisings of the Continental Bagaudae. The collapse in social order was colourfully described by the Anglo-Saxon monk Bede, writing in the early 8th century, when he tells us that even the pastors *"had given themselves up to drunkenness, hatred, quarrels and violence."* The civil disorder greatly compounded the damage caused by Pictish raids, and the result was a famine, again described by Bede. *"They [the citizens] were driven from their homesteads and farms, and sought to save themselves from starvation by robbery and violence against one another, their own internal anarchy adding to the miseries caused by others, until there was no food left in the whole land except whatever could be obtained by hunting."*

The already debased token money system was abandoned, and the British reverted to the Iron Age customs of barter, in which the basic unit of currency was a cow. The urban population was forced to seek food in the countryside, and whole towns started to be abandoned, including the city of York. And in those still inhabited, a lack of resources and civic disorder led to the collapse of the infrastructure. Sewers began to clog up, probably resulting in an increase in the rat population, which in turn may have been the cause of a contagion. Bede tells us *"Suddenly a terrible plague struck this corrupt people, and in a short while destroyed so large a number that the living could not bury the dead."* Certainly the archaeological record shows a significant population retreat in the early 5th century. The population of Britain at the end of the 4th century was probably 3.5 to 4 million, and it may have almost halved in the first decades after the departure of the Romans. As Nennius put it *"The Britons were once very populous, and exercised dominion from sea to sea"* – but clearly that was no longer true.

To Gildas, this plague was simply divine retribution for the sins of the people, one of the worst of which was their attachment to the doctrines of Pelagius (a monk of British origin who lived c.390 – 418). Pelagius opposed the ideas of predestination and 'original sin'. People needed no divine intervention to perform good deeds, he argued, and their actions and the outcomes of their lives were largely the consequences of the exercise of their free will. This was all heresy to the Catholic Church, and in 429, the Bishops of Gaul sent St Germanus, the Bishop of Auxerre, together with St Lupus, the Bishop of Troyes, on a mission to counter the deviants. Nennius reports that St Germanus debated the doctrinal issues in public and was successful in debunking the arguments of the Pelagian priests of Britain, owing to his superior oratory. Germanus and Lupus then returned to Gaul the following year.[19]

The biography of St Germanus by Constantius of Lyon also provides us with some evidence for a continuing Roman form of government in Britain. When Germanus visited Britain in 429, he is said to have restored the sight of a ten-year old girl who was described as a daughter of a man 'of tribunician powers'. A tribune, in the Roman system of government, was originally a cavalry officer, although the title later came to be used by the members of a senate or a civitas. The words of the biographer may therefore mean that officials holding such titles continued to exist in the 420s, but since he was careful to use the phrase 'of tribunician powers', he may have been signalling that titles of this sort no longer existed. Bede said simply that he was a tribune, but that can only have been his assumption. However, the clear implication of the original text is that individuals who held powers similar to, and who performed functions previously discharged by, Roman officials continued to be appointed, at least on a local basis.

In contrast, it is very likely that government at a national level had disappeared almost entirely. After the Roman towns were abandoned in the early 5th century, there would have been no formal seats of government, and as communication by road became perilous, such authorities as remained in each region would have felt almost completely isolated. Formally, and in terms of titles, the local governments may have been modeled on the Roman system, but with the very limited resources available to them, there would have been distinct limits to what the councillors could achieve.

2.2   The Groans of the Britons

So in the 430s, the island of Britain was suffering from the continuing raids of the Picts and Saxons, and from economic collapse, albeit interspersed with years of good harvests.[20] The task of defending

---

[19] Gildas, curiously, does not mention St Germanus, but Constantius of Lyon's 'Life of St Germanus' (c.480) is an even more contemporary source, apparently based on the recollections of Bishop Lupus.
[20] Gildas even managed to find the successful harvests a cause for concern, as a threat to the moral welfare of the people!

the north from the raids of the Picts and Scots was largely beyond the meagre resources of the residual Roman-style authorities, particularly because it proved impossible to recruit enough troops for the task from the shrinking indigenous population. Gildas, as usual, was scathing in his assessment of the British forces deployed to secure the borders: *"Moreover, having heard of the departure of our friends [the Romans], and their resolution never to return, they [the Picts] seized with greater boldness than before on all the country towards the extreme north as far as the wall. To oppose them there was placed on the heights a garrison equally slow to fight and ill adapted to run away, a useless and panic-struck company, who slumbered away days and nights on their unprofitable watch."*

Nevertheless, the British did enjoy occasional successes in these confrontations, one of which was described in the 'Life of St Germanus'. Constantius tells us that St Germanus led the British to a victory, now known as the 'Alleluia Battle', probably against the Picts and some of their Saxon allies. Bede wrote that this battle took place in Guidcruic in Flintshire, which is now called Mold, and about a mile from Mold there is indeed a Maes Garmon, the 'Field of Germanus'. According to the story, Germanus, who had been a soldier before entering the church, took command of the British forces and deployed them in a valley to ambush the raiders. At the approach of the enemy, he ordered his men to shout 'Alleluia', and the sound, reverberating around the hills, so unsettled the invaders that they fled, many of them drowning in a river in their hurry to escape.

Despite the fact that Constantius does not mention any dates, we happen to know that this visit of St Germanus took place in 429, because it was independently reported by Prosper of Aquitaine. However Constantius also tells of a second visit to Britain by St Germanus, on which Prosper is silent, and indeed we can deduce from Prosper's account that it is unlikely that such a visit took place. Prosper visited Rome in 431 to enlist the support of Pope Celestine in a campaign against Pelagianism, and reported that *"With as much vigour he [Pope Celestine] delivered the British isles of the same disease, in that he drove from that retreat of the Ocean certain individuals, enemies of Grace, who had taken possession of the land of their origins, and by ordaining a bishop for the Irish [presumably St Patrick], while striving to keep the Roman island Catholic he also made the uncivilised island Christian."* In the 'Life of St Germanus', the expulsion of the Pelagians from Britain followed the second visit of St Germanus to the island. But if this had happened by 431, as Prosper reported, there could hardly have been any time (after the first visit of 429) for the second visit to have taken place. Celestine died in 432, so Prosper's date for his visit to Rome is reliable.[21] As we shall see in due course, I believe that the 'second visit of St Germanus' was actually a visit to Brittany, made in about 447.

Despite the occasional British victory, the raids of the Picts and Scots became increasingly severe, and the British sent a message to the Roman general in Gaul, Flavius Aëtius (c.396 – 454), to ask him for military assistance. We can confidently say that this appeal happened after c.429, because Aëtius arrived in southern Gaul with an army of 40,000 Huns in 427. He relieved the city of Arles (which had been besieged by the Visigoths), and after defeating the Visigoths he drove them back into Aquitaine. Then in 428 he defeated some Franks who had crossed the Rhine into Gaul. In 430, the Visigoths again marched on Arles, and Aëtius defeated them a second time, before undertaking a campaign to re-establish Roman control over the Danube later that year. He returned to Gaul in 431 and defeated the Franks again in 432 – so he was clearly a busy man. It is hardly surprising that Aëtius rejected the British appeal for assistance, and not only because he had more than enough on his hands. He probably had little sympathy for the Britons, who he may well have associated with the usurper Constantine III.

Gildas describes this last appeal to the Romans in some detail: *"Again, therefore, the wretched remnant, sending to Aetius, a powerful Roman citizen, address him as follows:-"To Aetius, now consul for the third time: the groans of the Britons." And again a little further thus:- "The barbarians drive us to the sea; the sea throws us back on the barbarians: thus two modes of death await us, we are either slain or drowned." The Romans, however, could not assist them."*

The Winchester manuscript of the Anglo-Saxon Chronicle dates this appeal to 443, although that seems too late in view of the subsequent events. A date in the 430s seems more probable, possibly c.436 when Aëtius was campaigning in Armorica against the

---

[21] For a full discussion, see Anthony A Barrett, 'St Germanus and the British Missions', Britannia (Cambridge Journals), Volume 40 (2009) pp 197 – 217.

Bagaudae. It appears that the British had won a battle against the Picts in 429, and we can assume that Pictish raids continued in the following decade.

According to Gildas, the British did manage to win some battles against the Picts, despite the lack of support from Aëtius: *"the discomfited people, wandering in the woods, began to feel the effects of a severe famine, which compelled many of them without delay to yield themselves up to their cruel persecutors, to obtain subsistence: others of them, however, lying hidden in mountains, caves and woods, continually sallied out to renew the war. And then it was, for the first time, that they overthrew their enemies, who had for so many years been living in their country".*

But he tells us that the British were then faced with the threat of a massive invasion, which they feared would overwhelm them. He wrote that *"a vague rumour suddenly as if on wings reaches the ears of all, that their inveterate foes were rapidly approaching to destroy the whole country, and to take possession of it, as of old, from one end to the other."* In the face of the renewed threat, the British were to turn to an unlikely source for assistance, as we shall see in Chapter 3.

2.3   Climate Change

At the same time as these disasters were befalling Britain, rising sea levels were making inroads into the coasts of what are now Denmark, northern Germany and the Netherlands. These previously densely inhabited areas became progressively depopulated from the second half of the 4th century onwards, as a result of the changing environment. Coastal salt-marshes expanded and rivers broke their banks, depositing clay over the surrounding countryside and making the soil agriculturally useless. The climate of Europe became cooler and wetter, too, and marginal uplands in Scandinavia became untenable. Together, these developments contributed to a pattern of emigration from the Nordic countries and the coastal regions of the lowlands.

Nature abhors a vacuum, and the reduction in the population of Britain began to attract some of the displaced peasant farmers of the Continental North Sea coast. The eastern regions of what is now

England were of course already well-known to Saxon pirates, who had been raiding the coasts of Britain since the 3rd century. Indeed, as we have seen, the threat from this source had resulted in the construction of the Saxon Shore defences, from Brancaster in Norfolk, around the coast to the Isle of Wight and even as far as Topsham in Devon. But the impetus behind the Saxon migration of the 5th century was different: these people were not pirates – they were displaced farmers (although they were no doubt prepared to fight to defend themselves). We will return to this subject in 2.7.

Similar forces were at work in the areas to the west of the Saxon lands, and the Franks, who had formerly occupied the territory around the Rhine, had moved westwards to inhabit the former Roman province of Belgica Secunda (the Second Belgica) in the latter half of the 4th century. This meant, for the British, that the Continental ports at the eastern end of the Channel were controlled by the Franks, initially as Roman allies, but effectively as an autonomous power after the German invasions of Gaul of the early 5th century. Trade in general had reduced with the withdrawal of the Roman officials from Britain, but trade at the eastern end of the Channel must have almost ground to a halt. When St Germanus visited Britain in 429, he passed through Nanterre, to the west of Paris, so it seems certain that he crossed the Channel from a port in Normandy, rather than from Boulogne which was in Frankish hands. And for the port of London, the collapse of trade with the Continent would have been catastrophic.

2.4   Life After Rome in Brittany

At much the same time as the withdrawal of the last Roman governors from Britain, the Bretons had revolted against Roman rule (this first 'war of independence' is traditionally dated to the period 408 to 417). The Germanic invasions of the early 5th century had broken down the structures of government in much of Gaul, and the Third Lyonnais then become a magnet for displaced peasants, escaped slaves and vagabonds from the rest of the country. The Romans called these groups the Bagaudae, after the peasant insurgents of that name who had infested Gaul in the 3rd century.[22] It is probable that most of these people were from the less-Romanised areas of Gaul, and they may well have come from communities that remained predominantly Gaulish-speaking. In any case it seems they felt an affinity with the population of the relatively wild western peninsula.

Like their British counterparts, the Bretons objected strongly to the increasingly heavy burden of Roman taxation. But for the Bretons, the issue was more complicated, because, although most Roman forces had been withdrawn from the peninsula to help fight the tide of Germanic invaders, some troops continued to guard the coasts against Saxon pirates. And a significant number of British or Breton troops were serving in the Roman army, in the peninsula and elsewhere in Gaul. In 410, a British force of 1,000, under a commander called Luomadus, siezed Blois, a town to the west of Orléans, from a 'German' commander called Odo. Odo may have been an Alan, because we know that some Alans had allied themselves with the Romans after the invasion of 406, but he called himself a 'Roman Consul'. Quite what the motives of the British were, and in whose interests they were acting, are uncertain. If the British (perhaps still ruled by Conan Meriadoc) were asserting their control over the Third Lyonnais, this would tell us that the province still extended to include Brittany, Maine, Anjou and the Touraine. However if these were troops still loyal to the Roman authorities, they may have been deployed to Blois to safeguard the city from other threats. On balance, I think the former interpretation is the more likely, and that they were acting on the instructions of a British commander based at Tours, the capital city of the province.

Although it is hard to prove that there were direct links between the Bretons and the Bagaudae in the first half of the century, the uprisings of the Bagaudae coincided with the periods of Breton revolt (408 – 417 and 437 – 448), which surely cannot be a coincidence. The Romans themselves evidently connected the Bretons with the Bagaudae, and accused the Bretons of harbouring outlaws, by which they probably meant escaped slaves. And this highlights a philosophical dispute that went to the heart of the British campaign for independence. The Roman economy was dependent on slavery,

---

22 Today, a 'bagad' in Brittany is a musical band comprising bagpipes, bombards and drums.

but the British, who had seen the serfs of insular Britain freed after the departure of the Roman officials, seem to have regarded slavery as abhorrent.

Of course, the Bretons would not have been entirely of one mind on this issue because many of the soldiers from the army of Maximus had become landowners in the peninsula, and some may well have employed slaves. Towns like Nantes, Vannes and Rennes remained relatively Romanised, and the bourgeoisie had a vested interest in the continuation of the Roman lifestyle. But we have written evidence that slavery was an issue at the heart of the Breton revolt, from a source close to the Roman general who suppressed it.

In 417, the Romans mounted an expedition to recover the province, which was commanded by Exuperantius of Poitiers, the Praetorian Prefect of Gaul. He was probably the father of Palladius, the first Bishop of Ireland, and the poet Rutilius Claudius Namatianus wrote of Palladius; *"Even now his father Exuperantius trains the Armoric sea-board to love the recovery of peace; he re-establishes the laws, brings freedom back and suffers not the inhabitants to be their servants' slaves."*[23] To the Romans, the structure of a society based on the enslavement of its lowest class was fundamental to their way of life. And it was essential for the maintenance of a society based on slavery that there should be no refuges for escaped slaves – so that the slaves could be convinced that there were no alternatives to their condition (unless their masters chose to free them). And thus an independent and libertarian Brittany was a threat to the vital interests of the Romans in Gaul.

The uprisings of the Bagaudae are often described as peasant revolts, but Salvian, a Christian from Belgic Gaul of the early 5th century, claimed that the pressure of taxation had forced small landowners and even educated men from good families into the camp of the rebels.[24] It even seems possible that some of the outlaws had served in the Roman army, and since the Bretons had arrived in Armorica as Roman soldiers themselves, the forces of the peninsula proved to be capable warriors. They fought the Roman army to a standstill on occasions, and it seems that the Romans were thwarted for a long time in their efforts to take Nantes.

---
23 Rutilius, 'De Reditu Suo' (417).
24 Salvian, 'The Government of God', (c.440).

However, Exuperantius was eventually successful in re-establishing Roman control over the Loire Valley, which did not return to Breton rule until the 9th century. The Bretons lost control of a large part of the Third Lyonnais, and were confined within a border that generally followed the Vilaine River in the south and the River Rance in the north. Either the Romans did not consider it worthwhile to suppress this residual enclave, or they became distracted by other threats, because the Bretons were left as a quasi-Roman client state in the peninsula. The Romans certainly faced more significant problems at this time, with the Visigoths settling in Aquitaine in 418 and the sack of Trier by the Franks in 421. And we know that the morale of their army cannot have been good, because Exuperantius was killed by his own troops, in 424, in the course of an army mutiny at his capital in Arles.

As a result of the restoration of this quasi-Roman rule, the cities of Armorica continued to function much as before, and even at the end of the 6th century, officials with Roman titles continued to rule in the 'pagi' around Vannes, Nantes and Rennes.[25] Whereas no coins minted in Rome after 402 reached Britain, eighteen gold Roman coins dating from 395 to 491 have been found scattered around the peninsula, demonstrating that Brittany remained part of the economy of the Western Empire until its end. Moreover, frequent finds of 5th century pottery from Aragon and the Mediterranean in the peninsula show that the Atlantic trade routes continued to operate. Most of the trade, it is true, seems to have centred on Nantes, which was now back in Roman hands, so for example tin from Abbaretz and St Renan continued to be exported to other Roman provinces.[26] But in general it seems that the society of Brittany in the 5th century remained far more Romanised than that of Britain, and this is a matter of some importance to our understanding of the events of the Arthurian period at the end of the century. The British colony in Armorica was both economically and socially stronger than its parent country.

The Bretons had not been completely crushed in 417, and probably entertained ambitions to recover control of the Loire Valley,

---

25 Noël-Yves Tonnerre, 'L'Armorique à la fin du Vème Siècle', in 'Clovis, histoire et mémoire', editor Michel Rouche (1997), pp 145 – 146.
26 'Le commerce nantais à l'époque mérovingienne', in the 'Mémoires de la Société d'Histoire et d'Archéologie de Bretagne', vol LXI (1984) pp 3 - 28.

hoping that an opportunity to do so would arise while the Romans were distracted by the Franks. Appreciating the threat, in the 430s the Magister Militum of Gaul, Aëtius, settled some Alans in the Nantes area to consolidate his control. This was provocative, and as a result the restive Bretons replaced a leader called Salomon I, who was a Roman ally, with an insular Briton of a more independent spirit (possibly by assassinating Salomon). Gradlon was the elderly 'Count of Cornouaille', a retired soldier who had been a military commander under Meriadoc, and he was too old to lead an armed revolt himself. So he appointed a leader of the Bagaudae, called Tibatto, to the command of the Breton forces, and they rose in revolt in the mid-430s. According to the Chronica Gallica of 452, the Romans then sent a force under the command of a General called Litorius to suppress the revolt in 437, and Litorius eventually defeated the rebels in 439.[27] It seems that Tibatto was killed, but Gradlon remained in power.

Gradlon then appointed Eudoxius to lead the Breton army and launched an expedition to capture Tours in 444, but Aëtius responded and recaptured the city the following year. Sidonius Apollinaris tells us that Aëtius appointed his lieutenant Majorian to lead the campaign in 446, but apparently he was unsuccessful because, according to the 'Life of St Germanus', the following year Majorian instructed an Alan commander called Eochar (sometimes rendered as Goar), to suppress the Bretons. Goar would have done so, but for the intervention of St Germanus.

The involvement of St Germanus in this struggle might at first sight seem curious, but the church remained a strong link between the Bretons and Rome. There was a Council at Bourges in 444, attended by Léon, the Bishop of the city, Eustochius of Tours and Victor of Le Mans, and the instructions from this Council were sent to Desiderius and the other bishops and priests of the Third Lyonnais. Brittany remained under the rule, in religious matters, of the Roman metropolitan See of Tours, even as its leaders were expelling the Roman civil authorities. And it is probable that it was the Bishops who appealed to St Germanus to use his influence to broker a peace.

Breton legend has it that Gradlon died during these struggles, and was succeeded by Audren, a man who was to become a Breton national hero as the leader who restored peace on honourable terms.

---
27 Sidonius Apollinaris.

The Life of St Germanus tells us that Eochar's campaign occurred immediately after the saint's 'second visit' to Britain, but I believe that the campaign began immediately before a visit by St Germanus to Brittany, made with the objective of preventing an outbreak of war. The effect of his intervention was that Eochar agreed to call a halt to his campaign, on condition that St Germanus obtained 'a pardon' (presumably for the rebels) from the Emperor and from Aëtius. St Germanus set off for Ravenna to accomplish this task, but he died on the mission; and in the meantime, the Bretons (probably now led by Audren) had apparently expelled the remaining Roman officials from Nantes, Guérande, Alet and Léon.[28] The Chronica Gallica of 452 dates this rebellion to 448.

It was about this time that St Brieuc, the first immigrant among the seven 'founding saints' of Brittany, arrived in the peninsula from Cardigan in Wales. He was allegedly a disciple of St Germanus, and had been sent to Brittany at his command, possibly to help pacify the region. St Brieuc can be considered the pioneer for a third wave of British immigration into the peninsula, which really got under way at the end of the century.

2.5 The Intervention of the Huns

At the end of the 440s, the attention of the Romans was entirely absorbed by the threat to Gaul posed by the Huns, who rampaged across the Empire under the command of their fearsome leader, Attila. When Attila came to power, in 433, Aëtius was living with him as a hostage and the Hunnish empire extended into Germany, right up to the Baltic Sea. As H G Wells puts it, *"He [Attila] ruled not only over the Huns but over a conglomerate of tributary Germanic tribes; his empire extended from the Rhine across the plains into Central Asia."* [29]

In 447 Attila launched a devastating attack on the Balkans, which brought him to the walls of Constantinople. Here the Magister Militum of the Eastern Empire was forced to sign a humiliating treaty in 449, under which the Eastern Romans promised to pay the Huns

---

28 Nicolas Travers. 'Histoire civile, politique et religieuse de la ville et du comté de Nantes' (1836).
29 H G Wells, 'A Short History of the World (1922)

an annual tribute of 2,100 pounds of gold. Attila next turned his attention to the Western Empire, where a surprising development became the catalyst for an upheaval of seismic proportions. In the spring of 450, Honoria, the sister of the Western Emperor Valentinian III, sent Attila a plea for help, together with her engagement ring, in a bid to escape from an arranged marriage to a Roman Senator. Attila took this to be an offer of marriage, and promptly accepted, with a demand for half the Western Empire as a dowry. When Valentinian discovered what had happened, he exiled Honoria and wrote to Attila denying the legitimacy of the 'proposal'. But Attila rejected this contention, and replied that he would come to Ravenna to collect what was rightfully his.

However he then quarrelled with Aëtius over which of two candidates should succeed to the throne of a Frankish kingdom, and he invaded Gaul in 451 to impose his will. He marched across Germany and arrived in Gallia Belgica, with an army estimated by Jordanes to have been 500,000 strong (probably an exaggeration). In 451, he crossed the Rhine with this huge army of Huns and their Germanic allies, and devastated eastern Gaul, penetrating as far as the walls of Orléans. He was driven back by the threat of a coalition force assembled by Aëtius, which contained Franks, Alans and, crucially, the Visigoths. According to Jordanes, it also contained a contingent of Armoricans (whom he called 'Letavians', after an ancient name for Brittany), which indicates that the Bretons had returned to the fold after their rebellion. Faced with this coalition, Attila retreated eastwards to an area near Châlons (in what is now the Champagne district), which was then called the Catalaunian Plains. Even discounting the wild claims of Jordanes, it is probable that the two armies numbered something in the order of 100,000 men each, so the ensuing battle dwarfed any military engagement in medieval Britain. After a preliminary skirmish on the periphery of the battlefield, involving about 15,000 men on each side, the main battle lasted a day, and resulted in heavy casualties on both sides. But Attila's army had the worst of it, and after a day of fighting his forces broke up and began to retreat. Somewhat surprisingly, Aëtius chose not to press his advantage, but it may be presumed that he was concerned that, if his victory was too complete, the Visigoths would be left as masters of Gaul (although their King Theodoric I was killed in the battle). After the battle, Attila's core units remained with him to pursue an ultimately unsuccessful campaign in Italy, but many of the Germanic tribes returned home, and some of the captives of the Romans became militias in the service of Aëtius.

2.6   The Restoration of Roman Rule in Brittany

This victory at the battle of the Catalaunian Plains freed Aëtius from external threats for the time being, and altered the relationship between the Romans and the Bretons. As we have noted, troops from Brittany formed part of the Roman coalition, so it appears that at least some of the Bretons were reconciled to the Roman cause. But others clearly remained bent on independence, because Aëtius took military action to restore the province to Roman rule in 452-453, apparently using Germanic mercenaries (including captured Huns) for the task.

Brest was ruined in 452, to the extent that the bishopric remained vacant for 50 years, and in 453 Aëtius sent an army of Huns to retake Nantes, which may have been in Breton hands since 448. As a result of this campaign, Brittany was pacified and brought back under Roman control, but Aëtius was astute enough to respect the distinctive traditions of the Bretons. A fragment in Latin of the first written laws of Brittany, possibly promulgated by Aëtius before he died in 454, is contained in a document called 'Excerpta de libris Romanorum et Francorum', which was found in Ireland,[30] The terms of the law evidently reflect the customs and mores that the Bretons had brought with them from Britain.

The reconquest of Brittany may well have inspired a fear among the insular British that a similar fate awaited them. We will shortly meet the British king of the period, who was called Vortigern, and the Romano-British general who succeeded him, who was called Ambrosius Aurelianus, a man who may have been an exile in Brittany in the 440s. We are told by Nennius that Vortigern lived in dread of the Romans, which at first sight seems odd, given that the British had relatively recently appealed to Aëtius for help against the Picts and Saxons. But what the British presumably wanted on that occasion

---

30 L. Feuriot, ' Un fragment en latin de très anciennes lois bretonnes armoricaines', Annales de Bretagne, tome LXXVIII (1971), pp 601 – 660.

was military assistance, not a reconquest of the island. Nennius wrote that *"Vortigern then reigned in Britain. In his time, the natives had cause of dread, not only from the inroads of the Scots and Picts, but also from the Romans, and their apprehensions of Ambrosius."* The fear of the re-imposition of Roman taxation also appears to underlie the pronounced anti-Roman sentiment in Geoffrey's 'Historia Regum Britanniae', where Arthur's most important campaign is waged against a Roman Emperor whose officials have tried to collect the tribute due by Britain to Rome. But more of these matters later.

The reconciliation of the Armorican Bretons to Rome, after 453, is illustrated by their increasing participation in the affairs of the church. In 463 a Council of Bishops from northern Gaul was held at Vannes, in the south of Brittany, and no previous church Council had been held in Brittany itself. Indeed, only in 461 did a Breton bishop appear at such a Council for the first time, when Mansuetas attended the Council at Tours.

2.7   The Early Anglo-Saxon Settlers

The Anglo-Saxon immigration into Britain of the early 5th century seems to have been a peaceful process. It is particularly striking that some of the earliest settlements were located in the Upper Thames Valley, in places like Abingdon, Dorchester-on-Thames and Long Wittenham. If they arrived by sea, the ships that brought the settlers to these locations would have sailed (or more probably rowed) past London, and under London Bridge, which had existed since c. AD 55. They would have taken the flood tide over the ford that carried Watling Street across the Thames at Thorney Island, and under the Roman bridge at Staines. The migrants would have eventually reached Dorchester-on-Thames, which had been the headquarters of a Roman consular governor, and which became the first capital of Wessex (before the seat of government was moved to Winchester). Here, the immigrants formed a relatively cohesive community, which eventually became known as the Gewisse. Such a journey up the river would only have been possible either in a time of peace, or by force of arms in a time of conflict, and even if the Germans arrived overland, eg from Kent, the same considerations apply.

There has been much speculation as to what the Saxons were doing in the Upper Thames Valley, and it is often suggested that the early settlers were mercenaries, based on the evidence of some military objects found there, and the fact that one of the graves excavated near Dorchester appeared to contain a man in military uniform. Some have suggested that this may reflect a resurrection of tribal conflicts in an area that had historically marked the borders of three tribes, the Belgic Catuvellauni and Atrebates and the Celtic Dubonni of Gloucestershire. And certainly it is hard to imagine that the Saxons were stationed in the Upper Thames Valley in response to any external threat. Mercenaries may have been required in places like York and Richborough, but the threat of a Pictish invasion was slight in Dorchester or Abingdon.

The alternative explanation is simply that these migrants were not primarily mercenaries, although they may have included fighting men. Perhaps they were simply traders or farmers, possibly people from the Scheldt Estuary who were displaced when the Emperor Julian allowed the Franks to occupy Toxandria in 358 (the ancient trading connections between the area of Bruges and London are underlined by the former name of the Scheldt River – the Tamesis).

But from about 420, it appears that new Germanic migrants started to buy their passage to England, where agricultural land was known to be freely available. They arrived in whole families, probably sailing across the Channel at the shortest crossing points in the Straits of Dover and following the east coast northwards. Arriving in small groups and settling in communities of between 4 and 20 individuals, the migrants made their way inland on the waterways of the Ouse, the Trent, the Witham, and the Nene. They often settled near what had previously been Roman towns, but whether or not they mingled with the indigenous population, or whether the Roman towns had already been abandoned, is unclear from the archaeological record. There are very few sites that clearly demonstrate an unbroken continuity of occupation from the end of the Roman to the beginning of the Anglo-Saxon period, but establishing accurate dates for artefacts of the 5th century is notoriously difficult.

These settlements may even have been encouraged by the British authorities, such as they were, because the farmers were occupying relatively deserted lands in areas that had been vulnerable to the

The Age of Despair

predations of the Picts and Scots. The east coast of England was penetrated by several large rivers and marshes, which effectively divided it into a series of peninsulas and islands, forming a coast-line very different to that of today. These rivers had served as highways for Pictish and Saxon pirates to attack inland towns, reaching far into the interior to find high value targets. And they hampered the organisation of coastal defences, since road journeys north and south often involved long detours inland. The settlement of Germanic farmers in the river valleys would therefore have served the useful purpose of establishing a front-line of defence against such raiders.

So, if the British authorities had had any choice in the matter of where 'the Saxons' settled, they would probably have wanted them to choose the peninsulas and river valleys of Northumberland, Lincolnshire, East Anglia and Kent. The German farmers might then have given some protection to the main British centres of population, particularly York, Lincoln, Colchester and London. And these are precisely the areas where the Anglo-Saxon settlements of the mid-5th century were established. However, it would be rash to assume that the distribution of Anglo-Saxon settlements was a result of any strategic thinking on the part of the British. It was almost certainly simply a consequence of the fact that the settlers arrived by the same waterways that had brought the pirates, and the outcome was therefore, from a British perspective, merely fortuitous.

It would be immensely helpful to have more information on the development of the Saxon settlements, but the research has simply not been undertaken. The sites of more than 1,200 Anglo-Saxon cemeteries are known, but only a handful have been subject to a full excavation to modern archaeological standards. There is therefore probably an enormous amount of information buried in the ground, that would help to explain the Anglo-Saxon immigration, but only a tiny fraction of this has been recovered. Moreover, research of this kind is necessarily painstaking and slow, and it can take decades to evaluate a large site even after it has been excavated; so even where research has started, in many cases no conclusions have yet been published.

Because this period is so comparatively unresearched, archaeologists have not yet been able to create a chronological framework for the dating of early Anglo-Saxon ceramics, so for example pottery finds may be classified simply as 'Early Saxon '(450 – 650) or 'Middle Saxon' (650 – 850), which is unhelpful to anyone trying to understand the sequence of events between 420 and 600.

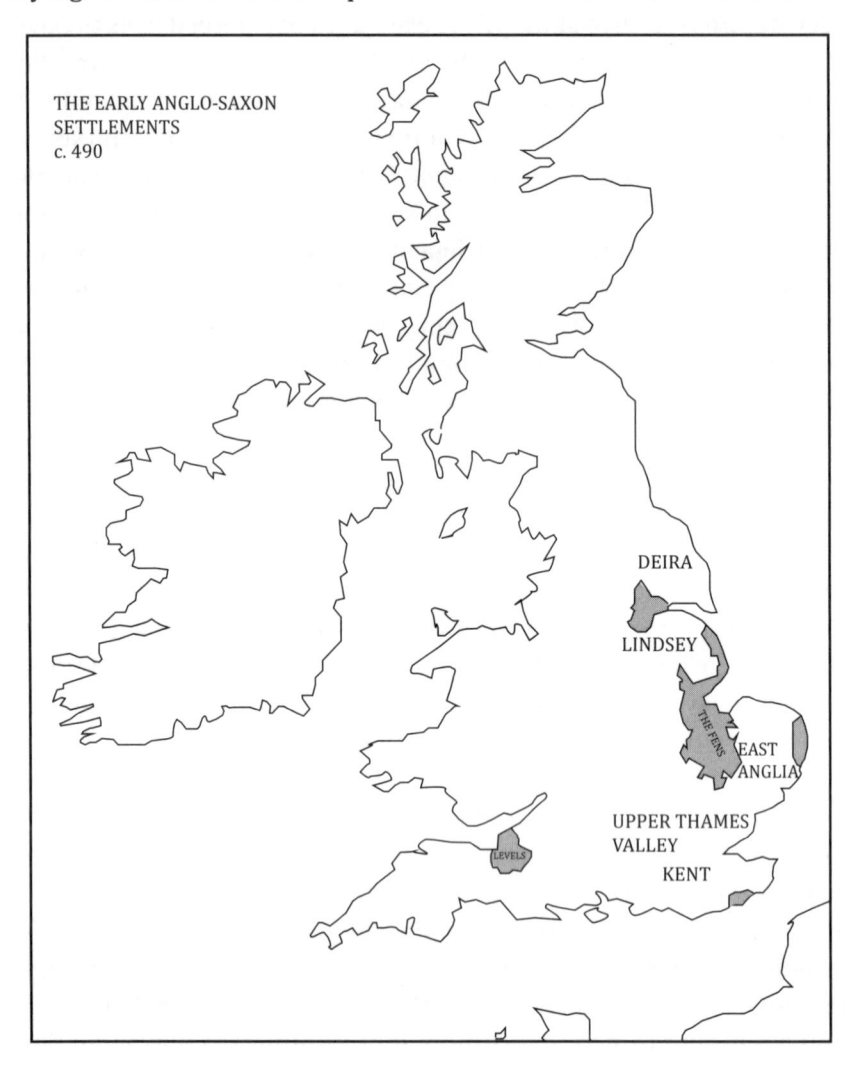

THE EARLY ANGLO-SAXON SETTLEMENTS c. 490

DEIRA
LINDSEY
THE FENS
EAST ANGLIA
UPPER THAMES VALLEY
KENT
LEVELS

By 490, there were 'Anglo-Saxon' settlements in all the peninsulas of eastern England, in addition to the original 4th century settlements in the Upper Thames Valley.

However, from the evidence available, it seems that the earliest 5th century settlements of Anglo-Saxons (in the period c.420 to c.450), took place in East Anglia. The Saxon settlement at Mucking on the north side of the Thames Estuary, developed on a site that had earlier been occupied by the Romans, and comprised about 90 people. At West Stow in what is now Suffolk, a village dating from c.420 developed to comprise 69 houses and 7 communal halls. A large cemetery at Spong Hill, near the river Wensum, in Norfolk contains at least 2,384 5th and 6th century cremations (ashes in cremation urns decorated with Germanic symbols – including the swastika symbol later misappropriated by the Nazis). From Spong Hill, the Wensum flows eastwards towards the inland port of Norwich, 16 miles away, which may have been where the Saxons arrived.

Elsewhere, the area south of the Humber is called Lindsey, after the Roman town of Lincoln ('Lindum Colonia'), which was the main town in the region. Small quantities of late 4th century Germanic metalwork (buckles and brooches) testify to the presence in the area of German mercenaries in the Roman army, but the evidence from cemeteries suggests that there was no substantial Anglo-Saxon settlement before the middle of the 5th century. By then, Lincoln had fallen into disrepair, and it may have been partly or wholly abandoned by the 430s. The Anglo-Saxons started to colonise the area some time thereafter, as evidenced by the Anglo-Saxon cemetery at Cleatham in northern Lincolnshire and the cemetery at Loveden Hill. North of the Humber there were settlements of Angles at West Heslerton in North Yorkshire from about 475 onwards, and therefore the colonisation here appears to have been slightly later than the settlements to the south of the river.

The early to mid-5th century Anglo-Saxon penetration into England, other than in the older colony of the Upper Thames Valley, does not appear to have been particularly deep. The main settlements were concentrated in the peninsulas of Norfolk and Essex, and even where they had pressed inland, up river valleys, the immigrants had not penetrated very far from the coasts.

Eventually some 35 tribes of Germanic immigrants became established in England (according to the 'Tribal Hidage', an Anglo-Saxon record compiled sometime between the 7th and 9th centuries). And these coalesced into half-a-dozen kingdoms by the end of the

6th century. But at the end of the 5th century it is probably more realistic to think of the settlers as a disparate, and not very numerous, collection of warbands and families, from widely different coastal regions of the North Sea, spread along a series of east coast enclaves. The result was more of a 'Balkans' type of political landscape that one where the 'British' and 'Anglo-Saxon' territories were clearly defined polities

2.8   Vortigern

Procopius of Caesarea (c.500 – 565) tells us that, after the Romans departed from Britain, the island was ruled by unnamed 'tyrants'. One of these seems to have been Coel Hen ('Old King Cole', of nursery rhyme fame), who may have ruled in Strathclyde and possibly northern England from c.412 to c.420. And he was followed by a Ceretic, who was accused by St Patrick of mounting raids into Ireland. But the first recorded ruler of lowlands England after the withdrawal of the Roman officials was Vortigern (*"the very thin",* according to a Welsh triad).[31] Conceivably he was the direct successor to Constantine III and his officials, but equally possibly he was a successor to several other 'tyrants' whose names are no longer known.

Vortigern is mentioned by Gildas, Bede, Nennius etc. as the British king at the time of the first major Saxon military immigration, in the 440s. For example, Nennius records that *"Vortigern reigned in Britain when Theodosius and Valentinian were consuls, and in the fourth year of his reign the Saxons came to Britain".* Theodosius was Eastern Roman Emperor from 408 to 450, and Valentinian was Western Roman Emperor from 425 to 455. In another passage, Nennius tells us that the Saxons came to Britain *"When Gratian Aequantius was consul at Rome, because then the whole world was governed by the Roman consuls, the Saxons were received by Vortigern in the year of our Lord four hundred and forty-seven."* Linking these two texts together, we might conclude that Vortigern came to the throne in the period 425 - 450, which is within the reigns of both the Emperors that Nennius names. There was no Roman Consul called Gratian in the relevant period, nor even a prefect of Gaul of that name, so this reference has caused much confusion.

---

31 Rachel Bromwich, 'The Welsh Triads', Triad 51.

Nennius also tells us that Vortigern was reproached for his sins by St Germanus, who, as we have seen, visited Britain in 429 and who probably died in 448. If St Germanus met Vortigern in 429, and if Vortigern was then already a king, he must have been crowned in the 420s at latest, so several authors ascribe a date of 425 to his accession. This date is supported by yet another statement in Nennius, *"Also from Stilicho to Valentinian, son of Placida, and the reign of Vortigern, are twenty-eight years."* Valentian III became the Western Roman Emperor in 425 and Stilicho became a Roman Consul in 400. We should not be too surprised by the inconsistencies in Nennius, because his book is a compilation of work from earlier sources, and the best we can really say is that it appears that Vortigern came to the throne in c.425.

Vortigern became infamous, and stands accused of a number of crimes, of which the most serious in the eyes of Germanus would have been Pelagianism. The British however most resented the fact (as narrated by Nennius) that one of his several wives was a daughter of a 'Saxon' called Hengist, and Vortigern was therefore a sort of traitor. It is further alleged that he had a son by one of his own daughters (who is not named by Nennius), and this son, Faustus, appears to have become the historical Bishop of Riez, in the south of France.

But Vortigern's name appears on the Pillar of Eliseg, a stone monument in Denbighshire, as an honoured ancestor of Cyngen ap Cadell (d. 855), King of Powys, so his reputation has not always been as bad as it now is.[32] It was probably also Vortigern who was eulogised as a saint in a Breton hagiography, the 'Vita Sancti Gurthierni', so some consider that the allegation of incest was simply a smear put about by his enemies. But if the story is true, and if he had a son called Faustus who really did become the Faustus of Riez, this is very useful information, because the dates of Faustus of Riez can be reasonably accurately estimated. And that would allow us to calculate some approximate dates for Vortigern – as I have done in Appendix 2.

On the basis of the chronology set out in that Appendix, Vortigern would have been about 50 in 425 and in his late 60s in 443, so it is tempting to assume that he might have become king earlier. Given that few people lived into old-age, and that weak leaders tended to

---

32 The Pillar also refers to a Britu, son of Vortigern, whose name does not appear in Nennius.

be deposed, we might generally imagine that the leaders of the post-Roman world would have come to power in the prime of their lives. And indeed there would be no reason, based on my chronology, why Vortigern could not have taken the reins of office immediately after the departure of the Roman officials in 410.

What seems clear is that Vortigern was a Celtic Briton, either from the north of England or from Brittania Prima in the west. The Welsh Triads suggest that he came originally from the north, but Nennius gives him a long pedigree stretching back to an alleged founder of the city of Gloucester. The idea that he had 'Celtic' roots would help to explain both the fact that his memory was recorded in Wales, and also his apparent antipathy for Ambrosius Aurelianus and the Romans. However, as we shall see, the 'vor' element of his name appears to be Belgic, so his ethnic origins are rather obscure.

What is also unclear is how much of England Vortigern actually ruled, and it is quite possible that he had effective control only over the southern counties. The eastern coasts were being colonised by Angles, in Lindsey and East Anglia, and the north of the country was infested by invading Picts and Scots, so it seems unlikely that Vortigern's writ ran much north of Staffordshire-Derbyshire-Nottinghamshire. Some light on this question would be shed by the 'Confession of St Patrick', if only we knew where the town of his birth was.

St Patrick lived in the 5th century, and was therefore a witness to, and indeed a victim of, the troubles of the times. His father was Calpornius, a deacon, and his grandfather was Potitus, a priest, who lived in a small villa near a place which Patrick called 'Bannavem Taburniae'. The location of this is uncertain, but its name must derive from the Latin 'taburna' meaning a shop, inn or tavern, and therefore we may suppose that it was located on a Roman road. Patrick was captured by Irish raiders near this place, when he was about 16, and taken into slavery in northern Ireland *"along with thousands of others"*.[33] According to the 'Annals of Ulster', he arrived in Ireland in 432, and died in 493, but these dates may not be reliable. It is possible that Bannavem Taburniae was the Roman fortified town of Bennaventa, which was situated on Watling Street in Northamptonshire. And if this was the case, we would have to conclude that even the English Midlands were not secure in the early 430s.

---
33 St Patrick's 'Confessio'

However, later tradition locates St Patrick's place of origin much further north, in Dumbarton. The gloss on Fiacc's Hymn on St Patrick says that *"Patrick and his father, Calpurn, Concess his mother.... and his five sisters...his brother, the deacon Sannan, all went from Ail Cluade (Dumbarton.) over the Ictian Sea[34] southward to the Britons of Armorica, that is to say, to the Letavian Britons, for there were relations of theirs there at the time."* A similar account also appears in Colgan's 'Trias Thaumaterga'.

Vortigern is named in only two of the surviving manuscripts of Gildas, and in the others he is referred to only as 'the proud usurper' or 'the unlucky usurper'. Gildas certainly does not describe him as a king, but then he would have regarded Vortigern as a usurper because he came to power without the blessing of the Roman Emperor. Moreover, his use of the term 'proud usurper' was clearly a satirical reference to the meaning of his name: Vortigern probably meant something like 'high king', as discussed below, and Gildas was mocking him. Bede names him as Vertigernus, probably on the basis of a lost manuscript of Gildas or another early Celtic source.

There does not seem to be any toponymic evidence of his existence to help us, but that may simply mean that he was an unpopular leader, or that any such evidence was subsequently obliterated by the Anglo-Saxons. Nevertheless, I think that the literary sources are sufficient proof that he existed, even if they are frustratingly short on detail about his life. And we can, perhaps, discern a little of his ethnic background by examining his name.

'Vortigern' is the Latin version of a name that is traditionally rendered as 'Guorthigern' in Breton or 'Gwythern' in Welsh, and the Latin name is clearly much closer to the Breton version. In the two manuscripts of Gildas that name him, he is referred to as 'Gurthrigern' (in Mommsens's MS X manuscript, in the library at Cambridge University) and 'Uortigerno' (in MS A, in Avranches). It seems improbable that the apparently Breton style of the name arose simply because the various manuscripts of Nennius were copied in Normandy or Brittany, but it also seems unlikely that Guorthigern came from Gaul. I suspect that the name came from a common Gaulish/Belgic root, and that there was no causal relationship between the Breton language and the British name. The 'vor' prefix

---

34 *the Sea of Ictis – ie the English Channel.*

appears to have been quite common, because we are told that one of Vortigern's sons was called Vortimer, and Gildas berates the 'King' of Dyfed in his own day, a Vortipore.

The same prefix occurs in Roman place names, for example Vorgium, which was the name of Carhaix in Brittany (a town which plays a prominent part in the Arthurian legends).[35] Carhaix was a civitas of some importance, possibly the capital city of the Osismes tribe in western Brittany, and situated at the junction of seven roads. It is possible that the name of the town is related to those of the towns of Vergium in Spain, Vergoanum in the Lérin Islands and Vorges in the Aisne Department, suggesting a Continental Celtic origin.

Some have suggested that the 'vor' element derives from a Gaulish word 'Worrike', meaning willow, but this seems scarcely credible. A more probable solution is that the 'vor' element indicated an exalted status, similar to the 'fore' element in the English word 'foreman' (which I suspect is of proto-Germanic origin – the word being 'voorman' in Dutch, and 'vormann' in German). The Breton equivalent 'guor' appears to have no known meaning in Breton or Welsh, and there are no towns in Brittany that have names which begin with 'guor', so a Brythonic origin seems implausible.

'Tigern' (tighearn, tighearna, tigernus in Old British etc) was a word in widespread use in the Celtic world, meaning lord or master.[36] So whether the name was a personal name or a title that he adopted upon his accession to power, 'Vortigern' probably meant something like 'Great King', 'High King' or 'Overlord'. This could either have been his original personal name, indicating that he came from a family of hereditary rulers, or it could have been a title adopted by Vortigern on his accession to power, but either way it seems fairly clear that the name belonged to a Celtic inhabitant of the 'land of cal'.

In summary, the fact that we know anything at all about Vortigern suggests that he was a 'King' of unusual significance: he possibly reunited the shattered and dislocated authorities of lowlands England after the relative anarchy of the post-Roman period. His misfortune, in terms of his reputation, was to have been the British

---

35 The name of the town was Vorgium according to the Peutinger Table, but Vorganium according to Ptolemy.
36 Alexander MacBain, 'An Etymological Dictionary of the Gaelic Language' (1896).

'high king' when the country suffered a series of set-backs as a result of the raids of the Picts and the Saxons, to which he appears to have had no effective answer, and a low-point of his career seems to have been reached in 441 or 442.

2.9   The Raid of 441/442 and the Second Wave of Emigration

If Vortigern was the British King in 429, when Germanus came to Britain, it is probable that he held that position when the country was subject to a massive attack by 'Saxons' in 441 or 442. We know about this event from a brief statement in both surviving editions of the Chronica Gallica (of 452 and 511). The edition of 452 says (of the year 442) *"Britain, which until this time had suffered various ills and reverses, fell under the power of the Saxons."* And the edition of 511 says *"AD 441; Britain, relinquished by the Romans, fell to the power of the Saxons".*

The date of this conflict is several years earlier than the dates of the arrival of the Anglo-Saxon warlords given by the Anglo-Saxon Chronicle (447), Bede (449) and Nennius (449) so this has caused much debate. Some scholars have pointed out that dates in the Chronica Gallica for years before 444 are often inaccurate (particularly in the edition of 452), and others have suggested that the Chroniclers made a systematic mistake in the reckoning of regnal years, which means we need to add 4 years to their dates.

However I think that the simplest explanation for the discrepancy is that the literary sources are describing two separate events. The date of 441/442 must be fairly reliable, because the event was first reported only 10 years later. But, on the archaeological evidence available, whatever happened could not have amounted to a conquest of the whole island – evidence of Anglo-Saxon occupation remains scant until the 470s. More likely, a large-scale raid was mounted, which resulted in a substantial loss of life and property but not the permanent seizure of territory. As for the location, the raid must have taken place in an area that was conspicuous to commentators on the Continent, which suggests it did not happen in the wilds of East Anglia or Lincolnshire. The most plausible candidate target is of course the Thames, and specifically London, which was by then half-abandoned in any case.

The Duke and the Decoy

THE MORBIHAN

Map labels: Oust, Ploermel, Aff, Saint Marcel, River Vilaine, Elven, Arz, Redon, Guérande

Many of those in the second wave of British emigrants settled in the fertile valleys of the Morbihan, in south-eastern Brittany.

However, if there was a separate raid in 441/2, it is curious that this is not reported in the early British literary sources. I suspect that the events of the 440s had simply become blurred into one episode, in the mind of Gildas, who was writing a century later. If I am correct in my belief that Gildas was a Celt, and therefore possibly not totally familiar with the history of the Belgic population in the front line against the Anglo-Saxons, this too would help to explain the omission in his account. But it is notable that Gildas also seems to have had an Anglo-Saxon source (because for example he tells of the first mercenaries arriving in *"three cyuls, as they call them, that*

The Age of Despair

is in their ships of war"), and evidently he did not learn of a raid of 441/442 from this source either. A possible explanation here is that the mercenaries whose arrival he reports were of a different tribal origin to the raiders of 441/2, and we will consider this shortly. Bede (writing in the early 8th century) and Nennius (writing in the first half of the 9th) can be excused for failing to precisely record all of the details of what Bede called 'the Anglo-Saxon adventus' in a strictly chronological order.

It is possible that corroboration of the fact of a raid in 441/442 is to be found in Breton tradition, because, according to Nicolas Travers [37] a large group of Britons arrived in Brittany and settled around Guérande and the Vannetais in 441. However, we cannot be certain that this tradition was not merely an extrapolation from the assertion in the Chronica Gallica. If we assume that Travers reflects an independent source of information, we may surmise that the Britons were probably fleeing from a military disaster in England, which would corroborate the date of the 'conquest' provided by the Chronica of 511. As we shall see, there is archaeological evidence of a migration of people from south-eastern England to Brittany, in the form of a cemetery in what is now called Saint-Marcel, in the Morbihan. This dates from the late 4th century until the end of the 5th century, and tends to corroborate that there was a second wave of migration in the mid-5th century (the first being the deployment of the British legions in Gaul on the orders of Maximus, in the 4th century).

The displaced Britons are very likely to have been farmers, and the archaeological evidence from Saint-Marcel shows that they came from the south-east of England. It appears that they chose the valleys of the Arz, the Oust and the Aff in the Morbihan region to settle in (Saint-Marcel is close to the Oust) and no doubt they did so because the land was fertile and the soil suitable for farming.

2.10   Vortigern's End

Vortigern may well have been the British King at the time of the raid of 441/442, but he was probably not a field commander. If the

---
37 'Histoire civile, politique, et religieuse de la ville et du compté de Nantes' (1836), p.43.

chronology suggested in Appendix 2 is correct, he would have been about 65 in 441, and therefore probably too old to have played a very active role in a battle at that time. In my view, it is more likely that he was a late participant in the second wave of emigration, and that he took refuge in Guernsey in the early 450s, on his way to Brittany.

Nennius tells us that he went to 'Guunessi' or 'Gueneri' (depending on the manuscript), and he may have stayed there for a time, uncertain what kind of welcome he could expect from the rulers of Brittany. Nennius further writes that Vortigern built a city called 'Cair Guorthegern' at Guunessi, which was one of the 33 cities of Britain. According to Nennius, this was a town on the River Towy in Wales, which flows from Llyn Brianne to Carmarthen, but this would be inconsistent with the evidence of Vortigern's hagiography.

The 'Life of St Gurthierni', written in the 12th century, claims that Vortigern sailed from the River Tamar and *"brought the boat to land at a certain island"*, where he lived for a period of time. *"After this, an angel came to him and said go forth to the other promised place which is called Anaurot....The angel of the Lord committed to him that whole region of Brittany in order that the whole domain of St Gurthiern, served Anaurot, because that city was chosen by God."* The Vita tells us that Vortigern was buried on the island of Groe (assumed to be the Île de Groix), so I now think that Anaurot was Auray. Auray is called 'An Alre' in Breton, meaning 'at the hall (or court) of the king' – where 'al' is derived from the Latin 'aula'. So I think that Anaurot was a corruption of 'An-aula-roi'.[38]

The Welsh claim that Vortigern ended his days in Wales, once more based on a text in Nennius, which in turn is based on the 'Life of St Germanus'. Nennius wrote: *"Again Vortigern ignominiously flew from St. Germanus to the kingdom of the Dimetae, where, on the river Towy, he built a castle, which he named Cair Guothergirn. The saint, as usual, followed him there, and with his clergy fasted and prayed to the Lord three days, and as many nights. On the third night, at the third hour, fire fell suddenly from heaven, and totally burned the castle. Vortigern, the daughter of Hengist, his other wives, and all the inhabitants, both men and women, miserably perished: such was the end of this unhappy king, as we find written in the life of St. Germanus."*

---

38 However, Bernard Merdrignac believes that Anaurot was Quimperlé – see his 'D'une Bretagne à l'autre' (2012), p.93.

The 'Life of St Germanus' says that Vortigern locked himself in his castle at Caer Beris in Gwertheyrnion for forty days and forty nights while St Germanus prayed that he might return to the true religion (ie to abandon Pelagianism). As we saw in section 2.4, St Germanus made a visit to Brittany in c.447 to broker a peace treaty between the Bretons and some Alans who had been sent by Aëtius to quash the Breton revolt. And it is tempting to think that this journey may have been the 'second visit to Britain' reported by Constantius – confusing the island with the peninsula would have been a mistake easily made.

On this second mission, St Germanus met a British *"chief of that region"* (per Bede) called Elafius, and cured his son by a miracle, which so impressed the population that they gave up Pelagianism. However, it seems that he did not meet Vortigern, which may indicate that his visit was not to Britain. As we will see in the next Chapter, Vortigern is alleged to have invited some 'Germans' to Britain as mercenaries in 447 – 449, so we can presume that he was not yet in Brittany at this time.

The decision to invite the mercenaries to Britain backfired, and Gildas blamed this mistake on Vortigern and his counselors. Gildas was almost certainly not alone in holding this opinion, and there seems no doubt at all that Vortigern became very unpopular in Britain as a result of his failure to deal with the external threats, and indeed because of his alleged relationship with a 'Saxon' girl.

According to Nennius, Vortigern abdicated and handed over the reigns of power in Britain to his son Vortimer, whose exploits we will consider in the next chapter, but he attempted to take back the throne after Vortimer was killed in battle. We are left to presume that Ambrosius was also waiting in the wings during the brief reign of Vortimer, and since there is no suggestion that Ambrosius ever challenged Vortimer for power, I think it is entirely possible that Ambrosius remained in exile in Brittany throughout Vortimer's reign. But when Vortimer died, Ambrosius was in no mood to allow Vortigern to return to power, and very clearly prevented him from doing so. Whether Vortigern died in a house fire, and if so, whether that fire was started deliberately, are probably questions to which we will never know the answers. But if his body was buried on the Île de Groix, it seems more likely that he died of natural causes.

Chapter 3
The Anglo-Saxon War

3.1   The Arrival of the 'Anglo-Saxon' Mercenaries

We have noted that there had been Saxon settlements in the Upper Thames Valley since the later years of the 4th century, and there was a migration of peasant farmers into the river valleys of eastern England during the early 5th century. There had also been piratical raids on Britain, some on a very large scale, in 409 and 441. But in the middle of the century, there was a further immigration of 'Saxons' of a very different kind, because mercenaries were deployed in East Kent, possibly to help protect the mouth of the Thames Estuary. We are given to understand that they were invited to England by Vortigern to defend the east coast against the Picts. However, in the light of the fact that Britain had suffered periodic raids by Saxon pirates, the mercenaries may equally have been employed to keep out other Saxons, perhaps following the maxim of 'setting a thief to catch a thief'. This explanation would be more credible if the mercenaries were perceived to be not of the same ethnic origin as the pirates, and it seems that this may have been the case. It is likely that they were in fact Danes (or Jutes as they were known at the time), because the area of Kent in which they became established was later identified as Jutish territory.

The early literary sources tell us that Vortigern sent an invitation to these people to fight for the British. As Gildas puts it, the leaders of Britain *"sealed its doom by inviting in among them like wolves into the sheep-fold, the fierce and impious Saxons".* But I cannot help wondering if some of the 'Saxons' arrived more as refugees than as soldiers of fortune. As we saw in 2.5, the empire of the Huns extended to the coast of the Baltic Sea by the 430s, and it is clear that any Germanic tribes along the North Sea coast who were not allied to Attila were in a very perilous position. An offer of employment in Britain may have been a very attractive proposition in the circumstances.

Indeed it is possible that some of the allies of the Huns settled along the North Sea coast at around this time. The Frisian book of laws called the 'Keran fon Hunesgena' (c. 1252) testifies that there was a Frisian tribe called the Hunesgena or Hunsings by the Late Middle Ages. Another Frisian tribe was called the Huntanga, and Bede mentions a tribe in Saxony called the Hunni.[39] Nobody knows whether any of these tribes were descended from the Huns, but it certainly seems possible.

The story told by Gildas is essentially consistent with that of Bede and the Anglo-Saxon Chronicles. They all recount that Vortigern took advice from his councillors on how to deal with the continuing and growing problem of Pictish raids, and that a decision was taken to invite some 'Saxon' warlords to establish a base at a place on the east coast of England, later identified as the Isle of Thanet. Gildas of course was scathing about this decision: *"Then all the councillors, together with that proud usurper Gurthrigern, the British king, were so blinded, that, as a protection to their country, they sealed its doom by inviting in among them (like wolves into the sheep-fold) the fierce and impious Saxons, a race hateful both to God and men, to repel the invasions of the northern nations. Nothing was ever so pernicious to our country, nothing was ever so unlucky! What palpable darkness must have enveloped their minds!"*

Gildas goes on to describe the arrival of the first of Vortigern's merceneries but is unspecific as to location or date: *"They first landed on the eastern side of the island, by the invitation of the unlucky king, and there fixed their sharp talons, apparently to fight in favour of the island, but alas! more truly against it."* Nennius provides a date for the arrival, in the same period as that given by the Anglo-Saxon Chronicle, give or take a couple of years: *"When Gratian Aequantius was consul at Rome, because then the whole world was governed by the Roman consuls, the Saxons were received by Vortigern in the year of our Lord four hundred and forty-seven, and to the year in which we now write, five hundred and forty-seven".* Nennius also supplies us with the location of the first mercenary base camp: *"Vortigern received them as*

---

39 T W Shore 'The Origin of the Anglo-Saxon Race' (1906).

friends, and delivered up to them the island which is in their language called Thanet, and, by the Britons, Ruym."[40]

Bede was the first writer to name the leaders of the mercenaries, as being two brothers called Hengist and Horsa. But since 'hengist' meant stallion and 'horsa' meant horse, in the language of the Anglo-Saxons, even Bede appears to think that this story may be apocryphal. In truth, the names of the individuals do not matter very much, but it is clear that, as a group, the mercenaries were very effective warriors. Even Gildas accepts that the policy of recruiting these heathens to fight against the Picts was initially successful, and we are told that the Saxons won several battles and drove the Picts away, apparently mounting raids on their homelands as far north as the Orkneys.

The relationship between the British and their mercenaries prospered for about 5 years, and the initial band of warriors were soon followed by further reinforcements. As Gildas puts it, *"Their mother-land, finding her first brood thus successful, sends forth a larger company of her wolfish offspring, which sailing over, join themselves to their bastard-born comrades."* Soon, however, the 'Saxons' began to see other opportunities in the land of their paymasters. They dispatched messengers, *"sending back news of their success to their homeland, adding that the country was fertile and the Britons cowardly.'*

The Winchester manuscript of the Anglo-Saxon Chronicle (which is the oldest version), derives partly from Bede, and confirms the story from the Anglo-Saxon perspective:

449 "Here Mauricius and Valentinian succeeded to the kingdom and ruled 7 years. And in their days Hengist and Horsa, invited by Vortigern, king of the Britons, sought out Britain in the landing place which is named Ebba's Creek, at first to help the Britons, but later they fought against them. The king ordered them to fight against the Picts, and they did so and had victory wheresoever they came. They then sent to Angeln and ordered them to send more help, and tell them of the worthlessness of the Britons and of the excellence of the land. They then sent them more help. These men came from three tribes of Germany; from the Old Saxons, from the Angles, from the Jutes. From the Jutes came the Cantware and the Wihtware – that is the tribe that now lives on Wight – and that race in Wessex that they still call the race of Jutes."

At the same time as the Jutes were establishing a foothold in Kent and the Isle of Wight, the older Anglo-Saxon colonies were also

---

40 'Rhium' meant 'promontory' in Latin.

expanding, as more Germanic immigrants arrived in Britain, and the colonists around the Wash started to penetrate deeper into the river valleys. An example of this was their expansion in the Nene Valley, which took place during the mid to late 5th century (although precise dates cannot be determined). Here the immigrants followed the tributary River Ise to its source in what later became known as Rockingham Forest in Northamptonshire. This wild area originally stretched from Stamford in the north to Northampton in the south, covering a large part of north-eastern Northamptonshire. And in the depths of the forest, the Anglo-Saxons settled in a former Roman village, which became Kettering ('the people of Ketter'). Here they were more or less out of sight of the natives living around Towcester (known as 'Lactodurum' to the Romans), Irchester and Water Newton ('Durobrivae'), all former walled Roman towns. Deep in the forest, the settlers were not depriving any natives of agriculturual land, and they must have cleared the terrain to make it workable for themselves.

The map overleaf shows the sites of pagan cemeteries and burials in the Nene Valley, dating from the 5th and 6th centuries, all of which are located just above the floodplain of the river. It will be seen that the interments mark a process of colonisation, that had taken the immigrants up the Nene Valley as far as Northampton and beyond. In this area, the Saxons gained control of the ironstone fields, and were probably able to start their own iron production. And they threatened the British control over Watling Street ('the street of the wealas, or Welsh', in their language).

3.2 The War of c.455 – 457

At first the warlords did not require much land, because they had arrived as mercenaries and not as settlers. The British, under Vortigern, agreed to provide them with food, so they had neither the need or the inclination to take up farming. And they were preoccupied with carrying the war to the Picts, so they did not have the time or resources to expand their territorial interests in Kent. But later, when the British failed to deliver the supplies that the mercenaries wanted (as they alleged) the 'Saxons' took to raiding the surrounding countryside, and gradually more and more of eastern Kent fell under

The Duke and the Decoy

their control. Presumably the British stopped paying the mercenaries, in an attempt to force them to go home, but the mercenaries simply decided to collect payment in a different way. Bede tells us that the Angles now formed an alliance with the Picts, and turned on their former paymasters: *"All of a sudden the Angles made an alliance with the Picts, whom by this time they had driven some distance away, and began to turn their arms against their allies."* This conflict appears to have commenced in c.455.

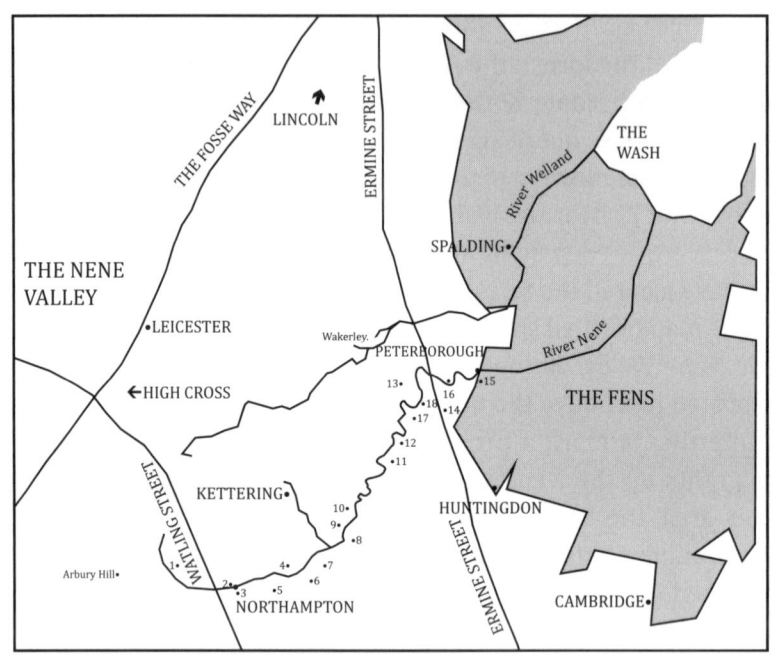

EARLY ANGLO-SAXON BURIAL SITES IN THE NENE VALLEY

1 Nether Hayford	6 Grendon	11 Tansor	16 Castor
2 Cow Meadow	7 Wollaston	12 Warmington	17 Woodstone
3 Hardingstone	8 Addington	13 Nassington	18 Lynchwood
4 Ecton	9 Great Addington	14 Alwalton	
5 Little Houghton	10 Aldwindle	15 Fletton	

The valley of the River Nene, from west of Northampton to Peterborough (where the river entered the Fens), is dotted with early Anglo-Saxon burials. At the head of the valley stands Arbury Hill, the highest hill in Northamptonshire, which is one of the principal sources of the river. The main Roman roads to Lincoln and York (Ermine Street) and to the north-west (Watling Street), cross the river Nene. Once Ermine Street was under Anglo-Saxon control, the main British line of communication from London to Lincoln and York was via Watling Street to High Cross and then along the Fosse Way. The point at which Watling Street crosses the Nene was therefore of vital strategic significance. {Data on burial sites from Ian Meadows 'Nene Valley Survey: Part 1, The Roman and Early Saxon Periods' Northamptonshire County Council (2002)}

The 'Saxons' began to seize land, and to establish camps in former British territory, and it is evident that the resulting settlements in Kent were significantly larger than the earlier settlements north of the Thames, although once again there is a severe shortage of good quality evidence. In 2012, the British Museum reported that there is a *"scarcity of fifth-century Anglo-Saxon material from Kent, especially from well-documented excavations"*, and therefore the excavation of a cemetery at *"Ringlemere has enormous potential to shed more light on the as yet poorly-understood arrival of Germanic settlers in the fifth century and their interaction with the local, Romano-British population"*.

On my chronology, Vortigern would have been about 80 by this time, and was clearly not the man to lead the British in a war. It seems that he abdicated in favour of his son Vortimer, who may have been about 50 years old, probably soon after the arrival of the mercenaries, and as explained in the last Chapter, I believe that he then went into exile, heading for Brittany by way of Guernsey.

Meanwhile the Anglo-Saxons were ravaging Britain. According to Gildas, their predations touched the whole country, and his account is positively biblical:

"For the fire of vengeance, justly kindled by former crimes, spread from sea to sea, fed by the hands of our foes in the east, and did not cease, until, destroying the neighbouring towns and lands, it reached the other side of the island, and dipped its red and savage tongue in the western ocean. In these assaults, therefore, not unlike that of the Assyrian upon Judea, was fulfilled in our case what the prophet describes in words of lamentation; "They have burned with fire the sanctuary; they have polluted on earth the tabernacle of thy name." And again, "O God, the gentiles have come into thine inheritance; thy holy temple have they defiled," &c. So that all the columns were levelled with the ground by the frequent strokes of the battering-ram, all the husbandmen routed, together with their bishops, priests, and people, whilst the sword gleamed, and the flames crackled around them on every side. Lamentable to behold, in the midst of the streets lay the tops of lofty towers, tumbled to the ground, stones of high walls, holy altars, fragments of human bodies, covered with livid clots of coagulated blood, looking as if they had been squeezed together in a press; and with no chance of being buried, save in the ruins of the houses, or in the

ravening bellies of wild beasts and birds; with reverence be it spoken for their blessed souls, if, indeed, there were many found who were carried, at that time, into the high heaven by the holy angels. So entirely had the vintage, once so fine, degenerated and become bitter, that, in the words of the prophet, there was hardly a grape or ear of corn to be seen where the husbandman had turned his back."

But from the Anglo-Saxon reports, it appears more likely that the war was confined to the far south-east of Britain. The Anglo-Saxon Chronicle tells us that, in 455, a battle was fought at Aylesford in Kent, and Horsa was killed in action (Bede reports that a monument to Horsa still stood in east Kent in his day). Hengist then shared power with his son Æsc, and the Anglo-Saxon Chronicle records that they fought against the British at Crayford, in north-west Kent, in 457: *"Here Hengest and Æsc fought against the Britons in the place which is called Crayford, and there killed 4,000 men, and the Britons then abandoned the land of Kent and in great terror fled to the stronghold of London."*

While the dates in the Anglo-Saxon Chronicle for the 5th and 6th centuries are dubious, it is hard to imagine that the authors of the Chronicle would have understated the achievements of Hengist, Horsa and Æsc. If they had driven the British into the Irish Sea, would the scribes not have said so? This passage confirms also that the British still held *"the stronghold of London".* But it is a reasonable deduction that London was exposed to an Anglo-Saxon blockade in the Thames Estuary, and in any case the ports of the eastern Channel (eg Boulogne and Richborough) were now under Saxon or Frankish control, so commerce through the city must have already withered on the vine.

In the end, according to Nennius, Vortimer enjoyed some successes in this war: *"At length Vortimer, the son of Vortigern, valiantly fought against Hengist, Horsa, and his people; drove them to the isle of Thanet, and thrice enclosed them with it, and beset them on the western side. The Saxons now dispatched deputies to Germany to solicit large reinforcements, and an additional number of ships: having obtained these, they fought against the kings and princes of Britain, and sometimes extended their boundaries by victory, and sometimes were conquered and driven back.*

Four times did Vortimer valorously encounter the enemy; the first has been mentioned [Thanet], the second was upon the river Darent [a Kentish tributary of the Thames], the third at the Ford, in their language called Epsford, though in ours Set thirgabail [Aylesford in Kent], there Horsa fell, and Catigern, the son of Vortigern; the fourth battle he fought, was near the stone on the shore of the Gallic sea [possibly Richborough], where the Saxons being defeated, fled to their ships."*

Whether the Saxons were in fact driven out by Vortimer is uncertain, because it is possible that they simply withdrew from England. Some Anglo-Saxons may have returned to northern Germany after the death of Attila in 453, and the destruction of his army by the Gepids at the Battle of Nadao the following year. Under their leader Ardaric, the Gepids appear to have restored peace to the former Hunnish empire, as described by Jordanes in c.551: *"But the Gepidae by their own might won for themselves the territory of the Huns and ruled as victors over the extent of all Dacia, demanding of the Roman Empire nothing more than peace and an annual gift as a pledge of their friendly alliance. This the Emperor freely granted at the time, and to this day that race receives its customary gifts from the Roman Emperor."* All we can say is that there appears to have been a reduction in the level of hostilities in Britain from the late 450s for about 20 years.

Nennius tells us that Vortimer died before his father (of what cause, he does not say), and suggests that Vortigern attempted to resume his reign in his old age, I suppose in the late 450s or early 460s. Nennius recounts that the Saxons offered a truce to the British, and invited Vortigern and his nobles to a feast to seal the peace. There they treacherously massacred the British nobles, leaving Vortigern alive as a puppet king. But I think that this story is based on the assassination of Odoacre, the last independent Western Roman ruler, together with his nobles, at a feast in Ravenna in 493, so I doubt that the tale has anything to do with events in Britain. Nevertheless, it is possible that Vortigern was still alive, in exile, when Vortimer died, and that he made moves to return to Britain with the intention of recovering his throne. If so, he was to be disappointed.

In the 'Life of St Germanus', we are told that the Saxons left Britain and did not immediately return after the death of Horsa, *"for five years they dared not enter the island until the death of Vortimer."*

The Duke and the Decoy

The only battle in Britain recorded in the Anglo-Saxon Chronicle for the years between 457 and 477 was an action in 465, so there certainly appears to have been a lull in the fighting. Nevertheless, the British victory in the war of 455 – 457 was not complete, if we are to believe the Anglo-Saxon Chronicle. Hengist and Æsc were not killed, because the same two chieftains were reported as leading the Saxons a decade later, at a place which has not been identified: *"465; Here Hengist and Æsc fought against the Welsh, near Wipped's Creek, and there killed twelve Welsh chieftains."* And yet again they were in action in 473, when they *"took immense booty"*, and *"the Welsh fled from the English like fire".*[41]

3.3   The Succession

Who was the British commander after Vortimer? The 'Life of St Germanus' tells us that Vortimer lived for five years after the war with the Saxons of Kent, and Nennius tells us that Vortigern (in exile) outlived his son. He wrote: *"After this [the death of Vortimer] the barbarians became firmly incorporated, and were assisted by foreign pagans; for Vortigern was their friend, on account of the daughter of Hengist, whom he so much loved, that no one durst fight against him."* But if Vortigern tried to return to power, Nennius and Geoffrey of Monmouth make it clear that he was quickly overthrown by Ambrosius Aurelianus. Vortigern would have been in his late 80s in the early 460s, on my reckoning, so it seems unlikely, although not impossible, that he still entertained ambitions of this sort.

We therefore have a clear indication that Ambrosius came to power at this time. Bede dates his victories to the reign of the (Eastern) Emperor Zeno (474 – 491), and the apparent time lapse can be explained if we assume that the Saxons started to return to Britain in the early 460s, but that no significant battle occurred until the mid-470s. Either Bede overlooked the supposed battle at Wipped's Creek in 465, or it was not that significant, and the first major confrontation occurred a decade later (the Anglo-Saxon Chronicle reports the next battle as taking place in 473).

---

41 'Welsh' was of course simply the Anglo-Saxon term for any foreigner or slave, the two senses being interchangeable as far as they were concerned.

But we cannot get too obsessed with this detail, because the dates in the Anglo-Saxon Chronicle for this period are simply not that reliable. Taking a broad-brush approach, the chronology just about works – Ambrosius Aurelianus took up the throne of England in the early 460s, after the death of Vortimer and after a brief power struggle with Vortigern, and did not have to fight many battles before the late 470s. He then led the British in a campaign against a new Saxon warlord who was threatening to conquer the country, who we will come to in due course. Firstly let us consider who Ambrosius was.

3.4 Ambrosius Aurelianus

The earliest mention of Ambrosius, occurs in Gildas, when he writes: *"But in the meanwhile, an opportunity happening, when these most cruel robbers were returned home, the poor remnants of our nation (to whom flocked from divers places round about our miserable countrymen as fast as bees to their hives, for fear of an ensuing storm), being strengthened by God, calling upon him with all their hearts, as the poet says, "With their unnumbered vows they burden heaven," that they might not be brought to utter destruction, took arms under the conduct of Ambrosius Aurelianus, a modest man, who of all the Roman nation was then alone in the confusion of this troubled period by chance left alive."*

Bede's account is obviously based on Gildas, and reads as follows: *"When the victorious invaders had scattered and destroyed the native peoples and returned to their own dwellings, the Britons slowly began to take heart and recover their strength, emerging from the dens where they had hidden themselves, and joining in prayer that God might help them to avoid complete extermination. Their leader at this time was Ambrosius Aurelianus, a man of good character and the sole survivor of the Roman race from the catastrophe. Among the slain had been his own parents, who were of royal birth and title. Under his leadership the Britons took up arms, challenged their conquerors to battle, and with God's help inflicted a defeat on them. Thenceforward victory swung first to one side and then to the other, until the battle of Mons Badonicus where the Britons made a considerable slaughter of the*

The Duke and the Decoy

invaders. *This took place about 44 years after their arrival in Britain; but I shall deal with this later."*[42] Gildas, writing in about 540, also tells us that Ambrosius's descendants were contemporaries of his *("and now his progeny in these our days, although shamefully degenerated from the worthiness of their ancestors"),* which is consistent with Ambrosius having been active during the reign of the Emperor Zeno, especially if 'ancestors' is translated as 'grandparents'. Nennius refers to Ambrosius as a young man during the reign of Vortigern, possibly even as a boy to whom Vortigern gave the western parts of his kingdom.

If we assume that Ambrosius lived from c.430 to c.490, consistent with an active military career from the mid 470s, his parents would possibly have been born before the withdrawal of the Roman officials from Britain and it is just possible that his father might have reached an age to hold a military commission at that time. If his father was born in say, 385, he could have been a young cavalry officer in 410. But the chronology does not allow much room for manoeuvre, and I conclude that Ambrosius must have been quite elderly by 493. This is a point of some significance, as we shall see.

The clearest fact known to us, however, is that Ambrosius was a Roman. His parents had worn the purple, and it seems likely that he grew up in a Roman household. But his parents had been killed in the *"same broils"* (Gildas), and according to Geoffrey of Monmouth, Ambrosius had been removed to Brittany for his safety, and placed in the care of his cousin King Budic. Geoffrey tells us (for what it is worth) that Ambrosius was the second son of Constantine, the younger brother of King Audren of Brittany

He then tells us that, after the death of Vortimer, Ambrosius returned from Brittany, where he had been a guest at the court of his cousin Budic or his uncle Audren, to take up the throne, usurping Vortigern. Nennius hardly mentions Ambrosius, other than in a fairy-tale context (which I describe below), and his confusing account suggests that Arthur succeeded directly on from Vortimer as a military commander. But the compilation that is attributed to Nennius contains many bizarre inconsistencies.

Nennius also tells us that, after the death of Vortigern, Ambrosius appointed one of Vortigern's sons, Pascent, to rule part of Wales.

---

42 He never returned to the subject.

The Anglo-Saxon War

This sounds like an astute diplomatic move to reconcile the family of Vortigern to the new regime, with Vortigern's other sons either dead (Catigern and Vortimer) or in a religious retreat (Faustus), Pascent was the only surviving claimant to the throne from that dynasty mentioned by Nennius.

It seems clear that Ambrosius had considerable military skills. He may have been trained at the court of Audren or that of Budic in Brittany, where the Roman military arts were still practised, as Geoffrey implies, but wherever he had studied warcraft, he was certainly no amateur. From the external context, it appears that he reorganised and trained an army in Britain that was able to contain the Anglo-Saxons in their eastern colonies for many years. However, we have little specific information on the battles that he fought. Gildas tells us, laconically, that: *"After this,*[43] *sometimes our countrymen, sometimes the enemy, won the field".* It is possible of course that Ambrosius was the British commander at some of the battles mentioned in the Anglo-Saxon Chronicle, such as the Battle of Mercred's Burn, but the Anglo-Saxons did not name the leaders of their opponents.

According to the Chronicle, Hengist and Æsc were still active in 465, and they fought another battle in 473, at an unnamed location. This too was claimed as an Anglo-Saxon victory *("And the Welsh fled from the English like fire"),* but these are the only two battles listed by the Chronicle in the twenty years from 457 to 477. Whether this was because there were no other battles, or because the Anglo-Saxons lost the others, is a matter of conjecture. I incline to believe Gildas that the course of the conflict swung one way and then the other, but the bigger picture seems to have been that the period was relatively peaceful, with intermittent skirmishes, and the British were able to keep the Anglo-Saxons confined to their eastern colonies. However the reduction of hostilities certainly came to an end in the mid-470s, by which time a more general war broke out, and this time the conflagration was not confined to Kent.

In his campaigns, Ambrosius may have been able to call upon the resources of Brittany. There is no way this can be proved, but Geoffrey of Monmouth wrote of the period that Ambrosius spent in exile in Brittany, and there was certainly a history of military assistance in

---

[43] the rise to power of Ambrosius.

the other direction. It seems to me unlikely that Ambrosius actually commanded the Breton forces, and Geoffrey does not suggest that he fought any battles (as opposed to duels) in Brittany, but Léon Fleuriot speculated that Ambrosius was one and the same person as a certain Riothamus, who commanded 'British' forces in Gaul at the end of the 460s.[44] I think this is most unlikely, and consider Fleuriot's opinions unreliable on several points, but we will come to Riothamus in 4.4.

To summarise his achievements, it appears that Ambrosius restored the British army, improved security and more generally restored social order. Nennius tells us that, after the departure of the Romans, the British *"were in alarm forty years"*, which suggests that the chaos came to an end in the 450s, probably initially under the regime of Vortimer. Moreover, Ambrosius evidently left a significant impression. He was described by Nennius as *"the great king among the Kings of Britain"*, and by Gildas as *"worthy"*, and since few people earned favourable reviews from Gildas, this was high praise indeed. He also left a substantial toponymical footprint, which we will come to shortly.

However his conduct did not always win approval from everyone, because Nennius reports that *"from the reign of Vortigern to the quarrel between Guitolinus[45] and Ambrosius, are twelve years"*. We know nothing more about this quarrel, but assuming that Vortigern abdicated in the early 450s, the disagreement must have arisen in the mid 460s, perhaps at around the time when the Anglo-Saxons claim to have won a victory at Wipped's Creek, in which they slew 12 Welsh chieftains. Was Ambrosius away in Brittany?

In Geoffrey of Monmouth's work, Archbishop Guithelinus of London was the man who appealed to King Audren in Brittany for assistance, and persuaded him to send his younger brother Constantine to become king of the island. He then introduced Constantine to his future wife, and they produced three sons, one of which was Ambrosius. So the Bishop may have had a role as a kind of godfather to Ambrosius, which perhaps made him feel at liberty to criticise any lapses of duty.

---

44 Leon Fleuriot, 'Les origines de la Bretagne: l'émigration' (1980).
45 Archbishop of London, according to Geoffrey of Monmouth.

3.5 The Family of Ambrosius

An early Irish translation of Nennius refers to Ambrosius as *"King of the Franks and the Armorican Bretons"*, and while it is inconceivable that he had any authority over the Franks, this text demonstrates that from very early on there was a tradition that Ambrosius had jurisdiction in Brittany. Geoffrey of Monmouth tells us that he was an exile in Brittany for a period during the reign of Vortigern, and that he returned to Britain at the head of a Breton army. So he seems to have had strong Breton connections, and may even have originated in the peninsula. Perhaps his name can provide us with some clues as to his origins?

The 'Aurelian' name was carried by a number of other figures from the relevant period in history, for example Paul Aurelian, one of the founding saints of Brittany, who was a companion of St Sampson, and who is thought to have died in 575. However this may not be surprising, since the soubriquet 'Aurelian' was applied to many people whose families had acquired Roman citizenship by virtue of the Edict of Caracalla in 212.

One of the most interesting of these other 'Aurelians', for our purpose, is Aurelius Conanus, whom Gildas addresses as one of the five 'tyrant' kings whose sinful lives besmirched the name of Britain. He was apparently the sole survivor of his family: (*"now left alone as a withering tree in the midst of a field"*). Gildas preached to him: *"remember (I beseech thee) the vain and idle fancies of thy parents and brethren, together with the untimely death that befell them in the prime of their youth"*. The kingdoms of the other four tyrants can be identified in Wales, from Welsh sources, but those sources contain no references to Conan's kingdom, so it appears possible that he was a Belgo-Roman. His name also recalls the name of another military commander who was almost certainly a Belgo-Roman – the legendary figure of Conan Meriadoc. It is therefore possible to imagine a family tree stretching from Conan Meriadoc (if he was an historical figure), through Ambrosius Aurelianus, down to Aurelius Conanus. If Breton folklore is to be believed, Ambrosius was a descendant of Conan Meriadoc, and the possible family tree I have described would certainly help to explain the apparent connections of Ambrosius Aurelianus with Brittany. Gildas described Conanus as the *"lion's whelp",* but was clearly no fan of his parents, which suggests that he was the grandson of Ambrosius.

Ambrosius' lineage appears to pass rapidly out of the pages of history, and none of the accounts describes any subsequent leader who appears to be a member of the same family. But that would not be surprising if Conanus was his only surviving grandson.

3.6   Ambrosius in the Legends

Nennius recounted a fairy tale, in which Vortigern was on the point of sacrificing a young boy called Ambrose, the son of a Roman Consul, to enable him to complete a castle that kept collapsing during construction. The boy showed Vortigern and his advisers that there was a spring under the foundations, and the resulting pool of water was the source of their problems. Vortigern then gave the boy *"that city and all the western provinces of Britain"* before going off to Guunessi (or Gueneri). Geoffrey of Monmouth wrote that Vortigern had a number of visions before he left, sitting by the pool that had been drained, which were interpreted as prophesies by Merlin. This is the first passage in which Merlin is introduced into the legends, and in Appendix 2, I explain why I do not think he had an historical role in Arthur's lifetime. Geoffrey dwells on the prophesies in some detail, but since I do not think that any historical value can be attributed to either the story of the 'sacrificial lamb' or the prophesies, I do not propose to spend further time on them.

Chapter 4
Northern Gaul; 450 - 475

4.1   The Invasion of Gaul by the Franks

The Franks were originally a disparate group of Germanic tribes from the area east of the Rhine. The meaning of the name 'Franks' has been much debated by scholars, but without a conclusive result. The question is not really important to us, but we need to note that the Franks are today usually classified into two groups, the Salian Franks ('the salty Franks') who lived near the coast, and the Ripuarian Franks ('the riverbank Franks') who lived further inland. In reality they were members of a number of tribes called variously the Saliens, Chamaves, Bructères, Tenetères, Ampsivariens, Chattuaires, Tubantes and Usipètes, but these distinctions do not greatly matter to us. We should merely note that, given this background, it is not surprising that the Franks spent almost as much time fighting among themselves as fighting together against common enemies.

The origins of the Franks were a mystery even to Gregory of Tours, who wrote a history of them in the 6th century: *"The historians whose works we still have give us all this information about the Franks, but they never record the names of their kings. It is commonly said that the Franks came originally from Pannonia and first colonised the banks of the Rhine. Then they crossed the river, marched through Thuringia, and set up in each country district and each city long-haired kings chosen from the foremost and most noble family of their race."*

Nevertheless, they were closely connected to the other Germanic tribes of northern Europe, and crucially for the Arthurian period, they were for the most part allies of the Saxons. The Salian Franks were next-door-neighbours to the Frisians, and these two peoples enjoyed close relationships throughout the period covered by this book. Indeed, by the end of this period, the Anglo-Saxon High King of

England, in Kent, was married to a Frankish princess. And Frankish objects appear in the archaeological record of East Anglia and Kent for the 5th and 6th centuries, so we know that there were substantial cultural exchanges between the Anglo-Saxons and the Franks. The histories of events to the north and south of the Channel also bear a striking similarity to each other, with the Germanic Saxons and Franks pushing westwards into the territory of the Romans in the central areas, so events of this period on one side of the Channel are often mirrored in those on the other.

The Franks had become allies of the Romans in Gallia Belgica by the 4th century, and had been settled as confederates on the Rhine, where they were left literally 'holding the fort' when Stilicho withdrew the legions from that frontier to defend Italy. In the ensuing mass invasion of Gaul in 406, the Salian Franks had been brushed aside, but since the restoration of Roman rule in northern Gaul, some of them had resumed their status as allies of the Romans. However, in 444, they had crossed the Charbonnière Forest and seized the cities of Amiens (the former capital city of the Ambiani), Tournai and Cambrai from the Romans. Aëtius, the Magister Militum of Gaul, was powerless to prevent this invasion, but when the Franks sent an army across the Somme to mount an attack on Soissons in 447, he defeated them. Both sides then appear to have accepted the status quo, and the Salian Franks renewed their pledges of loyalty, in return for Roman acceptance of their territorial gains.

4.2   Merovech

In 449, according to French tradition, a king called Merovech succeeded to the throne of the Salian Franks, but almost the only thing we know about this individual is that he agreed to join the coalition assembled by Aëtius to confront Attila the Hun, at the Battle of the Catalaunian Plains in 451 (see 2.5). Despite the lack of historical evidence, however, Merovech is celebrated in French history as the founder of the Merovingian dynasty of kings, which ruled northern France, and eventually most of Gaul, throughout the remainder of the period covered by this book.

4.3 Childeric

Merovech was succeeded by his son Childeric I in c.458. Childeric's private life was described by Gregory of Tours as *"one long debauch"*, but he was an effective war-leader and a cunning diplomat, who extended and consolidated the Frankish Empire in northern Gaul. In the immediate vicinity of his kingdom in Gallia Belgica, his most important competitors for power were the remains of the Roman province and the Saxon colonies along the Channel coast. The history of the reign of Merovech was essentially concerned with his relationships with these two powers, which he skillfully played off against each other. And from a British perspective, his relationship with the Saxons in Gaul is of particular interest.

In 454, Aegidius had succeeded his father Aëtius, and had been appointed the new Magister Militum in Gaul, although the territory under his command was an increasingly isolated outpost. The northern 'province' was essentially cut off from Gallia Narbonensis, the province along the south coast of France, by the territory of the Burgundians (in the upper Rhône Valley) and the expanding kingdom of the Visigoths in Aquitaine. So for example, when Aegidius wanted to send envoys to the Vandal King Geiseric in North Africa in 465, he had to do so *"by the Atlantic sea route"*.[46] Childeric's Salian Franks effectively controlled the territory north-east of a system of Roman defences that stretched from Cologne to Bavay. His capital is presumed to have been at Tournai, in what is now Belgium, because that is where he was buried, but we have no proof that Tournai was the centre of his government. To the south, the Ripuarian Franks controlled what had been Gallia Belgica I, with its capital at Trier. The city itself had been overrun at least four times by the Franks in the early 5th century, and, as a consequence, the capital of the Roman province in Gaul had been transferred from Trier to Arles (at some time between 395 and 418). But when Childeric came to power Trier was still nominally in Roman hands, and was to remain so for another 20 years, albeit governed by Romanised Franks.

To their south-west, the area under the control of Aegidius was essentially the Second, Third and Fourth Lyonnais, and he made his capital at Soissons, in the extreme north-east of this territory (in fact just over the border in Belgica Secunda).

---

46 Hydatius, 'Episcopi Chronicon'.

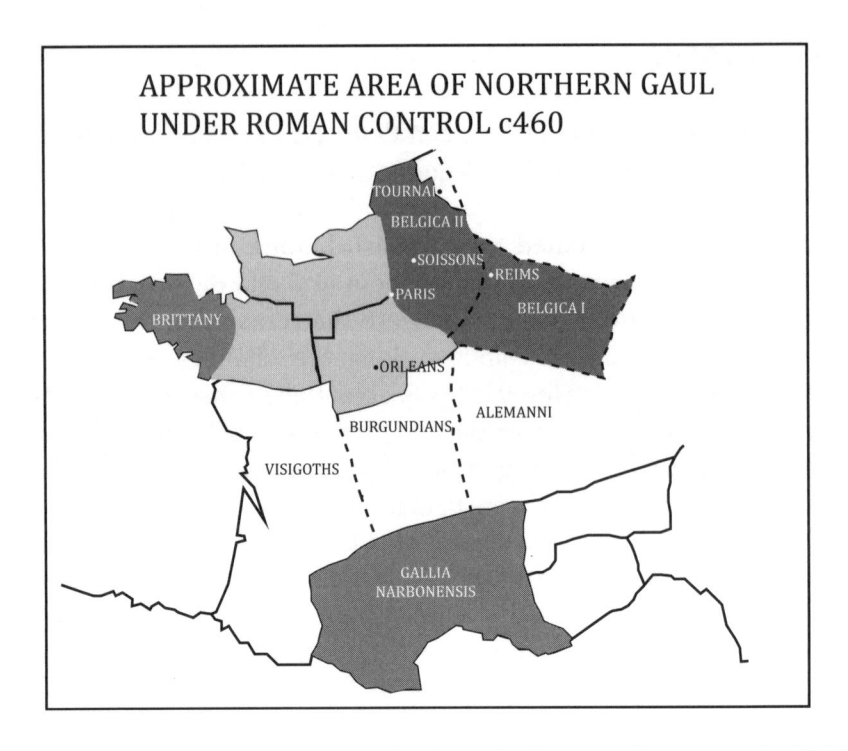

APPROXIMATE AREA OF NORTHERN GAUL UNDER ROMAN CONTROL c460

The kingdom of Aegidius comprised essentially the Second Lyonnais, the Third Lyonnais east of the Vilaine and the Fourth Lyonnais (Lugdunensis Sensona), although he had nominal control of Brittany, Belgica I and the southern part of Belgica II. He was increasingly dependent on the Franks for his authority in Belgica, entirely so north of the Somme. The Romans in northern Gaul were cut off from their compatriots in the disintegrating southern province by a phalanx of Germans.

Aegidius remained a loyal servant of Rome through the short reign of the Emperor Avitus, to whom he owed his appointment as Magister Militum, and through that of his successor Majorian. Indeed he expanded his province southwards by taking Lyon from the Burgundians in 458. But when in 461 Majorian was murdered by Ricimer, the Magister Militum in Rome, Aegidius refused to recognise the authority of his successor. He remained in Soissons, where he effectively established an autonomous 'kingdom'.

The hold of the Empire over most of Gaul had therefore effectively disappeared, and King Euric of the Visigoths took the opportunity to establish a de facto independent state in Aquitaine. He was territorially ambitious, and hoping to extend his kingdom into the Fourth Lyonnais, he took an army north to seize Orléans in

463. But the attack was beaten off by Aegidius with the assistance of some Franks, and Euric's brother Frederic was killed in the fighting. Orléans was close to the vital interests of Aegidius, but the territory further west was of less concern, and the Romans were powerless to prevent the Visigoths from seizing Tours, on the north bank of the Loire, a few years later. It is a matter of debate how much more territory they acquired north of the Loire.

However, Aegidius was killed in 465, either by poisoning or in an ambush, and possibly on the orders of Ricimer. He was succeeded in turn by his son Syagrius (apparently a family name, because the are several later reports of Syagrii in Burgundy). What little we know about Syagrius is derived from Gregory of Tours, because he is mentioned by no contemporary sources. Gregory describes him as a King of the Romans ('rex Romanorum'), and because of this, historians often refer to 'the kingdom of Soissons', but it is hard to discern exactly what his status was or what territory he ruled. Unlike his father, he never had any official appointment from Rome. He was not a 'Comes', a 'Patrician' or a 'Magister Militum', and may not even have recognised the authority of the Roman Emperors of his time.[47] And it may have been partly for this reason that the Franks declined to recognise him, but in any case the change of regime represented an opportunity that Childeric could not resist.

With Aegidius dead, Childeric immediately seized the territory to the north-east of Paris, and effectively put Paris itself under siege with a blockade, which started in 465. The city was home to a woman called Genevieve, who had met St Germanus when she was a young girl, and she had been inspired to a life of Christian virtue by his words. She now rose to the challenge and rallied the population. Being herself half Frank and half Gallo-Roman, she embodied the ethnic divisions within the city that divided the loyalties of its citizens. To avert a civil war, Genevieve effectively made Paris a neutral zone, and, negotiating directly with Childeric, she used her personal charisma to keep the Frankish army at bay. The embargo lasted a decade, during which the citizens of Paris were several times brought close to starvation, but Genevieve organised relief convoys of food in boats from Troyes to keep the city alive. Childeric held her in enormous respect, and it was partly their relationship which effectively prevented him from

---

47 Edward James, 'The Franks' (1988).

bringing the stand-off to a conclusion. Doubtless, however, he had plenty of other projects to keep himself occupied, because it must be presumed that he was busy annexing the rest of the Second Lyonnais, in Normandy, and preventing the Visigoths from seizing any more territory north of the Loire.

So Syagrius was left ruling a much reduced Roman enclave to the south of the Marne river and east of Tours: and even that 'kingdom' was threatened by Saxons advancing up the Loire. They seized Angers, and in the mid-460s Count Paul was killed in fighting for the city. Childeric and his army had circled around Paris to Maine, where he had installed his cousin Rignomer at Le Mans, and he was not prepared to tolerate competition from the Saxons in the Loire Valley. So he briefly re-allied himself with the Romans in a joint effort to expel the Saxons from the Valley. Angers was retaken, although the city was burned in the process, and the Romans then completed the elimination of the Saxon intruders by destroying the bases that they had established on some islands in the upper Loire. This campaign ended the territorial ambitions of the Saxons in Gaul, and we will return to the consequences of this shortly. The Bretons appear to have been largely spectators in these events, and to have played no part in the struggles for Gaul since the Battle of the Catalaunian Plains, but they now became caught up in a Roman intrigue involving not only control over Gaul, but of the Western Empire itself.

4.4 Riothamus

Ricimer's grip on power was reduced in 467, when the Eastern Emperor Leo appointed one of his generals, Anthemius, to succeed the Western Emperor Libius Severus (who had died 18 months earlier). The following year, Arvandus, the Praetorian Prefect of Gaul, overwhelmed by debt and desperate for any initiative that could save him, wrote to King Euric of the Visigoths, urging him not to make peace with the new Roman Emperor Anthemius. Instead, he suggested, Euric should destroy the British 'above the Loire', because they were a strong bulwark of the remaining Roman regime in northern Gaul *("Brittanos supra Ligerim sitos impugnare oportere demonstrans"*). This would pave the way for a division of Gaul between the Burgundians and the Visigoths, which he considered to be the natural order of things. It is possible that Arvandus, who was from Gaul, hoped thereby to create a coalition which would allow him to overthrow Anthemius. But his letter was intercepted and Arvandus was tried for, and convicted of, treason (the sentence of death was commuted to exile upon the pleas of Sidonius Apollinaris).

The Emperor Anthemius then wrote to the Bretons requesting their assistance in a campaign against King Euric, and in response a force of 12,000 men, under the command of one Riothamus, was sent to Berry. Whether the expeditionary force was actually 12,000 men we cannot be certain, because Jordanes, our source (infra), was prone to exaggeration. And whether the force came from the island of Britain or the peninsula of Brittany will be discussed shortly. But clearly the force was of substantial size, and the 'British' concerned were still allies of the Romans.

However, when the British arrived in Berry, they found themselves kicking their heels, waiting to be joined by the other forces that Anthemius had promised to bring to the coalition. And before they were able to unite with these other reinforcements they were lured into battle by the Visigoths in 469/470. The result was a hard-fought, but ultimately catastrophic, defeat. According to Jordanes, the remnants of the British army retreated into Burgundy, and it is striking that there is a town called Avallon, about 30 miles east of Bourges, which was in the kingdom of Burgundy at the time.[48]

This event is well attested in Gallic sources, in particular in Jordanes's 'The Origins and Deeds of the Goths' (c.551): *"Now Eurich, king of the Visigoths, perceived the frequent change of Roman Emperors and strove to hold Gaul by his own right. The Emperor Anthemius heard of it and asked the Brittones for aid. Their King Riotimus came with twelve thousand men into the state of the Bituriges (Berry) by the way of Ocean, and was received as he disembarked from his ships. Eurich, king of the Visigoths, came against them with an innumerable army, and after a long fight he routed Riotimus, king of the Brittones, before*

---

48 Little is known of the history of Avallon before the 10th century, but who is to say that it was not named after the Island of Apples, of Arthurian fame, by some of the survivors of the battle?

The Duke and the Decoy

the Romans could join him. So when he had lost a great part of his army, he fled with all the men he could gather together, and came to the Burgundians, a neighbouring tribe then allied to the Romans. But Eurich, king of the Visigoths, seized the Gallic city of Arverna (Bourges); for the Emperor Anthemius was now dead."[49]

The episode is also referred to in Gregory of Tours' 'The History of the Franks': *"The Bretons were expelled from Bourges by the Goths and many were killed at Bourg-de-Déols."* There is considerable uncertainty over whether the British force was drawn from the island of Britain or from Brittany, with some commentators arguing that the former is more likely, because of the reference to the arrival of Riothamus *"by the way of Ocean",* and his disembarkation from ships. But it is possible that the *"Ocean"* referred to was the River Loire, and certainly Brittany would have been a more convenient source of troops for a campaign in Berry than the island of Britain. Moreover, the Bretons had a motive to become involved, because they had heard of the treachery of Arvandus and his correspondence with Euric. It is hard to see why the insular British would have been so passionate about defending an Empire that had abandoned them and refused their pleas for help in the 430s.

Against this, some commentators have questioned whether such a large force could have been recruited in the peninsula, because they believe that the main British migration to Brittany did not occur until the 6th century. This is disputed by others, who argue that the British military migration of the late 4th century continued into the 5th century, even after the abandonment of Britain by Rome. In my view there is evidence to support the idea that there was a second British migration to Brittany in 441, following the devastating Saxon invasion of Britain in that year, and this could account for the fact that the peninsula was able to produce a large army by the end of the 460s.

If part or all of the force was indeed recruited from the island of Britain, it would have significant implications for our assessment of the situation on the island. It would suggest strongly that the threat from the Anglo-Saxons was considered to be in abeyance. But Hengist and Æsc were still alive, and still fighting a battle in 473 according to the Anglo-Saxon Chronicle, and even after a long period of relative

---
49 Anthemius died in 472.

peace under Ambrosius Aurelianus, it seems improbable that the British would have been willing to take the risk to their own security of mounting an expedition on the Continent.

So I incline to the view that the expeditionary force comprised Armorican Bretons, for the most part, perhaps with an insular British contingent. However, either way, the campaign demonstrates that the British were still capable of transporting an army by water, in the late 460s. And whether the troops came from the peninsula or the island, the principal consequence of the heavy defeat is likely to have been a shift in the balance of power on the island. If the army that was destroyed came from Britain, the defeat would have directly depleted the British defences, but even if it came from the peninsula, the defeat would have reduced the capacity of the Bretons to provide their insular cousins with military support. And the Saxons would have been well aware of what had happened.

Despite the defeat, we may suppose that the British had given their opponents a terrible mauling, because the following year, Syagrius was able to defeat the Goths and put an end to their ambitions in the Fourth Lyonnais. And we know that Riothamus himself survived the battle, because in 472, Sidonius Apollinaris, who made a visit to Bourges to try to sort out the succession to the vacant bishopric of the city, had cause to write *"to his friend Riothamus"* in the following terms:

"I will write once more in my usual strain, mingling compliment with grievance. Not that I at all desire to follow up the first words of greeting with disagreeable subjects, but things seem to be always happening which a man of my order and in my position can neither mention without unpleasantness, nor pass over without neglect of duty. Yet I do my best to remember the burdensome and delicate sense of honour which makes you so ready to blush for others' faults. The bearer of this is an obscure and humble person, so harmless, insignificant, and helpless that he seems to invite his own discomfiture; his grievance is that the Bretons are secretly enticing his slaves away. Whether his indictment is a true one, I cannot say; but if you can only confront the parties and decide the matter on its merits, I think the unfortunate man may be able to make good his charge, if indeed a stranger from the country unarmed, abject and impecunious to boot, has ever a chance of a fair or kindly hearing against adversaries with all the advantages

he lacks, arms, astuteness, turbulences, and the aggressive spirit of men backed by numerous friends. Farewell".

It seems clear that Sidonius already knew Riothamus, and considered him a man of honour. But, as we have seen, there was evidently a sharp difference of opinion between the Romans and the British on the acceptability of slavery, and the insular British and the Bretons of Armorica both seem to have given up the practice at the start of the century. So the response of a British army in central Gaul to the discovery of slaves in the territory under their influence is easy to imagine, and unlikely to have been pleasing to the Roman aristocrat Sidonius. Suffice it to say that I doubt that the letter procured the response that the author was hoping for, if he got a reply at all.

The letter is significant from another point of view. As mentioned in 3.4, Léon Fleuriot speculated that Riothamus was in fact Ambrosius Aurelianus. And it is certainly true that Ambrosius was another historically attested British commander of the same period. But Ambrosius was a Roman, and I cannot see why Sidonius would have addressed him as 'Riothamus' if he had a perfectly good Roman name. This would then have been a letter from one Roman gentleman to another, both from senatorial families. Supporters of this identification argue that 'Riothamus' was the Latinisation of a Brythonic title, 'Rigotamus' being said to mean 'most kingly' or 'high king', and they would therefore argue that Sidonius was addressing Ambrosius by his title. But I cannot believe that Sidonius would have preferred to use a Breton title to the name used by Gildas, the distinguished name of a previous Bishop of Milan, and a name signaling the Roman citizenship of the bearer.

Geoffrey Ashe, rather less convincingly, considered that Riothamus might have been the historical King Arthur.[50] But if Arthur died in 535 (per Nennius) or 542 (per Geoffrey of Monmouth), he is hardly likely to have been fighting a battle in 469/470. To resolve these problems, Ashe has to argue that the dates of the Battle of Camlann have been miscalculated, and that it took place in the early years of the 6th century. However, while it is certain that the dates in the histories of this period are vague and only reliable within a certain margin of error, I see nothing in the chronology to suggest that the dates in the early sources were wrong by decades. In fact, in

---

50 Geoffrey Ashe, 'The Discovery of King Arthur' (1985).

general I have not found it difficult to reconstruct the history around the dates that we are given, and I suspect that the chroniclers of the Early Middle Ages were better at reckoning time than many have given them credit for.

Naturally, Breton opinion claims Riothamus (or 'Riotime', following Jordanes) as one of their own. The name is said to have been used by other personages of significance, for example, it is claimed that it was the name of St Radimius, who was allegedly appointed Bishop of Rennes in 385.[51] Nicolas Travers claimed that Riotime was a brother of Budic and son of Audren, possibly on the basis of the 12th century (and therefore rather late) Cartulary of Quimperlé (he did not cite his authority). We have such a vague understanding of the ruling elite of Brittany at this time that I would not care to guess where Riothamus actually fitted into the various dynasties of the peninsula, but I think it likely that he was a member of a Breton royal family, and therefore quite possibly a relative of Ambrosius.

It seems to me that a more likely candidate for the identity of Riothamus is Uther Pendragon, the legendary father of Arthur. At least he was of the right generation. Moreover, if we accept that 'Rio' was a title, meaning king, 'Thamus', 'Uther' and 'Arthur' clearly have a strong family resemblance. In 'Lancelot du Lac', Uther assisted King Aramont of Brittany (more usually called Hoël) in a campaign in Bourges and Berry, so there is at least a legendary connection between Uther and Bourges, near the scene of the destruction of the army of Riothamus. Moreover, we have very little evidence to support the supposed identification of Arthur's father, being only a few slight references in Welsh poems before Geoffrey of Monmouth's 'Historia', and I have a low level of confidence in his name.

However, leaving the identity of Riothamus aside, the critical point is that the defeat at Bourges left Britain's defences weakened, at a time when the territorial ambitions of the Saxons in Gaul had been thwarted. And this combination of factors was to have grave consequences for the island.

---

[51] The claim is made by Albert Le Grand, Malo-Joseph de Garaby and the Bollandistes. Robert de Langres and the Saint-Marthe brothers also recognised Radimius as a saint.

4.5 The Saxons in Gaul

The Saxons had been established at Vron, in Picardy, since c.370, and by the early 5th century, they had settled in colonies at Boulogne, Ponthieu and Bayeux. Then, in the middle of the century, 'Saxons' established a base on the peninsula of Le Croisic at the mouth of the River Loire. I have put the term 'Saxons' here in inverted commas, because it is said that the migrants arrived in boats made of skins, and we know that the Saxons used clinker-built wooden boats (ie constructed with overlapping planks). The only people in northern Europe who are on record as using boats made of animal skins, apart from the British and Irish in their curraghs, were the northern Scandinavians who used boats constructed of a wooden frame covered with seal-skins. So, while it is possible that these 'Saxons' came from the British Isles, I think it more likely that they came from Norway. At the time, the Romans and British would have called any pagans from the east 'Saxons', and we know that the population of Norway was under pressure from climate change, as much as any of the Germanic coastal tribes.

Nicolas Travers, writing in 1836, thought that the Saxons were invited to Gaul as mercenaries by the Franks, but it is much more likely that they arrived either of their own accord or as foedarati of the Romans. Since their base at Le Croisic seems to have been essentially piratical, I assume that they were there to suit their own purposes, and were probably not concerned with the power politics of northern Gaul until they became allied to the Franks. They became a menace to the whole Atlantic seaboard of Gaul, including Brittany, which was to continue for many years - for example, Saxons were recorded as raiding the village of Marsas in the Garonne in the middle of the century.[52]

We have some quite good descriptions of the Saxons of the third quarter of the 5th century from Sidonius Apollinaris, written at a time when he was visiting Bordeaux. Sidonius was a Roman Gaul, of a senatorial family, whose life had taken him to the highest levels of society in Rome, and who eventually became the Bishop of Clermont. His letters contain the only surviving contemporary accounts that describe the people who were invading Britain at this time, so it is

---
52 Vita Viviani, ch.7.

worth dwelling briefly on this material. Sidonius mentioned the threat the Saxons posed to civilian life in Gaul, in a letter that he wrote in c.480 to Namatius, a Visigoth commander of the naval forces in the Garonne. These forces had been stationed there precisely to protect the region against the Saxon menace:

"Just as I was on the point of ending a letter which had rambled on long enough, lo and behold! a courier from Saintonges. I whiled away some time talking with him about you; and he was very positive that you had weighed anchor, and in fulfilment of those half military, half naval duties of yours, were coasting the western shores on the look-out for curved ships; the ships of the Saxons, in whose every oarsman you think to detect an arch-pirate. Captains and crews alike, to a man they teach or learn the art of brigandage; therefore let me urgently caution you to be ever on the alert. For the Saxon is the most ferocious of all foes. He comes on you without warning; when you expect his attack he makes away. Resistance only moves him to contempt; a rash opponent is soon down. If he pursues he overtakes; if he flies himself, he is never caught. Shipwrecks to him are no terror, but only so much training. His is no mere acquaintance with the perils of the sea; he knows them as he knows himself. A storm puts his enemies off their guard, preventing his preparations from being seen; the chance of taking the foe by surprise makes him gladly face every hazard of rough waters and broken rocks.

Moreover, when the Saxons are setting sail from the continent, and are about to drag their firm-holding anchors from an enemy's shore, it is their usage, thus homeward bound, to abandon every tenth captive to the slow agony of a watery end, casting lots with perfect equity among the doomed crowd in execution of this iniquitous sentence of death. This custom is all the more deplorable in that it is prompted by honest superstition. These men are bound by vows which have to be paid in victims, they conceive it a religious act to perpetrate this horrible slaughter, and to take anguish from the prisoner in place of ransom; this polluting sacrilege is in their eyes an absolving sacrifice."

As we have already seen, the Saxons penetrated deep into France on the River Loire in the 460s, and were only expelled by a combination of the Romans and Childeric's Franks in 469. The Saxons in the Loire were led at this time by one Odoacre ('Adovacrius', according to Gregory of Tours), who may or may not have been the individual that Gregory mentioned a little later, called Odovacrius.

The second Odovacrius was a Germanic commander, with whom Childeric entered into an alliance, after the expulsion of the Saxons from the Loire, and he was almost certainly the Odoacre who went on to depose the last Western Roman Emperor in 476. The main purpose of the treaty between Childeric and this Odoacre was an alliance for a campaign against the Alamanni, whose territory to the south of the Franks held an obvious attraction to Childeric.[53] But I suspect that the treaty also settled the interests of the Franks and the Saxons in northern Gaul, where the annexation of the Second Lyonnais (Normandy) had brought the Franks into proximity to the Saxon colonies at the Vron, Ponthieu and Bayeux.

A logical agreement might have left the Saxons in peaceful occupation of their colonies along the southern coast of the English Channel, in return for their acknowledgement of the sovereignty of the Franks and their commitment to abandon any further territorial ambitions in Gaul. As subjects of the Franks, the Saxons would then have been expected to provide military assistance when required to do so by Childeric.

Whether or not such an agreement was reached, the parties certainly behaved as if it had been from that point onwards. Thereafter, the Saxons only featured in battles in Gaul as allies of the Franks, or as allies of one Frankish faction against another. And the Saxons appear to have redirected their appetite for conquest to the northern side of the Channel, because the Anglo-Saxon Chronicle tells us that in 477 the Saxons of the south-east were joined by fresh reinforcements, quite possibly from Gaul.

The archaeological evidence also suggests that Anglo-Saxon immigration into Britain increased sharply from around 470. Moreover, in showing us that there were substantial contacts between the Saxons of Kent and the Saxons of north-eastern France, especially those around Vron, throughout the second half of the 5th century and into the 6th century, it suggests where the newcomers may have originated. The cemeteries of Kent and Picardy contain many objects which evidence a system of cross-Channel exchange in this period, for example button or disc brooches of an insular Saxon design, which have been found in graves in north-eastern France.

---

53 The 'Alamanni' was a term applied to them by others. They called themselves the Suevi, and they inhabited the area to the south of the Franks, including what are now Alsace, southern Germany and northern Switzerland.

There also seems to have been a change in the style of goods found in northern France at the end of the 5th century, which French archaeologists characterise as the difference between 'Saxon' and 'Anglo-Saxon' design.[54] This development appears to reflect a subtle change in the character of the Germanic colonies in Britain at that time, as it seems that the insular Saxons gained a new cultural assertiveness, a new confidence in their art. And these changes tie in with the literary record, which tell us that in the 470s, a new and more terrible Saxon warlord arrived in Sussex, the first to be called the 'High King' of England, or 'the Bretwalda' in their language.

4.6 Ælle

The Saxons who arrived in 477 were led by a warlord called Ælle, who arrived in Britain with his three sons, Cyman, Wlenking and Cissa, in three ships (so perhaps with a force of 250 – 300 men). The immigrants immediately fought with 'the Welsh', slaying many and driving the remainder into the woods called Andred'sley (ie near Pevensey in Sussex). We can therefore deduce that they landed on the south-eastern coast of Britain, in territory to the west of the Jutes of Kent.

The invaders were clearly Germanic, rather than Danish, and in my opinion it is very likely that they included Franks. This would not necessarily have been the first Frankish incursion into Britain, because there is potentially archaeological evidence of an earlier Frankish influence in East Anglia, but the Frankish contribution to the foundation of the kingdom of Sussex was significant, because it later led to the development of a close alliance between the 'Anglo-Saxons' of the south-east and their Germanic cousins in Gaul.

Ælle became King of the new colony of the South Saxons (Sussex), and Bede claims that over the next decade he established himself as the ruler of all the Anglo-Saxon colonies to the south of the Humber River. The Anglo-Saxon Chronicle merely states that he was the first of the Anglo-Saxon kings to hold the title of Bretwalda (High King of England), but is unspecific as to the extent of his realm. The Chronicle

---

[54] Jean Soulat, 'La Pénétration des Groupes Saxons et Anglo-Saxons dans le Ponthieu entre la fin du IVème et le Milieu du VIème Siecle' (2009).

records him fighting two further battles against 'the Welsh', one at Mecred's Burnsted in 485 (which may have been the name of an earthworks now called Town Creep, situated between Ashburnham and Penshurst in East Sussex) and one at Pevensey Castle in 490, when all of the occupants of the castle were slaughtered. The locations of these battles again strongly suggest that Ælle had not advanced out of Sussex by 490.

It seems probable that the British commander at this time was Ambrosius Aurelianus, although the Anglo Saxons either did not know or did not record the names of the Generals commanding their opponents. But the Celtic histories suggest that, by the end of this war, the British had a new commander to replace or support the ageing Roman. And we will come to him in Chapter 5.

4.7 Description of the Franks

Sidonius gives us an eyewitness description of a Frankish prince, in 470, which allows us to form a very clear impression of the appearance of the nobility who surrounded Childeric and Clovis. The young prince was on his way to pay court to his (probably Burgundian) fiancée in Lyon, when Sidonius happened to witness his arrival. Sidonius described the scene to his friend Domnicius, in a letter, as follows:

"You take such pleasure in the sight of arms and those who wear them, that I can imagine your delight if you could have seen the young prince Sigismer on his way to the palace of his father-in-law in the guise of a bridegroom or suitor in all the pomp and bravery of the tribal fashion. His own steed with its caparisons [horse blankets], other steeds laden with flashing gems, paced before and after; but the conspicuous interest in the procession centred in the prince himself, as with a charming modesty he went afoot amid his bodyguard and footmen, in flame-red mantle, with much glint of ruddy gold, and gleam of snowy silken tunic, his fair hair, red cheeks and white skin according with the three hues of his equipment. But the chiefs and allies who bore him company were dread of aspect, even thus on peace intent. Their feet were laced in boots of bristly hide reaching to the heels; ankles and legs were exposed. They wore high tight tunics of varied colour hardly

descending to their bare knees, the sleeves covering only the upper arm. Green mantles they had with crimson borders; baldrics supported swords hung from their shoulders, and pressed on sides covered with cloaks of skin secured by brooches. No small part of their adornment consisted of their arms; in their hands they grasped barbed spears and missile axes; their left sides were guarded by shields, which flashed with tawny golden bosses and snowy silver borders, betraying at once their wealth and their good taste. Though the business in hand was wedlock, Mars was no whit less prominent in all this pomp than Venus."

Sidonius was evidently struck by the bare legs of the prince and his companions, which is not surprising since the Romans generally identified all northern barbarian men, including the Celts, by their trousers and tunics. The northern tribes were also distinguished by their hairstyles, north-eastern Gaul being known to the Romans as Gallia Comata (long-haired Gaul). Many Germans could be distinguished by their fair hair colouring and pale eyes, and Sidonius later referred to the *"blue-eyed Saxon".*

The reference to *"much glint of ruddy gold"* is probably a description of the gold and garnet ornamentation that was so popular among the Germanic tribes of the first millennium, eg, for men, on sword hilts. The combination of gold and garnets is seen in the ornamental bees with which Childeric I was buried at Tournai (481/482) and it remained fashionable for many centuries, as we can see in the objects recovered in the Staffordshire hoard of Anglo-Saxon gold (6th – 8th centuries). Brooches were essential items in both male and female clothing, to pin cloaks or robes at the shoulder, and the detailed variations in design can often assist us in identifying the tribal origins of the wearer.

The wearing of animal skins was typical throughout northern Europe, and a source of much curiosity to the Romans. Clearly, the wearing of furs, such as bear skin, would have been unnecessary (and indeed unpleasant) in the warmer climate of the Mediterranean. But fur cloaks were practical in the north (including in *"these islands, stiff with cold and frost",* as described by Gildas), both for their thermal qualities and for the protection they could provide against light blows. Gregory of Tours reported encountering a Breton pilgrim called Winnoch, who stopped at Tours on his way to Jerusalem. This man practised extreme abstinence, and Gregory found it remarkable that he *"wore no clothes except for sheepskins from which the wool had been removed."* As, Sidonius noted, the upper parts of the shoes of the Franks were also made from fur (while the Romans wore sandals made from leather).

The missile axe described by Sidonius was known in Iberia as a 'francisca', from the days when the Franks had invaded Spain. The Saxons were more typically associated with a large single edged dagger called the 'seax', from which these tribes obtained their nickname. But from their graves in Britain, we know that their warriors carried long-swords and spears, as well as these weapons. And like other soldiers of the era, they carried shields and wore helmets for protection.

The Saxons and Franks were allies for much of the 5th century and beyond, so we may imagine that some of the features of Frankish dress observed by Sidonius would have been shared by Saxon warlords. But Saxon society in Britain and northern Gaul seems to have had a relatively 'flat' structure, during the 5th and early 6th centuries, with little to differentiate the graves of the early immigrants. Certainly we do not see, in the archaeology of the 5th century, the type of princely burial found in the 6th and early 7th century Anglo-Saxon cemeteries at Sutton Hoo, so Arthur's opponents may have been clothed in relatively drab materials, compared to the young Prince Sigismer.

4.8 Clovis

In 481 Childeric died and was buried with great pomp at Tournai. His grave was furnished with a great quantity of treasure, in gold and garnet ornaments, and 20 horses were slaughtered and buried in two nearby graves to accompany him into the afterlife. The ornaments interred included some 300 gold and garnet bees, which may have decorated the tack of his horses, and which Napoleon later adopted as a symbol of his empire.

Childeric was succeeded by his son Clovis who was only 15, but who had nevertheless attained the Frankish age of majority. Bishop Remigius of Reims wrote a letter to the young Clovis, congratulating him on his coronation, which contains several points of interest: *"A strong report has come to us that you have taken over the administration* of the Second Belgic Province. There is nothing new in that you now begin to be what your parents always were." The clear implication is that Childeric, the father of Clovis, had ruled over Belgica Secunda, the province in which Soissons and Tournai were situated. The capital of this province was Reims, the city where Remigius was the Bishop, so he must have known the political situation in the region. But what did the letter really mean? And why, of all the letters that must have been addressed to Clovis, is this one of only two that have survived?

I think the lightly coded message of this letter, from a Roman Catholic bishop to a supposedly pagan or heretical Clovis, was a blessing from the Catholic church for a campaign by Clovis to get rid of Syagrius. This message may even have been conveyed with the approval of the powers in Rome, which would have seen Syagrius as a rebel, like his father before him. In 476, Odoacre had deposed the last Western Roman Emperor, Romulus Augustus, and thereafter ruled in the West, ostensibly in the name of the puppet Emperor Julius Nepos until 480, and then 'on behalf of' the Eastern Emperor Zeno. As we have seen, he may well have been the Odoacre who formed an alliance with Childeric after the Saxons were expelled from the Loire in 469. If so, it is not hard to imagine that he remained an ally of the Franks in the 480s, and that he may have foreseen a fruitful partnership with the young Clovis.

What are slightly more surprising are the religious implications of the letter. Syagrius, we might presume, was at least nominally a Roman Catholic, and at first sight it is hard to see why Remigius should have encouraged a Frank to depose Syagrius, if the Frank was a pagan. Clovis was not baptised into the Catholic Church until the end of the century. But we have no proof that Syagrius was a Roman Catholic, or that Clovis was a pagan in the 480s. In fact we know almost nothing about Syagrius, beyond the little that Gregory of Tours tells us. But the text of Remigius's letter strongly suggests that Clovis was on good terms with the Catholic episcopate in Belgica Secunda from the start of his reign. The letter continued *"You should defer to your bishops and always have recourse to their advice."*

The second letter to King Clovis, which has survived to us, was written by Bishop Avitus of Vienne, shortly after the baptism of Clovis (on either 25 December 496 or 499). This strongly suggests that Clovis was an Arian Christian before his conversion: *"Many others,*

The Duke and the Decoy

in this matter, when their bishops or friends exhort them to adhere to the True Faith, are accustomed to oppose the traditions of their race and respect for their ancestral cult; thus they culpably prefer a false shame to their salvation. While they observe a futile reverence for their parents unbelief, they confess that they do not know what they should choose to do." We may therefore suppose that Childeric was also an Arian Christian and probably not a pagan – after all, amongst many grave goods, he was buried with a cruciform brooch.

Clovis was no doubt pleased to receive encouragement from Remigius for his imperial ambitions, but could not confront Syagrius on his own. He therefore formed an alliance with Ragnachar, the Frankish king of Cambrai, and together they sent a challenge to Syagrius in 486 (according to Gregory). As we have seen, the Franks had probably not accepted the legitimacy of the succession of Syagrius to the realm of his father Aegidius, in any event, and Childeric had already made substantial inroads into what was once the Roman province. Syagrius had attempted to push the Franks back into the territory east of the Somme, but had failed, and Clovis decided that the time had come to bring the simmering feud to a head. Syagrius had no option but to accept the challenge, and the result was the 'Battle of Soissons'.

In the resulting engagement, it seems possible that Syagrius had Breton support.[55] The Bretons had fought for the Romans against the Visigoths in 469/470, five years after Syagrius had come to his throne, and we have no reason to believe that they had fallen out with him since. This is significant to our appraisal of the Arthurian legends, because Geoffrey of Monmouth tells us that Arthur fought against a Roman army led by a tribune called Frollo, in the service of the Emperor Leo (467 – 474), in a battle at Paris, after the 'Battle of Bath'. This is plainly nonsense on many counts, not the least of which is that if a British commander (whether Arthur or anyone else) took part in the Battle of Soissons, it is likely to have been on the side of the Romans against the Franks. But Geoffrey's version of history may reflect a folk memory that the British were involved in a battle near Paris, in which the Romans were among the protagonists, and that the Romans lost.

At any rate, the result of the battle was a defeat for the Romans,

---

55 L. Fleuriot, 'Les origins de la Bretagne (1980), pp 174 – 175.

although we have no details of the course of events. Syagrius survived, and fled to the court of King Euric in Toulouse, with whom he seems to have had at least a non-aggression pact since his victory over the Goths in 470 (after the British defeat at Bourg-de-Déols). His choice of place of refuge is interesting, because he evidently elected not to fly to the much closer territory of the Burgundians, where it is believed that he had family connections, and we can only assume that he perceived the Burgundians to be closer to, and more under the influence of, the Franks. Or perhaps he feared that he was the victim of a conspiracy orchestrated from Rome, in which case he may have felt that the Burgundians were too close to the Roman authorities for comfort. But whatever his thinking, the Visigoths proved no more helpful to him than the Burgundians might have been. Under threat from Clovis, King Euric imprisoned Syagrius and then handed him back to the Franks, who had him secretly murdered.

As a result of his victory over the Romans, Clovis immediately absorbed the 'kingdom' of Syagrius into his expanding Frankish empire, and 'Roman Gaul' effectively expired. Clovis may also have felt that his victory gave him title, by conquest, to Brittany, but he probably had enough on his plate in the short term, in absorbing his latest acquisitions.

4.9 The Franks and the Bretons

After the Battle of Soissons, the Franks set about consolidating their control over the north of France and Clovis spent some time establishing a structure of government in the areas which he had acquired. As an example, the Gallo-Roman castle at Le Donjon de Vez was made the capital of the Val d'Automne in the Oise Department. It is unclear exactly how much territory the Franks controlled west of the Seine (ie in Armorica), but they certainly had a kingdom at Le Mans and we can presume that they held Normandy. The Visigoths held Tours, on the north bank of the Loire, and commanded the whole of Aquitaine. An area in south-eastern Brittany was called Alania, at this time, having been held by Alans in the Roman cause since the revolts of the Bagaudae, and the lands under this vestigial 'Roman' control included Nantes. My assumption is that the Bretons swiftly capitalised on the demise of Syagrius and seized Nantes, because the defences of the city were commanded by Count Eusebius in 490,[56] and it appears that he may have been a Breton (see below).

The defeat of Syagrius had left the remaining Roman forces in northern Gaul in a somewhat stateless condition. Many of them did not want to submit to the pagan or Arian Franks, Alamanni or Visigoths, so those that had not surrendered to the Franks now put themselves at the disposal of the Bretons. Procopius tells us that *"Other Roman soldiers were also garrisoned on the Gallic extremities to be watched over. As they had no way of returning to Rome, and did not want to surrender to their enemies who were Arian, they gave themselves up to the Arborykhes (the Armoricans) and to the Germans with their military standards and the lands they had guarded before for the Romans; and they handed down to their offspring all the customs of their fathers, which were thus preserved, and this people has held them in sufficient reverence to guard them even up to my time. For even at the present day they are clearly recognized as belonging to the legions to which they were assigned when they served in ancient times, and they always carry their own standards when they engage in battle, and always follow the customs of their fathers. And they preserve the dress of the Romans in every particular, even as regards their shoes."*

We may therefore suppose that the Bretons were joined by the Duke of the Armorican Tract (if such a post-holder still existed) and his garrisons around the coasts of western Armorica. Quite how far to the east the Breton rule prevailed, we cannot tell, but there was certainly an outpost at Blois. This had been established by Luomadus in 410, possibly originally to defend the eastern border of the Third Lyonnais when Brittany first declared itself independent. But since the Visigoths had seized Tours, I suspect that the garrison in the town had served the Romans as a border defence to protect Orléans from the Visigoths, and that it had found itself isolated after the fall of the Kingdom of Syagrius.

To Clovis, this would have been an untidy remnant, and he began by expelling the Bretons from Blois in 490, although we have no details

---
56 Nicolas Travers.

of the event.[57] And in the same year he sent a Saxon ally called Chillon or Marcel Chillon to take Nantes, probably by sea. Chillon put the city under siege for two months, and it appears that Count Eusebius was killed in the course of these events, because he disappears from the record. The 'Chronicle of Anjou' tells us that Clovis encountered Bretons scattered all along the Loire Valley between Orléans and Tours in 491, so the Bretons had evidently not abandoned the Third Lyonnais during their pacification by Aëtius in the early 450s.

The siege of Nantes by the Saxons was clearly a critical event in this Frankish campaign, and the city may have been defended by a coalition of Romans and Bretons. According to the second 'Life of St Melaine', Eusebius was a Breton, but his supposed title of 'Count' suggests that he held a Roman appointment. In any case, the outcome was a set-back for Clovis, because the siege was apparently relieved by King Budic of Brittany, and the Bretons thereby retained control over the Pays de la Loire. This siege is described in more detail in the following section.

In the meantime, Clovis was also engaged in fighting the Visigoths in the Touraine, a struggle which eventually developed into a full-scale war and which culminated in the destruction of the Visigoth kingdom in c.510. However in the early 490s, this was a conflict of a much more local nature, focused on control of the city of Tours, which changed hands several times. In all of these events we can see that Clovis had a plan to complete his control over Armorica, ie the part of France north of the Loire, and he was picking off his opponents one at a time, in a process which would inevitably lead to an assault on Brittany when the time was ripe.

However, Clovis had in the process opened up a second front against the Visigoths, who fought tenaciously to retain the city of Tours, and he found himself dragged into a campaign in Aquitaine, probably before he would ideally have wished. We have little detail on the course this war, because Gregory of Tours simplifies the whole period into a single decisive battle at Vouillé in 507. But we know for example, that the Visigoths retook Saintes from the Franks in 496 (which means that the Franks had invaded Aquitaine by then), and

---

57 It is also unclear to what extent the Bretons were actually expelled; the 'Life of St Delmas' tells us that there was a 'Legio Britannica' stationed near Orléans in c.530.

that the Franks took Bordeaux in 498. However around the end of the century, it seems that the Franks were driven back to the Loire, because a temporary peace treaty was negotiated on an island in the river at Amboise in 502. So clearly the tide of this war ebbed and flowed for about 15 years.

At some point in the early 490s, presumably having secured at least a temporary advantage over the Visigoths, Clovis then moved westwards to relaunch the campaign against the Bretons. According to Abbot Dubos,[58] this happened immediately after the marriage of Clovis to the Burgundian princess Clotilde, a marriage which took place in c.493. The fact that Clotilde was a practising Roman Catholic (unusual for a German princess at that time) has a significant bearing on the course of the subsequent events.

Dubos tells us that the grounds for the war with the Bretons were that Clovis wanted to punish the Armoricans for not having sufficiently observed the terms of the treaty mediated by St Germanus of Auxerre – presumably because they had taken Nantes and other territory east of the Vilaine River. But we may suppose that the real reasons were political ambition and pecuniary advantage. Clovis was trying to build an empire, and there were only two possible sources of funds to sustain a large standing army, being taxation and war booty. So unless Clovis could extract sufficient revenue from his subjects, the only way that he could maintain his military capability was to mount a series of campaigns of conquest. Like a shark, his army had to keep moving forward to survive, and the Bretons looked like a tasty morsel.

Procopius, writing in Constantinople, tells us that: *"The Franks began to pillage their lands [the lands of the Bretons], then, very bellicose, marched against them with all their people. But the Arborykhes [or Arborychoi] proved their valour and their loyalty to the Romans and showed in this war that they were very brave. The Germans not having won by force, considered it advisable to make an alliance with them and to unite the two peoples by inter-marriage. This suggestion the Arborykhes received not at all unwillingly; for both, as it happened, were Christians. And in this way they were united into one people and came to have great power."* In reading this, we must bear in mind that the source of Procopius's information was a Frankish ambassador to

---

[58] 'Histoire critique de l'etablissement de la monarchie françoise dans les Gaules' (1734).

the court of the Eastern Emperor, Justinian, and that this version of events is almost certainly the interpretation most favourable to the Franks. So when we are told that the Germans had not won by force, we can assume that they had been soundly defeated. And when we are told that the treaty which concluded the conflict brought the Bretons into the Frankish fold, this is almost certainly an exaggeration. It is far more likely that the Franks accepted the de facto independence of Brittany in return for a nominal acknowledgement of the sovereignty of Clovis (as successor by conquest to Syagrius) and the cession by the Bretons of the territory which they had acquired east of the Vilaine River (other than Nantes, which they refused to give up). Procopius is specific in stating that the treaty created an 'alliance', rather than a seigneur/vassal relationship, and that the Bretons did not pay tribute to the Franks. He wrote *"These people are submissive to the Franks in other respects, but they never paid them any tribute."* And this point was later confirmed by Ermold the Black, who reported a complaint to the same effect made by King Louis the Pious, after Ermold had accompanied Louis's son Pippin on a campaign in Brittany in 824.

The 'treaty' between the Bretons and the Franks does not survive in written form, if indeed it was ever committed to writing, so the details are uncertain. But we can speculate on when the agreement was made, within a margin of error of a couple of years, with some confidence. Abbot Dubos suggests that the Bretons were willing to enter into such an agreement only because the Franks had become Christians.[59] Clovis was baptised in either 496 or 499, so Abbot Dubos dates the 'treaty' to 497, which is certainly plausible, and I refer to it as the Treaty of 497. The date may be reasonably accurate, but I doubt that religious considerations had much influence on the decision by either side to accept a peace treaty. Far more likely, the Franks found that the Bretons were a much harder nut to crack than they had expected, and that the region was so poor that it was not worth fighting over.

According to Albert Le Grand, St Melaine, a Gallo-Roman from the Vannes area who became Bishop of Rennes in 505, played a key part in forging the union of Brittany and Francia, which resulted from

[59] Fleuriot goes further, and suggests that the baptism of Clovis was a condition of the treaty, which in my view is most improbable.

the Treaty of 497.[60] Some historians consider this to be evidence that the Treaty was not made until after 505, but it does not follow that Melaine was already Bishop of Rennes when he became an intermediary between the Bretons and Clovis. I think it more likely that he was rewarded by Clovis for his efforts, with the appointment to the episcopate in 505. Prior to that it appears that Melaine, who had been born on the Breton border at Brain-sur-Vilaine (between Rennes and Redon), where he founded a monastery, had been a counsellor to King Hoël.

Of the events in Brittany, Gregory of Tours writes not a word, despite the fact that the whole of Brittany was within his diocese. But then he never took much interest in Brittany – over which his influence was more nominal than real (for example, we never read of him appointing any Breton clergy). As a Roman Catholic, Gregory was understandably more interested in the fact of the baptism of Clovis than in any war in the western peninsula, but in any case, he never mentioned any defeats suffered by the Franks.[61] To Gregory, the Bretons were uncouth and insubordinate barbarians, and a defeat for the Franks at their hands would have been an embarrassment, best swept under the carpet. But the silence of our most complete literary source of this era is extremely frustrating. We have to reconstruct the timeline of the period from what Gregory tells us of the surrounding events, and his chronology was vague, to say the least. Gregory tells us that Clovis agreed to be baptised after a battle against the Alamanni at Tolbiac, during which his spontaneous prayer in a moment of crisis resulted, as he saw it, in the turning of the tide. If the war with the Bretons followed after the baptism of Clovis, therefore, it also followed after the victory at Tolbiac, which Gregory dates to 496. However, Theodoric the Great, who ruled Italy from 493, referred to a victory of the Franks over the Alamanni in a letter dated 506, and this might or might not be the same event.

Nevertheless, while it is far from certain that the war with the Alamanni did precede the campaign in Brittany, I think it is fairly clear that the Breton campaign took place after 493, because until then Clovis was preoccupied with the Visigoths (and his marriage).

---

60 *"Saint Melaine fut l'un des principaux agents de cet événement capital".*
61 Incidentally, the hagiographies of the 6th century are curiously silent on Clovis and his baptism, but by the 7th century this seems to have been accepted as a fact.

And as we shall see, the date of 493 was significant in the history of the war between the British and the Anglo-Saxons, as indeed it was in the history of the Western Roman Empire, being the year when the last independent ruler of that Empire was assassinated.

Why did the Franks lose a war against the Bretons? The army of Clovis had defeated Syagrius. It had more recently defeated the Thuringians (of central Germany), and it was engaged in an ultimately successful war against the Visigoths. In roughly the same period as the Breton war, it defeated the Alamanni, and subsequently, in c.500, Clovis defeated the Burgundians. No power in Gaul was able to resist him, and yet his army was brought to a shuddering halt in Brittany. The central question is, what was it about the Breton forces that enabled them to defeat this formidable war machine?

4.10   Archaeology in Brittany

Knowing that the Franks fought a campaign in Brittany in the late 5th century, we might hope to find some archaeological evidence of it, particularly in cemeteries, just as we may hope to discover more about the progression of the Anglo-Saxon conquest of England from graveyards. And compared with England, we have the advantage in Brittany that the area to be searched is much smaller. But we are also faced with the same obstacles:

- Almost nothing was constructed in stone
- The invading 'Germans' eventually overran the territory, and therefore Frankish relics may be found over a wide area
- Securely dating artefacts of the period is very difficult

What is clear is that, as in Britain, mass graves of fallen warriors have not yet been found; but this should not be a surprise. Firstly, in Roman times, the Germanic tribes left the corpses of their fallen enemies on the battlefield to rot, and the Romano-British may have done exactly the same thing. Tacitus described the scene after the Roman defeat at Teutoburg Forest (AD 9) in these terms: *"In the middle of the plain, bones lay either spread out or heaped, depending on whether they had fled or resisted. Next to the bones lay bits of spears and horse limbs, and there were also human heads nailed to trees."* And secondly in Brittany, the civil funerary customs of the Early Middle Ages also militate against the preservation of the mortal remains of the dead, because the use of stone sarcophagi was virtually unheard of west of the Vilaine Valley. The dead were cremated or buried, either directly in the ground or in wooden coffins, and in the acidic soil of Brittany, wooden coffins and other organic matter generally decompose rapidly.

The only graveyard of the Early Middle Ages that has been found and archaeologically excavated in western Brittany is located at Saint-Marcel, in the Morbihan, just south of Ploërmel, and this was in use from the second half of the 4th century until the end of the 5th century (see map on page 52). In a dig in 2006, led by Françoise Le Boulanger, 45 graves were found in ranks, orientated north-west/south-east. Twelve of these showed evidence of a coffin or casket, and 18 contained sufficient evidence to show that the deceased was buried clothed, with his or her personal effects and grave goods (eg a glass goblet). The metal objects recovered included belt buckles, hair clips, a knife and bracelets. These objects are all typical of artefacts found in the south-east of England in the 5th century, and especially interesting are some brooches in the Quoit Brooch Style. Other examples of these have been found at Pont-de-Buis (Finistère), Réville (Manche), Bénouville (Calvados), Amiens and Thennes (Somme), and St Herpes (Charente).[62] The Quoit Brooch Style pieces are evidence of a widely dispersed exodus from the south-east of England in the sub-Roman period, which I think can be clearly linked to the expansion of the Anglo-Saxon kingdoms in Kent and Sussex.

The Quoit Brooch Style exhibits features of both Continental (particularly Scandinavian) and Romano-British origin, and it developed exclusively south of the River Thames. It therefore seems to have emerged from a society that was subject to both indigenous and Continental cultural influences, indicating a significant degree of cultural exchange with immigrants. The archaeologist Seiichi Suzuki writes that *"we may infer that the production of Quoit Brooch Style objects, particularly belt equipment, would have been initiated and supported by people who held an allegiance to Romano-British*

---

[62] 'Les influences culturelles à la fin de l'Antiquité: l'exemple de Saint-Marcel' by Institut national de recherches archéologiques préventitives (2009).

traditions as part of their socio-cultural identity. At the same time they expressed relative independence from the tradition by constructing their own distinct style. In this light it may be plausible to conjecture that the bearers of this style were a ruling elite of sub-Roman society which was being formed in southern England in the early 5th century, following the dissolution of Roman order in England".[63] The presence of these objects in Saint-Marcel testifies that at least one community of refugees from the south-east of England was established in the Morbihan in the middle of the 5th century, and the likelihood is that this was one of many. The find at Pont-de-Buis also demonstrates that other south-eastern refugees settled in Finistère, but it is interesting to note that no similar objects have yet been found in Dumnonée, and it may be that northern Brittany was settled by Britons from other parts of the island.

As I have said, these people arrived in what I call the second wave of British migration, after the military migration of the 4th century. They were Belgo-Romans who had been displaced by the first Anglo-Saxon incursions into Kent, and their presence in Brittany can be detected in the geography as well as the archaeology of the Morbihan – for example the church in the town of Elven, between Ploërmel and Vannes, is dedicated to the first British martyr, St Alban.[64]

It is not hard to see why a number of these emigrants ended up in south-eastern Brittany (although others were dispersed widely over other parts of northern Gaul). They were farmers from Kent, 'the garden of England', and from the Isle of Wight, who had been driven out by the Jutes. The areas from which they came are among the warmest and driest parts of Britain. It was logical that the migrants should seek out good agricultural land in the sunniest parts of Brittany, and some of the very best land in the peninsula is to be found in the valleys of the Arz, the Aff (which was then called the Aua) and the Oust (called the Ult in 834). There is a river called Ower, which flows into the Solent from Hampshire, a river Alt in Merseyside and several British rivers called Ouse, including one in Sussex, so I think that these names alone give us some clues as to where the

---

63 Seiichi Suzuki, 'The Quoit Brooch Style and Anglo-Saxon Settlement' (2000).
64 There is also a village called Saint-Alban near Pléneuf-Val-André on the north coast of Brittany, and several other dedications in France which attest to the presence of British troops at later periods in history.

migrants came from. For example, if the Ult was named after the Alt, it was probably named by some of the military migrants of the first wave, men from the Roman fort at Chester.

These were people from what is now England, and they were Arthur's people, although he was not necessarily from the same part of the country. It is quite possible that he was ethnically a member of the Catuvellauni from north of the Thames, the tribe which had the strongest military tradition among those of lowlands England. But the migrants were Belgic Britons, like him, and he would have felt a strong affinity with them, alongside his duty to them as a commander of the British army.

Unfortunately, however, it seems that he was unable to save them all from the predations of the Franks. The archaeological record at Saint-Marcel came to an end at the close of the 5th century, and we must assume that the village was abandoned at that point. It would be nice to think that the villagers had some positive reason to move to another location, but unfortunately it is very likely that they were swept away by the tide of war.[65]

An earlier (late 4th century or early 5th) cemetery of 'Germanic' soldiers was found at Guer in the Morbihan, also south of Ploërmel, in 1968, and this is thought to be associated with the Frankish laeti in the *"civitas of the Riedones"*, as recorded in the Notitia Dignitatum.[66] In addition, a few burials of 'Germanic' individuals have been excavated which have been identified as 'Merovingian' in period. This of course does not necessarily mean they are of the late 5th century, but greater precision in terms of dates is unlikely to emerge in the present state of knowledge. In general it may be said that these have been found around the borders of Brittany, although that does not necessarily mean that the deceased were invaders. The interior was largely uninhabited. For example, near the cathedral at Alet, a dozen bodies were arranged in a circle, one of them holding the antlers of a stag in his arms. They were clearly not Christians, who would have been buried in an east-west orientation, and they were probably soldiers

---

[65] Saint-Marcel is interesting in several other respects. Two chapels of the parish are dedicated to St Ambroise and St Geneviève. And old habits die hard – Saint-Marcel became the centre of the Breton resistance in World War 2, and was burnt to the ground by the Germans!

[66] Michel Petit, 'Sépultres du Bas Empire à Guer' (Annales de Bretagne, 1970, no 77, pp 273 – 278).

who died defending the city, because aggressors would probably not have been buried at all, and certainly not near the cathedral. So perhaps they were Franks.

Evidence of another battle of the Merovingian period was found in the burial mounds at Rallion, La Bouëxière, to the east of Rennes. Nearby fields are called 'Le Champs de la Bataille' ('the battlefield), through which runs the 'Ruisseau de Sang' ('the stream of blood').[67] While the site was almost certainly a battlefield in a war between the Bretons and the Franks, the date is uncertain – there were numerous conflicts between the Franks and the Bretons between the mid-5th century and the mid-8th century.

Somewhat later is the possibly mid-6th century sarcophagus of a British king found in the 17th century chapel at Lomarec, just south of Auray. Inside the sarcophagus there is an inscription which reads "IRHAEMA(chi rho)INRI". This is believed to mean "Here lies the king", in a language which predates the Brythonic tongue of the modern Bretons. The chi rho symbol of Christianity was common in the 5th and 6th centuries, and leaves no room for doubt that the deceased was a Christian, but sadly the inscription does not tell us his name. It is believed by some that the sarcophagus was the final resting place of Waroch I, the king of Vannes who died in c.550, but it could have been that of any British king of that period, and indeed it is not out of the question that this could be the tomb of Arthur. However the royal connections of Auray are clear from its name ('aula ri', the court of the king) and the town was evidently a seat of the rulers of the Vannetais for many years, so the king concerned could have been any one of a number of monarchs. Lomarec, a charming spot on the coast just south of the town, is in exactly the sort of location that one would expect to find the country villa of such a king.

In terms of coins, the castle Kerandroat at Plésidy, south of Guingamp, has yielded both a coin issued by the Emperor Zeno (474 – 491) and an aureus minted under Julius Nepos (474 – 475), so the site was probably occupied in the Arthurian period. Indeed, the name Plésidy is said to derive from 'Plou Seidi' (the parish of Seidi) and Seidi, according to the late 11th century Welsh prose text 'Culhwch

---

[67] Philippe Guigon, Jean-Pierre Bardel and Michael Batt 'Nécrepoles et sarcophages du Haut Moyen Age en Bretagne', Revue Archéologique de l'Ouest, vol 4 (1987).

The Duke and the Decoy

and Olwen', was the father of three of Arthur's warriors, Alun of Dyfed, Cadrieth and Cas. Kerandroat means 'the village of Androat', but this name is not recorded anywhere else in Brittany. The name may simply be a derivative of Audren, or a variation on Andros, an early form of the name Andrew

Chapter 5
Arthur

5.1   Introduction

Since there are almost no historical references to Arthur, at least under that name, his very existence is much debated. But I believe that the events of the late 5th century demonstrate that there was a strong commander of the forces both of insular Britain and the Breton peninsula, and that unless such a person existed, it is impossible to explain the historical events of the period. From these events, therefore, we are able to reconstruct the outlines of the military career of this 'missing link'.

The only near contemporary British literary source is Gildas, who does not mention Arthur. But then Gildas was more interested in villains than heroes, as he explains at the outset: *"it is my present purpose to relate the deeds of an indolent and slothful race, rather than the exploits of those who have been valiant in the field."* How much more interesting his work would have been if he had reversed his priorities! As we shall see, it is also possible that Gildas knew of Arthur, but had reasons to dislike him and deliberately refrained from mentioning him. But what seems certain is that Arthur was not from the same Celtic ethnic background as Gildas: it is highly likely that he was a Romanised Belgic Briton.

Moreover, if Geoffrey of Monmouth is to be believed, Arthur came from a family with connections in Brittany, and it is possible that this too might have counted against him in the eyes of Gildas, who does not mention any figures from Brittany or anything of the history of the peninsula. This is curious, because Gildas is supposed to have had strong connections with Brittany, according to the authors of the two hagiographies written about him.

The first of his 'Lives' was written by a monk of the abbey at Rhuys in southern Brittany in the 9th century, and the second by Caradoc of Llancarfan in Wales in the 12th century. According to the earlier hagiography, Gildas was born in Alt Clut, in the Brythonic speaking part of the north of England known as Hen Ogledd. He was educated at a Welsh monastery, at Llan Illtud Fawr, and worked in Ireland before travelling to Rome. He then retired to the Rhuys Peninsula in southern Brittany.

The second 'Life' does not mention Brittany at all, although it says that Gildas was educated in Gaul. According to this version, Gildas became a monk at Street, near Glastonbury, where he died and he was eventually buried at Glastonbury Abbey. However, many scholars now doubt that Gildas the author was the same person as Gildas the saint who established a monastery in the Rhuys Peninsula, and it is quite likely that the author of the 'De Excidio' never left Wales. In Breton tradition, there were several saints called Gildas (Gildas des Sources, Gildas des Bois, Gildas de Rhuys) so it is highly possible that the stories of the lives of several individuals have become confused in the hagiographies. For these reasons, we should not presume that any views Gildas may have had on a person called Arthur were tainted by any prejudices, either for or against the Bretons.

More substantially, Caradoc suggests another reason why Gildas may have ignored Arthur. He tells us that the brothers of Gildas rebelled against Arthur, and that Arthur killed the oldest of them, Huail ap Caw. This enmity between Arthur and Huail is also mentioned in a Welsh tale called 'Culwch and Olwen', written in c.1100, and tradition in North Wales holds that Huail was beheaded at Ruthin in Denbighshire. Since this feud seems to be corroborated by several Welsh sources, there may be more substance to the theory that this explains the silence of Gildas, and incidentally the stories would also corroborate the theory that Arthur was not Welsh (indeed that he fought against them).

Nevertheless, the earliest surviving reference to Arthur by name occurs in the compilation made by Nennius in c.830, although a passing reference in the 'Y Gododdin', a Welsh poem, is potentially older (in this passage, a warrior is praised, *"Though he was no Arthur"*). Nennius introduces Arthur with these words: *"Then it was, that the magnanimous Arthur, with all the kings and military force of Britain, fought against the Saxons. And though there were many more noble than himself, yet he was twelve times chosen their commander, and was as often conqueror."*

His name is also mentioned in the 'Annales Cambriae' (the Annals of Wales), of which the earliest manuscript dates to the 12th century and which is therefore of the same vintage as Geoffrey of Monmouth's pseudo-history. The pronounced Welsh characteristics of these sources has, I believe, misled many historians to assume that Arthur had strong Welsh connections, but I think they are simply an accident of fate. The Welsh produced most of the few written records of Britain in the Dark Ages that have survived, and the powerful Arthurian folklore had simply been absorbed into Welsh tradition by the time that these were written. For reasons that will become apparent, I do not think that the history originated in the Principality.

After the Welsh histories, the next earliest sources are the medieval romances about Arthur and the knights of the Round Table, and the dilemma, for the student of this period, is how much weight (if any) to give to these. To most serious historians the answer is probably 'none', but in the near total absence of other literary sources, many have searched this material for clues. In my assessment, parts of the legends were not entirely without foundation. Geoffrey of Monmouth had a vivid imagination, and filled in large tracts of the narrative with reported speech, which he invented, and colourful anecdotes, but I do not think he was deliberately lying about the essentials. He probably genuinely believed that the megaliths of Stonehenge had been magically transported to Britain from Ireland by Merlin. And in fact, the blue stones had been brought to the site from Wales, so even in this most bizarre of passages there was a grain of truth. Geoffrey was a man of religion, and no doubt believed that liars would be sent to hell. We have already seen several other examples where corroboration has recently been found for apparently strange or even outlandish accounts in his 'Historia', and in my view this calls for a reappraisal of the historicity of the book. The problem is that the piecemeal substratum of fact is now buried deep beneath piles of fiction, and we therefore have to sift through copious amounts of nonsense to find any historical nuggets.

Fortunately there is a certain amount of external evidence that helps us to understand the literary sources. This is to be found in the historical context, the geography of the time, both physical and political, in the names of people and places, and in language. These clues enable us to interpret the traditions, and draw some rational inferences about the historical truth, but it must be stated at once that there are no 'magic bullets': it is unlikely in the extreme that any undiscovered literary source which explains the history of the Early Middle Ages in northern Europe will emerge. And we are not likely to find any relics that conclusively prove that Arthur existed. We are dealing in percentages of probability, and lines of best fit, which together build up a picture in shades of grey, not black and white. It is for each one of us to form our own view on how accurate that picture may be, and all I can do is to set out the evidence, as I see it, and provide my interpretation of it.

5.2 Name

Even the origins of the name of Arthur are uncertain. Early Celtic names were often formed by compounds of two words (see Appendix 4), and some commentators claim that 'Arthur' derives from the Welsh words for 'bear', (arth), and 'king' (rix), or from 'arth' and 'gwr' (meaning 'man'). The argument for the 'arth' prefix appears to be solidly grounded, but the suggested suffixes seem less so. However even the 'arth' element appears to have evolved in different ways, because 'Artur' appears as a Celtic name very early in time, and in Brittany the word 'arth' sometimes became 'arz'. In the legends, 'Arthur' appears in a bewildering array of spellings, ranging from Arther to Artuz, and the name appears to be closely related to another popular Welsh name, Arthmael, which meant 'bear prince'. Although Arthur does not appear in the legends under the name Arthmael, it may be that his memory is preserved in place names reflecting Arthmael, if only because the meaning of the name seems so appropriate to the legend.

However the name may not have been a compound of Welsh words at all. Some have suggested that the original name was Arturios, a Roman family name known from the 4th century (see 1.4). And another, smaller, minority believes that the name derives from the star called Arcturus. Certainly the idea that Arthur was a Roman and would therefore have had a Roman name has its attractions, but there were many historically significant British figures of the time who did not have Roman names (eg Vortigern and Riothamus).

Since I believe that Arthur was a Belgic Briton, whose legend was subsequently incorporated into Welsh folklore, I think it possible that Arthur and Arthmael are simply Welsh equivalents for his original name. For example, it is possible to imagine that his original name was something like Ather, and that this was subsequently assimilated into Anglo-Saxon as Athel, meaning 'noble'. The name Athel appears in the names of many Anglo-Saxon kings, such as Athelstan, Ethelred, Æthelwulf etc. Then, when the legends were adopted into Welsh, the name would have been assimilated to Artur and Arthmael, and it is in these forms that the name survived in Welsh literature. And, as a consequence of the Welsh migration to Brittany in the 6th century, most of the 'Arthur' place names in the province reflect one or other of the Welsh forms.

There are several 'ather' and 'athel' place names in England, but they are usually explained as being of Anglo-Saxon origin. I suspect that this attribution is wrong, at least in the case of the 'ather' names, because 'ather' has no meaning in Anglo-Saxon. There is no obvious reason why such names should not pre-date the Anglo-Saxons, especially when found in earlier contexts. We know that a lot of British place names survived the Anglo-Saxon conquest (London, Durham, Cambridge, any name involving chester, caster or cester etc).

To give an example, Atherstone in northern Warwickshire dates back to Roman times, and I believe the name means 'Ather's Town', rather than 'Ather's Stone'. An important fort called Manduessedum ('city of chariots') was constructed nearby, and Watling Street ran through the middle of the town, so the name could easily predate the Anglo-Saxons. It therefore seems possible to me that it was named after an Ather. A small fly in the ointment in this case is that Atherstone was called Aderestone in the Domesday Book, but this may simply have been an error by a Norman scribe.

Near Atherstone is a town called Wall. The British Library has a Welsh genealogy,[68] which contains a passage that is generally translated as saying that the people of Wall relocated to the Somerset Levels (*"funt glastenic qui uenerunt que uocatur loyt coyt"* – Caer Loyt Coyt was the name of Wall). And curiously there is an Atherstone in

---

68 Harleian MS 3859 Pedigree 25

Somerset, a hill that would have been an island in the salt-marshes during the first millennium. About 15 miles to the north is another place called Athelney, also an island in the Somerset Levels, which later became famous as Alfred the Great's place of refuge from the Danes. This is really little more than idle speculation, but I think it possible that these 'Athers' and 'Athels' may derive from the original name of Arthur. However, I cannot prove it; so for the purposes of this book, it is simplest to accept the Welsh 'Arthur' as his name, because that is the name by which he is universally known.

5.3   Ethnic Origin and Family

I have already expressed my view that Arthur was a Belgic Briton, raised in the Roman military tradition. But it is also possible that he had family connections in Brittany, as alleged by Geoffrey of Monmouth, who makes him the grandson of Constantine, the younger brother of Audren. Great Britain and Little Britain were regarded as two parts of the same country at the time, and people from the south-east of England had been fleeing from the war zones to Brittany since the middle of the 5th century. So by the end of the century, there must have been many people in Britain who had relatives on the Continent.

I think it significant that Nennius does not provide Arthur with a lineage, unlike many of the other figures in his 'Historia', because he certainly would have done had he known it. This reinforces my opinion that Arthur was a Belgic Roman, whose antecedents were unknown to the Welsh bards. We are not introduced to the legendary Uther Pendragon, Arthur's supposed father, until the 'Historia Regum Britanniae' of Geoffrey of Monmouth, written in the 12th century. Since Uther was supposedly the son of Constantine, the younger brother of King Audren of Brittany, Geoffrey portrays Arthur as a prince of the royal blood, albeit one conceived out of wedlock. I think it highly unlikely that Geoffrey had any historical information on Arthur's breeding, and therefore assign a low level of confidence to these passages, particularly because they may have been a product of political spin. Geoffrey may have wished to present a parallel with William the Bastard, later William the Conqueror, as part of his plan to give legitimacy to the Norman Conquest.

Nennius may not have known anything of Arthur's family, but he does provide Arthur with a whole new Celtic context, with a dog called Cabal and a son called Amr, (who, we are told, was killed by Arthur, for unexplained reasons). In the 'First Continuation' of 'Percival', by Chrétien de Troyes, we are told that Arthur had a child by his half-sister, a lady named in that account as Orcades, who became Morgause in later romances. This son was Mordred, the man who eventually rebelled against Arthur, leading to the battle in which he was mortally wounded (according to Geoffrey of Monmouth). Mordred was allegedly killed in the same battle. While we do not need to attach any great significance to any of this, it is to be noted that none of the sources suggest that Arthur had any children who survived him. Indeed, according to the legends, he killed them. And it is clear that, if there was an historical Arthur, he did not found a dynasty of British kings.

The Celtic context has since been expanded to provide Arthurian associations to numerous stones, caves, hills and glens in Welsh, Dumnonian and even Scottish, kingdoms, from Merlin's Rock in Cornwall to Arthur's Seat in Edinburgh. There is hardly a county in western Britain, south of Edinburgh, which does not claim some kind of association with Arthur. Conversely (and ironically) there are only a handful of places in Belgic Britain which assert such an association, and then seldom under the name 'Arthur'. (We have considered the Ather place names above). However this does not necessarily mean that Arthur did not exist, because it is plausible that almost all traces of him in central and eastern England have been obliterated by the Anglo-Saxons, along with most of the rest of the history of Britain in the 5th and 6th centuries. However, as we shall shortly see, Geoffrey of Monmouth maintained that Arthur fought a campaign in Gaul, and if that was the case, a search for evidence of the existence of Arthur in the toponymy of Brittany may be more productive. It would be particularly interesting to find traces of Arthur in a context which included Hoël, the Breton king who was, according to Geoffrey, Arthur's cousin and co-commander.

5.4 Arthur the Soldier

Nennius twice refers to Arthur as *"the soldier"*, and at first sight it might appear that Arthur was of common origin, especially as Nennius goes on to tell us that *"there were many more noble than himself"*. Arthur is further described as a 'Dux Bellorum' (war leader) in the following passage, which makes a clear distinction between Arthur's position and that of the kings of Britain: *"Then Arthur along with the kings of Britain fought against them [the Saxons] in those days, but Arthur himself was the Dux Bellorum"*. In my opinion, the distinction that Nennius is drawing here is not so much between Arthur as a minor noble, compared to the royal status of the kings of Britain, but rather between Arthur as a comparative foreigner and the native chieftains. The surprise implicit in the second clause is that a noble with Breton connections was allowed to command the British army, not that a mere commoner was allowed to give orders to British kings.

Nennius also makes it clear that Arthur assumed command of the British army by the will of the army itself, rather than by royal command. When Arthur is first introduced in this account, we are told *"And though there were many more noble than himself, yet he was twelve times chosen their commander"*. Readers may recall that, in Roman military terms, a Dux (or Duke) was the commander of the Roman forces in a particular province. A Dux was therefore junior to a Count, (who might have had command of several provinces), and, in the Empire, he was under the overall command of the Magister Militum (commander-in-chief) of the relevant prefecture. While the imperial structure would have broken down in the Britain of the late 5th century, I think that the choice of the term 'Dux' is instructive, indicating both the approximate seniority of his command, and the order of magnitude of the forces at Arthur's disposal (a Duke would typically have had command of one or two legions).

The expression *"he was twelve times chosen their commander"* is also very telling. The Roman army, especially in Britain (the *"land fertile in tyrants"*), had a tradition of choosing its own leaders. The army in Britain had indeed attempted to raise three 'Emperors' at the start of the 5th century (Marcus, Gratian and Constantine III), and the appointment of Arthur to the command of what may well have

The Megalithic Alignments at St Just, with the fertile agricultural land of the Morbihan in the background.

Quoit Brooch Style Brooch, 5th century, found in Kent.
(Courtesy of British Museum).

The Chapel at Lomarec (1606), home to the sarcophagus of a 6th century British King.

The Cathedral at Dôl, 13th to 15th centuries.

Arbury Hill, looking west, scarred by a motocross track.

Arbury Hill, looking north-east towards the valley below.

The remains of part of the east wall and a tower of the Camp de César, at Binic.

The Jesse Tree window at Ploërmel church. The Virgin Mary and Jesus are shown top centre, but below that King Jesse, seated under a canopy, is surrounded by his Biblical descendants. The figures are all in medieval costume, and the scene could equally well depict King Arthur surrounded by his courtiers.

been a combined British/Breton force appears to have been made as a consensus decision of the troops under him.

This kind of selection process had been characteristic of the Roman Empire itself since the end of the Severan dynasty of Emperors, and was commonplace among the less hierarchical barbarian tribes. The northern nations were typically governed by the consensus of a council, and even Clovis felt obliged to ask his men if his share of some war booty could be increased by one ewer, which he wished to return to the bishop of the church from which it had been stolen.[69] In parts of the Anglo-Saxon world a civil council was called a 'wapantake', an assembly of the men of the community able to bear arms, who expressed their votes on any particular issue by holding up their weapons to be counted (so 'weapon take').

In this context, it is not at all surprising to learn that the British army chose Arthur as its leader. He was clearly a competent and respected soldier (known in French tradition as 'Artur le preux' – Arthur the valiant), and his military training was no doubt thorough and extensive. He may have studied under Ambrosius, and indeed may have already have earned a reputation in battle in northern France, eg at the Siege of Nantes. Conceivably he was present at the 'Battle of Soissons'.

Given the words of Nennius, it is doubtful that Arthur was a 'king', but we need to be careful when using this term in any case. This word was introduced into English by the Anglo-Saxons, and would certainly not have been adopted by the British of the 5th century. The native British would have used the Latin 'rex' and 'regina', or the Celtic 'rix' (or 'ri') and 'rigan', for 'king' and 'queen'. Moreover, all of these terms were much less exclusive in the Early Middle Ages than their modern equivalents. Riothamus was a 'king' in the sense that the Brythonic personal name 'rigotamus' meant 'most king-like'. And the Riocatus to whom Bishop Faustus of Riez entrusted a letter to 'his Britons' had a 'royal' name, even though he was a monk and cleric. The 'ri' element in any name of the period probably implied an association with a tribal chieftain, but the chieftain may have been of purely local consequence, and the association might have been quite remote.

---

69 Gregory of Tours, "The History of the Franks", Book 2, Chapter 27

5.5 Arthur in Brittany?

Is it plausible that the insular British and the Bretons maintained a military alliance during the late 5th century? Yes, it certainly is. As we have seen, the British and the Bretons had remained close allies since the British colonisation of the peninsula in the late 4th century. Breton 'kings' like Conan Meriadoc and Gradlon are supposed to have been insular Britons in origin, and others like Budic are supposed to have spent part of their lives in Britain. British monks like St Brieuc and St Gwenole evangelised the province, and British troops had been deployed in Brittany by the Romans. Moreover, it appears that Brittany had remained economically stronger and socially more cohesive than the motherland of Great Britain during the 5th century. It is entirely possible that soldiers from the peninsula had supported Vortimer and Ambrosius Aurelianus against the Saxons, and that soldiers from the island of Britain had supported Riothamus in a war in Gaul against the Visigoths.

But most importantly, the Bretons and insular British faced common enemies, in the Franks and the Saxons, whose efforts against them may have been co-ordinated. We have seen that the arrival of Ælle and his sons in Sussex appears to have followed on from an alliance between the Franks and the Saxons in Gaul. And who is to say that the Saxons fighting under Chillon at Nantes in 490 did not retreat to England after their defeat? They were clearly sailing up and down the Channel from their bases in Germany to the mouth of the Loire, and must have passed within a few miles of the coast of Sussex. If the campaigns of the Saxons and Franks were co-ordinated, those of the insular and Armorican Britons would have had to be as well.

5.6 Arthur's Personality

Several of the legends relating to Arthur paint him as a cruel despot. We have already seen that Nennius wrote (without explanation) that he killed his own son, and when Arthur is mentioned in the 'Lives' of various saints (seven in all) it is often in unflattering terms. The earliest 'Life' to refer to Arthur was the 'Life of St Gwynllyw', which concerned an unsavoury King of South Wales, who was in the habit of raiding his neighbours. This account says that this King, 'St Gwynllyw,' eloped with a young maiden called Gwladys, the daughter of King Brychan of Brycheiniog, and their union produced St Cadoc. But according to the 'Life of St Cadoc', Gwladys was abducted in a raid, which resulted in a battle that only came to an end when Arthur intervened on Gwynllyw's side. This was decent of Arthur, because he had previously considered abducting the maiden for himself! In the 'Life of St Padern', Arthur covets the saint's cloak and is swallowed up by the earth, up to his chin, after seizing it. And so on and so forth – Arthur sometimes appears almost as an Anti-Christ.

The legends tell some tales which are even more lurid. According to Sir Thomas Malory, Arthur, having heard from Merlin a prophesy that a child born on May Day would destroy his kingdom, rounded up all the babies born in the kingdom on that day and sent them to sea in a ship with no crew. The ship hit a rock and sank and Mordred was the only baby to survive. Arthur was therefore depicted as a kind of King Herod, but I think we can ignore this tale as the product of an active imagination.

Arthur received a passing reference in the Y Goddodin, but was not otherwise named in surviving Welsh sources before Nennius, writing in c.830. And I put this down to the fact that he was a 'foreigner', from lowlands England. But the hostility of the Welsh monks may have run deeper than a mere tribal prejudice. There were significant doctrinal differences between the Christian rites of the Celtic west and the 'Roman' church of lowlands England. These differences emerged after St Augustine of Hippo (354 – 430) developed the concept of the Catholic Church, and fathered the Nicene Creed. The Trinitarian doctrine, and the concept of original sin, which he espoused, rapidly became the orthodoxy of the Roman church, but ran counter to the views of the Pelagians in Britain. St Germanus had brought the Christians of Roman England 'on side', but the Celtic churches maintained their own traditons, and a schism developed that still existed when St Augustine of Canterbury undertook his mission to England at the end of the 6th century. Indeed, it was only finally healed at the Synod of Whitby in 664.

Whether Arthur was perceived by the Welsh clergy as being a Roman in this respect, or whether he was simply not very observant at all, it seems they did not regard him as one of their own. If the former, we might have expected that at least Gildas would have been supportive, because Gildas seems to have taken the Roman line (and not only in religious matters). I therefore conclude that Arthur was not seen by contemporaries as a model of Christian virtue, although the Annales Cambriae tell us that he *"carried the cross of our Lord Jesus Christ on his shoulders for three days and three nights"* at the Battle of Mount Badon and Nennius says that he carried the image of the Virgin Mary on his shield at the Battle of Gurnion (or Guinnion). Gildas may have paid him a grudging and impersonal acknowledgement as one of *"those who have been valiant in the field",* but that was as far as he was prepared to go.

In truth we can know little or nothing of Arthur's personality, but it may safely be assumed that he was a fearsome and brutal warrior. Combat in former times was not the detached experience of the sniper or the bomb-aimer – it was, in modern parlance, 'up close and personal'. Any man that led that sort of life would emerge fairly desensitised, but we have no reason to suppose that Arthur was any more savage than other soldiers of his time, or that he did not have any virtues. In fact, judging by the impact of the legends, it appears that he commanded immense respect and loyalty among his soldiers, and inspired terror in his enemies. Could any soldier wish for a better epitaph?

Chapter 6
Arthur's Campaigns

6.1 Battles Identified by Nennius

The details of the battles set out in the account of Nennius are not reliable, but should nevertheless be noted. He tells us of 12 battles, in which Arthur led the British against the Anglo-Saxons: *"The first battle in which he was engaged, was at the mouth of the river Gleni. The second, third, fourth, and fifth, were on another river, by the Britons called Duglas, in the region Linuis. The sixth, on the river Bassas. The seventh in the wood Celidon, which the Britons call Cat Coit Celidon.*[70] *The eighth was near Gurnion castle, where Arthur bore the image of the Holy Virgin, mother of God, upon his shoulders, and through the power of our Lord Jesus Christ, and the holy Mary, put the Saxons to flight, and pursued them the whole day with great slaughter. The ninth was at the City of Legion, which is called Cair Lion. The tenth was on the banks of the river Trat Treuroit. The eleventh was on the mountain Breguoin, which we call Cat Bregion. The twelfth was a most severe contest, when Arthur penetrated to the hill of Badon ['Mons Badonicus']. In this engagement, nine hundred and forty fell by his hand alone, no one but the Lord affording him assistance. In all these engagements the Britons were successful."*

Some of these battles appear to relate to other conflicts in history or to mythology, and none of the sites can be identified with certainty, but I will briefly rehearse a few of the most popular theories. There is a river Glen in Lincolnshire, and Linuis is often taken to be Lindsey, so the first five battles are often assumed to have taken place in Lincolnshire. The river Bassas has never been identified, but 'bassas' meant 'short and stout'. That would rule out rivers like the Humber, Severn or Thames, but it might have been a description of a river like the Welland, for example.

---
70 'the Battle of Celidon Wood'.

The Duke and the Decoy

POLITICAL MAP OF BRITAIN c.540

By the end of Arthur's reign, the area directly under his control was probably the shaded area, defined by Watling Street, the Welsh border and the borders with the Cornish and the West Saxons. However he also had alliances with King Cado of Dumnonia (d. 537), the Welsh Kings and Mordred, who ruled the area between the northern British kingdom of Hen Ogledd and Watling Street from his court at Moddershall in Stafford.

The forest of Celidon is said to be the Caledonian Forests, and hence in Scotland, but this seems most improbable on any rational analysis of the geopolitical situation. It is far more likely that Celidon was in 'the land of cal,'[71] perhaps at Calverton in Milton Keynes (the

---
71 'Cal-y-don', the fort of the stone, perhaps.

site of an ancient forest on Watling Street) or in Rockingham Forest in Northamptonshire (the previous name of which is unknown). Gurnion Castle has never been identified – I suggest possibly Gildenburgh, a name for Peterborough, found in local 12th century histories; the 'burgh' element was added by the Anglo-Saxons, and stripping that away, 'gilden' is fairly similar to 'gurnion'.

The City of Legion is usually said to be Caerleon in Monmouthshire, but it could have been any Roman legionary base (eg Chester, Carlisle, York or Colchester), and it is likely to have been one a good deal closer to where the Anglo-Saxons were. One possibility is Longthorpe in Cambridgeshire, a former base of the Roman Legio IX Hispana, which was in or near the probable conflict zone. And neither Trat Treuroit (in some manuscripts Tribruit) nor Breguoin (in some manuscripts Agned) have been persuasively identified. 'Traith', in the Gaulish language, meant a bay or tidal estuary, so perhaps Trat Treuroit was an inlet around the Wash or Thames Estuary. The battle is corroborated in a Welsh poem, possibly dating to the mid-9th century, called the Pa Gur, which talks of a Battle of Tryfrwyd. Bregouin appears in other early sources as a battle fought by Urien of Rheged. Rheged was a British kingdom of the Hen Ogledd (in northern England and southern Scotland). 'Bre', in Celtic, has a sense of 'hill' or 'fort' and 'guoin' is a personal name, commonly found in Armorica. Agned could possibly have been Andred – ie Pevensey Castle.

However it is possible to find modern locations for all of these names to support the various theories that Arthur's battles were fought in Brittany, in almost every part of England and Wales or in Scotland. It is simply not worth paying too much attention to such details. The battle in the list provided by Nennius that is most likely to be an historical fact is the Battle of Mons Badonicus, which may have been fought by Ambrosius Aurelianus or by Arthur (or by both). The remainder of the places may be names of mythical or real battles, but we cannot hope to securely identify them. What is important is simply to understand the historical context. It is likely that battles between the Anglo-Saxons and the Britons, and between the Franks and the Bretons, took place in the 480s and 490s, and by understanding the geo-political situation at that time, we can make educated guesses as to where those battles might have taken place.

The political geography of Britain in the late 5th century is fairly easy to reconstruct. The east of England was a patchwork of Romano-British towns (like Lincoln) and Anglo-Saxon hamlets (like Mucking), and places where the two peoples appear to have cohabited, eg in Kent. In section 10.2, we will see that the toponymic evidence suggests that Ambrosius ruled a kingdom in what is now southern England, and we can assume that he would have re-used existing Iron Age and Roman roads and forts in his defences. An example would have been Watling Street and the numerous camps and forts along it, which would have enabled the British to move troops up and down the country to meet any threat from raiders from the North Sea. To the east of Watling Street, the coastal regions were penetrated by many inlets, rivers and swamps, and it appears likely that the Anglo-Saxons had control of Ermine Street by the later years of the century. This may have allowed them to communicate by land between their settlements in Lindsey and East Anglia, but London was a major obstacle to any attempts to unite the 'kingdoms' of Kent and Sussex with those further north.

We saw in 3.1 that the Saxon settlements in the Nene Valley were encroaching into the former territory of the Catuvellauni, and threatening the British control over Watling Street. Indeed, by the late 5th century, they were established to the west of Northampton, and close to the very source of the River Nene, at Arbury Hill. The Angles had meanwhile colonised much of Lindsey and East Anglia, and their growing numbers created a demand for more land which could only be satisfied at the expense of their neighbours. Ælle established a Saxon kingdom in West Sussex in 477, and a significant increase in immigration from the Continent into that area followed.

This then was the background to a war that broke out in the 470s, a war which was essentially fought over land resources, and which therefore must have been a war fought in the east of England. If, as many assume, the 'Linuis' region was Lindsey, and the river Gleni mentioned by Nennius was the Glen in Lincolnshire, the first five battles listed by Nennius were fought in Lincolnshire, a distribution entirely consistent with the geo-political realities of the period. Although Nennius claims that Arthur was victorious in all of his battles, Gildas is more circumspect (*"Sometimes our countrymen, sometimes the enemy, won the field"*), and it would be unsurprising if the battlefields shifted west with the tide of war. As I have said, it is possible to come up with various theories about where the rest of the battles were fought, but some of the names are of doubtful historicity, and there can be no certainty about the details. The strong probability is that the conflict spread from West Sussex north to the East Midlands, but it would be very surprising, to me at least, if the front line got anywhere near Bath, at any time in the 5th century. While there had been pagan settlements in the Upper Thames Valley since the end of the 4th century, these seem to have been peaceful, and I suspect that they were of a different, possibly Toxandrian, character. Only in the latter part of the 6th century do we read of battles in the Cotswolds, and find archaeological evidence of a conflict in the west, eg in the Wansdyke. So in my view, we should look for the site of Mount Badon among the Downs, the Chilterns and the hills of the East Midlands, not in Somerset.

6.2   Mount Badon

Mount Badon is the only battle mentioned by Gildas (*"the last almost, though not the least slaughter of our cruel foes"*), and the only battle that we can be reasonably certain was as an historical event. Geoffrey of Monmouth placed the battle at Bath, but the Roman name for Bath was Aquae Sulis, and it is most unlikely that Gildas would have referred to the city by its Anglo-Saxon name 'Badon'. For this reason, as well as the geo-political logic, I reject the idea that Mons Badonicus was the Hill of Bath.

Polydore Vergil, an historian at the court of King Henry VII, wrote a history of England called the 'Anglica Historia' (manuscript completed by 1513), based on unknown sources, some of which are probably lost.[72] In it, he wrote that *"Not long afterwards [after the Alleluia Battle] they [the Saxons] occupied a high mountain in that part of the island which faces Germany, called at the time Badonicus".* (He dated the battle to 491). So Vergil believed that the battle was fought on the east coast of England, possibly on the basis of a manuscript that was lost in the Dissolution of the Monasteries by King Henry VIII.

Following the principle that it probably took place somewhere

---

[72] He was accused by contemporaries of burning manuscripts *"that the faults of his own work might pass undiscovered"* – John Caius, 1574).

along the border zone between the Britons and the Anglo-Saxons, as it was in 493, I think that a good candidate for the location is Arbury Hill in Northamptonshire. This site was called Badden Byrig in a charter of 944, by which King Edmund I gave some lands to Bishop Aelfric of Hereford. 'Byrig' was an Anglo-Saxon term meaning 'borough', or fortified place, but it was also their version of a much older Proto-Indo-European word 'berg', meaning a fortified hill. Badden Berg could have been translated literally as Mount Baden.

We have already come across Arbury Hill as the principal source of the River Nene, but it is also a source of the Thames (via the Cherwell), the Ouse and the Avon and accordingly it may have had a religious significance in pre-historic times. It is the tallest hill in Northamptonshire, at 738 ft, and it is located about five miles to the west of Watling Street. By one of those strange quirks of historical repetition, it is about 3 miles to the west of the most plausible candidate for the site of Boudicca's Battle of Watling Street, which underlines the strategic importance of the area.[73]

The hill is surmounted by the vestigial remains of an Iron Age hillfort, which appears to have formed one of a chain of forts along the valley of the River Nene. The fort is a square shape, with sides about 200 metres in length, protected by a ditch and single embankment that have been almost erased, to the point that some surveyors considered the fort to be a natural feature. The main episode of destruction must have been deliberate, and I take this as circumstantial evidence in support of the identification, because wherever Mount Badon was, we know that within 50 years or so of the battle, it had fallen into the hands of the Anglo-Saxons. They would hardly have wanted to leave intact a fort that was both a monument to their greatest defeat, and a potential rallying point for further resistance. The remains have however been further eroded by ploughing, and by the current use of the site as a track for motor-cycle scrambling.

So the Saxon colonisation of the Nene Valley had brought them within touching distance of Arbury Hill by the end of the 5th century (eg at Duston), and in fact an early Saxon burial in the context of a Roman villa site at Borough Hill, five miles to the north and clearly visible from Arbury Hill, demonstrates that the Saxons must have crossed Watling Street at about this time. Quite apart from any

---

73 John Pegg, 'Landscape Analysis and Appraisal, Church Stowe, Northamptonshire as a Candidate Site for the Battle of Watling Street' (2010).

religious or military significance that either side may have attached to the upper Nene Valley and Watling Street, the area was important for its ironstone fields and consequent metal production, so it is easy to see why men might have fought over it.

Gildas described the battle as the *"obsessio Badonici montis"*, meaning that it was a siege, but it is far from clear who were the besiegers and who were the besieged. As described by Geoffrey of Monmouth, it was the Saxons who were defending the top of the hill. In any case a siege would be consistent with the battle lasting a long time, and the Annales Cambriae suggest that it lasted for three days. In an entry for the year 516, the Annales tell us that there took place: *"The Battle of Badon, in which Arthur carried the cross of our Lord Jesus Christ on his shoulders for three days and three nights and the Britons were victors."* The words for 'shoulder' and 'shield' in Old Welsh were very similar – 'scuit' meant shield and 'scuid' meant shoulder– so the entry probably means that Arthur had a cross or chi-rho symbol painted on his shield (Roman soldiers had fought under Christian symbols since the time of Constantine the Great).

What is suspect about this entry is the date, which cannot be reconciled with the account of Gildas (or that of Bede, who clearly relied on Gildas). And as we shall see shortly, I do not think that a date of 516 can be reconciled with dates of related events on the Continent, so I am inclined to believe that the Annales are simply incorrect in this respect. Gildas tells us that the battle took place *"forty-four years and one month after the landing of the Saxons, and also the time of my own nativity"*, but he does not tell us when the Saxons landed. Bede dates the arrival of the Saxons to 449, and echoes Gildas in saying that Mount Badon took place 44 years after their arrival, which dates the battle to 493. A range of dates have been suggested for the battle, from c.480 to c.520, but I am content to accept the suggested date of 493, give or take a little. I think it unlikely that the battle was fought before 490 or after 496.

There is no corroboration for any of these events in the Anglo-Saxon Chronicle, because of course the Chronicle does not report any British victories. However, some support for the British view of events may be derived from the fact that Ælle disappears from the record after 490, and in 495 appears to have been replaced by Cerdic and his son Cynric, who arrived with five ships at a place called

Cerdic's Ore. One explanation for the change of leadership could be that the defeated Anglo-Saxons had to summon reinforcements to prevent their complete annihilation by the British. In any event, the battle seems to have established a new status quo, and the result seems to have been an extended period of armed peace.

While the chronology of the Anglo-Saxon Chronicle is uncertain for this period, and Cerdic and Cynric may not be historical figures, it appears that by the time that Gildas was writing (possibly c.540) Britain had enjoyed a long period with few outbreaks of hostilities. Indeed this peace had lasted so long that Gildas tells us the contemporary rulers of Britain had forgotten their religious and moral duties. By the time he was writing, *"our foreign wars have ceased"* and new leaders had emerged who had no memory of this time of troubles, having *"only experience of the present prosperity"*. We are therefore left with the impression that a generation had elapsed, consistent with a date of the battle at the end of the 5th century.

Although the outcome of the war was successful from a British point of view, in that the British won a victory and that the expansion of the Anglo-Saxon colonies was halted, I think it unlikely that the British succeeded in recovering any lands under Anglo-Saxon occupation. In the absence of coin and dated pottery evidence from the 5th or 6th centuries, it is impossible to tell the exact details of the progression, but it is obvious that at some point in time the Anglo-Saxons had broken out of their eastern enclaves, and it seems unlikely that they were driven back to them. The main period of conquest occurred in the second half of the 6th century when the Anglo-Saxons won battles at Sarum (552), Bedford (571) and Dyrham in Gloucestershire (577), but it appears to me probable that the 'front line' was considerably further west after the war of the 480s and 490s than it had been before. London appears to have collapsed as a trading centre by the end of the 5th century, which is unsurprising given that the Saxons had control over the Thames Estuary. It seems that the Saxons established their own settlement about a mile upstream of the Tower at the mouth of the River Fleet, at a place they called Lundenwic. The earliest Saxon material found in London consists of a few 5th century finds from Billingsgate and from St Brides and a small 5th to

6th century assemblage from St John's Clerkenwell, a short distance up the River Fleet.[74]

So we can form a reasonably accurate picture of the history of the period, and we know for certain the name of the main battle. But does Mount Badon prove that Arthur existed? The only early literary sources which identify him as the British commander are Nennius and the Annales Cambriae, both written centuries after the event. However, the British army must have been led by someone, and the two main candidates are Arthur and Ambrosius Aurelianus (or the same person, if they were one and the same). Those who support Ambrosius as the hero at least have the advantage that their candidate is an undoubted historical figure. It is also possible to read Bede as saying that Ambrosius was the British commander at Mount Badon, but that reading is not unquestionable.

Against that, if Ambrosius was the commander of the British forces after Vortimer (ie in c.460) he must have been quite elderly in 493, probably in his 60s, and this suggests that it is unlikely that he would have been capable of climbing a substantial hill and fighting a battle at the top of it. So I prefer the view that Arthur was the British commander

And I believe that corroboration for this, at least in outline, is to be found in the history of Brittany. It should come as no surprise that we need to look abroad for evidence of the British history of this period, because our main sources for the whole of the 5th century are to be found in Gaul. As we have seen, a Romanised lifestyle continued in Brittany long after it had collapsed in Britain, and a great deal of literature from Gaul in the 5th and 6th century survives. Moreover Brittany was not overrun by the Franks, in the way that England was conquered by the Anglo-Saxons (for example the Breton aristocracy was not displaced), so we would expect more of the evidence to have survived. Brittany also became a repository of the Welsh literature of the first millennium, including the oldest known manuscript of Nennius, so on both counts it is more likely that any historical traces will have survived there, rather than in Britain.

---

74 Les Capon, 'Saxon Activity at 15 – 17 Long Acre, City of Westminster', London Archaeologist, Winter 2006, p.172.

6.3   The Breton Campaign

Apart from the medieval Arthurian legends, there is one written source that tells us that Arthur fought battles in Gaul, which is a fragment of the preface of a 'Life of St Goeznou' [see Chapter 8 for details], which survives in a manuscript of the 'Chronicle of St Brieuc'. It contains the following passage: *"The Saxons, pagans and instruments of the devil, thirsting for blood, never ceased to mistreat the Britons. Their tyranny was then defeated by the king of the Britons, Arthur, who drove most of them out of the island and reduced them to submission. But after numerous victories in Britain and in Gaul, he left this human life: the way was once more open to the Saxons to enter Britain, so that the churches were destroyed and the saints persecuted...."*

On the evidence of a date provided in the preface to this document, it was written in 1019, and therefore long before Geoffrey wrote his 'Historia'. However the date has been questioned, and some think it is a medieval forgery. But even if the ostensible date is unreliable, the internal evidence of the contents of the work (eg the place names) suggests that it was based on 10th century sources, so it appears to be 'pre-Galfridian' in origin. And clearly the author believed that Arthur had "*numerous victories in Britain and in Gaul*", apparently not relying on Geoffrey for this view.

However, the bulk of the evidence to support the theory that Arthur fought battles in Gaul is contained in the accounts of Geoffrey and his successors. Although this material comes with the usual health warnings, it seems fairly clear that the legends, which have become known in France as the 'matière de Bretagne', are largely Breton in origin, and it is their provenance as much as their contents which convinces me that there is a historical basis to them. To evaluate the legends of this episode, we need to compare them with the historical evidence of the war between the Bretons and the Franks, and to consider whether there is any circumstantial evidence in terms of place names or personal names to support the hypothesis that a British commander called Arthur was actively involved.

In the medieval Arthurian romances, Arthur's campaign in Gaul is a centrepiece of the stories. Geoffrey of Monmouth tells us that, some time after winning the battle of Mons Badonicus, Arthur crossed the Channel. He made a brief detour in an attempt to save a maiden from a foul monster on an island near Le Mont St Michel, and then joined forces with the Armorican Bretons led by Hoël, in a battle against the Romans. Indeed, Geoffrey devotes only one page to the Battle of Mount Badon (which he calls Bath Hill), whereas he takes a full ten pages to describe the final battle of Arthur's campaign in Gaul, which he located at a valley called Saussy, near Autun. Clearly he thought that the campaign in Gaul was altogether on a larger and more significant scale than the battle at Mount Badon.

Geoffrey's account demonstrates a remarkable knowledge of the geography of Brittany, including a reference to the tiny island of Tombelaine near Le Mont St Michel, consistent with the view that he was a scion of a Breton family. But his descriptions of all the Arthurian battles are very obviously pure fiction, and it is clear that he invented this material. Despite this, it seems to me that in some essentials he may well have been correct: a British commander may have fought alongside the Bretons; the Bretons may have been commanded by Hoël; 'Romans' could well have been involved; and the scale of the war in Gaul is likely to have been significantly greater than the conflict between the British and the Anglo-Saxons in England. None of these propositions stand in obvious conflict with known history.

On the other hand Geoffrey clearly knew neither the names of Arthur's opponents, or the places where the battles were fought. He names Arthur's opponent at the supposed Battle of Autun as Frollo, but history reveals nobody of that name who could have been involved, and there is no way that a British commander could have been fighting battles in Burgundy in the 490s. But, fortunately, subsequent contributors to the legends were able to fill in a little of the missing information, and I believe that Arthur's opponent was (almost) correctly identified as 'Claudas', in the Vulgate Merlin (c.1230s), which was the second part of the Vulgate Cycle.[75] The stories relating to Claudas have often been interpreted as being located in England, but there are ample references in them to *"litill Bretayne"* (as mentioned in the translation at Corpus Christi), so I think it is clear who Claudas was.

According to the Vulgate Merlin, King Claudas held the lands of Bourges and Berry from Aramont (more usually referred to as Hoël), in the time of Arthur's father (Uther Pendragon). But he transferred

---

[75] The original was written in French prose, and there is an incomplete English translation, of the 1420s, in the library of Corpus Christi College, Cambridge.

his allegiance to the King of Gaul, and in response Aramont and Uther invaded Berry and laid waste the land (which became known as 'The Desert' or 'The Land Laid Waste', in consequence). After the deaths of Uther and Aramont, Claudas attacked Benoic and Gannes, which were ruled by Ban and Bors (or Bohors) respectively, and, in return for assistance that they had previously furnished to him in his wars in Britain, Arthur agreed to help the Bretons against the invader. Arthur, Ban and Bors won a victory against Claudas at the battle of Trèbes. *"Thus was the kynge Arthur in the reame of Benoyk, he and his men a moneth, and ronne euery day in to Claudas londes, and wasted it so that longe tyme after myght he haue no power to a-rise vpon the kynge Ban"*, continued the translation of the Vulgate Merlin. But subsequently, at a time when Arthur was preoccupied with a war in Britain, Claudas attacked again and both Ban and Bors were killed. *"King Bohort fell into a great sickness, and lay long in the city of Gannes, for which King Ban, his brother, was very sorrowful and in great distress; for he could not be with him as his will was, on account of a neighbour of his, who bordered on him, and who was very fell and cruel. This was King Claudas of the Desert, who was so grieved and angry (about his Castle which King Arthur had caused to be levelled), that he was nearly going out of his senses; and he did not know on whom to take vengeance, except on King Ban of Benoyc, and on King Bohort, who bordered on him, because they were King Arthur's men."* Arthur returned and defeated Claudas, and entrusted the lands he thereby acquired to Lancelot, before his return to England. Claudas fled to Rome and was never heard of again.

If we simply substitute 'Clovis' for 'Claudas', this mostly makes sense. And since Clovis was known to the Franks as Chlodowech (or, in Latin, Chlodovechus), it is not hard to see where the 'd' of the legendary version of the name came from. We know that, in the time of Arthur's father (whoever that may have been) the British fought a battle near Bourges, where they were crushed by the Visigoths (in 469 or 470). The Romans defeated the Visigoths the following year, and it is quite likely that considerable destruction was visited on the region of Berry in the course of these events.

Sixteen years later, Clovis had defeated Syagrius. Then in 490 he began his campaign against the Bretons, putting Nantes under siege. According to Procopius, the Franks wanted to subdue the 'Arborykhes', *"who had become Roman soldiers"* because their *"territory was adjacent to their own and they had changed the government under which they had lived for a long time."* It is clear that the 'Arborykhes' were the Armoricans, and it seems probable that they had assumed control of the western part of the former kingdom of Syagrius. Procopius then describes the events which followed: *"the Franks began to pillage their lands, then, very bellicose, marched against them with all their people. But the Arboykhes proved their merit and their loyalty to the Romans and showed in this war that they were very brave. The Germans not having won by force, considered it advisable to make friends with them and get closely connected."* The outcome was an alliance under which the Bretons were left largely autonomous in their peninsula, and free from any obligation to pay tribute to Clovis.

In 4.9, I asked how this could have happened. Clovis had an all-conquering army, and it seems almost inexplicable that he should have lost to the Bretons. Well, if we interpret the legends as I have suggested above, the answer is that the Bretons were reinforced by a British expeditionary force led by Arthur. And there is nothing in the history of the relationship between the Bretons and the British of the 4th or 5th centuries to suggest that this is implausible.

Indeed, since the Battle of Mount Badon evidently took place in c.493, and the truce between the Bretons and the Franks seems to have been made in c.497, there is a remarkably good 'fit' for a British campaign in Brittany. The introduction of battle-hardened British troops into the conflict between the Bretons and the Franks, together with the element of surprise, would have been just the sort of development that could have swung the war in favour of the Bretons. And this precise moment in the history of the Anglo-Saxon conquest of England is probably the only time when the British would have felt secure enough to mount a Continental expedition.

We may even have a report from a witness to Arthur's arrival in Brittany, although this is speculation on my part. It is a reasonable assumption that, if he fought a campaign in Brittany, he must have disembarked his troops in the peninsula (all the ports to the east being under Frankish control). And there is a strange account in Albert Le Grand's 'Life of St Gwenole' which cannot be wholly accurate, but which might shed some light on the events of the 490s. Gwenole lived from 460 to 532, and his father was Fragan, who made his home at Ploufragan, just to the west of St Brieuc. According to Le Grand, Fragan took part in a battle against a large force of Saxons near L'Aberwrac'h in 388, the arrival of the Saxon fleet having been reported to Fragan by an observer who told him *"Me a vel mil guern" ("I have seen a thousand masts"* in Breton).

If Gwenole lived from 460 to 532, it is obvious that his father was not fighting battles in 388, so if there is a grain of truth in the story, we need to reinterpret it. In terms of the probable time-frame of Fragan's life, the event described could plausibly have been the arrival of a fleet in c.495, and it must have been of very unusual significance for this report to have survived to us. A massive invasion of Finistère by Saxons in the late 5th century is always a possibility, but the Anglo-Saxon Chronicle describes them as arriving in Britain in fleets of three ships (in 449 and 477) or five ships (in 495), not in fleets of a hundred. The only people in northern Europe who are known to have been capable of transporting a large army by sea in the 5th century were the British. Could the event reported have been the arrival of such an army?

While I am engaged in speculation, I will just mention another episode that is equally mysterious. Most of Geoffrey's account of Arthur's campaign in Gaul is highly fanciful, and it is most improbable that Arthur fought outside Brittany. But a possible explanation of Arthur's supposed battle at Autun may be found in a fragment from Gregory of Tours. In a very succinct report of an event on an unspecified date (but probably in the late 6th century), Gregory tells us that *"Two swarms of locusts appeared at this time. They passed through the Auvergne and the Limousin, and are said to have penetrated as far as the plain of Romagna.*[76] *There they fought a great battle and many were killed."* It is just possible that this event found an echo in Geoffrey's book, because Autun is about 100 miles from Clermont Ferrand (and incidentally about 40 miles from Avallon). But since Gregory does not tell us who these 'swarms of locusts' were, we cannot make further progress.

The period is a tricky one for historians, falling just after the death of Procopius, so there are few sources to tell us what happened after Count Belisarius's campaign to recapture Italy from the Ostrogoths in 535 – 554. The Ostrogoths were finally defeated in Italy at the Battle

---
76 Romagnat, near Clermont-Ferrand.

of Mons Lactarius in 552 or 553, and surrendered on condition that they would be allowed to leave the country safely, but what happened to the remnants of their army is unknown. The Franks attempted to seize Italy after the Ostrogoth regime was destroyed, but failed, so an unrecorded battle between Franks and Ostrogoths in Burgundy is not out of the question. And Geoffrey may later have confused this battle with the events of Arthur's lifetime.

6.4   Toponymy of a Breton Campaign

As we have seen, Claudas is said to have invaded Gannes and Benoic. Gannes is presumably Vannes, and I believe that Benoic was the area around Binic on the Côtes d'Armor (see 'Lisia: Vortigern's Island'). We know from Procopius that Clovis made a number of forays into Brittany, and quite obviously the areas most likely to have been attacked were the eastern parts of the peninsula, with Vannes in the south and what is now St Brieuc in the north. To this day, this is the linguistic border of Brittany, with the Breton language spoken mainly to the west of the boundary and the (nearly extinct) Gallo language spoken mainly to the east of it. We know that the Franks were attacking Nantes in the south, and it is very likely that they had a base at Rennes, from which to launch their invasions.

Trèbes, the legendary location of the decisive battle, is however more difficult. The most prominent Trèbes in France today is a town near Carcassone in the far south-west, but traditionally the Arthurian town of that name is supposed to have been situated on the Loire and the only place with a similar name on the Loire is Chênehutte-Trèves-Cunault. However, it seems fairly clear that the Bretons had been driven out of the Loire valley (except for the city of Nantes) by 492, so it seems very improbable that Trèbes would be found there.

There are many places in France named Trèves or Trèbes, which both seem to derive from a Gaulish word 'treb', meaning habitation, cognate with the Breton word 'treb', meaning a sub-division of a parish. This therefore precludes any positive identification of the place in the Arthurian legends.

Rationally, we should look to Brittany to discover where the battles of the 490s took place, and many of the place names in the legends do indeed clearly relate to Brittany. As we have seen, Gannes seems to be Vannes, and the legends refer many times to Carhaix, which still bears the same name. Using this as a guide, we can note that there is a village called Trévé, near Loudéac, which was spelt Treves in 1274. This is in the right area to have been a possible scene of events during the Frankish campaign in Brittany, since it is a town on the road into the centre of the peninsula from Rennes. And the adjacent village of La Motte confirms that there was an ancient earthwork castle nearby. While these villages may today simply be sub-divisions of the parish of Loudéac, it is tempting to think that they may have been the site of a battle, and subsequent truce, in the war between the Franks and the Bretons.

The toponymic evidence for the existence of Hoël is set out in Appendix 2 and my conclusion is that he was probably an historical figure. But the other characters in the legendary accounts are much more elusive. The names of Ban and Bors may be reflected in Bannalec (near Concarneau), Plobannalec-Lesconil (Finistère) and Kerbors (Côtes d'Armor), but there is no solid evidence to support any such etymology. And indeed, since Ban was allegedly the king of Benoic (probably in the north) and Bors was supposedly the king of Gannes (probably in the south) the distribution of these names, if they were related to these persons, seems perverse.

My conclusion is therefore that there is so little evidence for a Ban or Bors (or Bohort) that these names are probably fictional. Similarly I think Lancelot is fictional (see Appendix 2), although it is just possible that he was the Duke of the Armorican Tract. The evidence for a campaign by Arthur in Gaul therefore rests on the toponymic evidence in Brittany for Arthur himself, together with the essential elements of the narrative in the 'Historia' and a few fragments in other documents (particularly the 'Life of St Goeznou'), viewed in the historical context.

6.5   Arthur's Last Battle

After the conclusion of the Treaty of 497 between the Bretons and the Franks, any troops from the island of Britain that may have taken part in the war would no doubt have returned home. Geofffrey of Monmouth describes Arthur's campaign against the Romans as

Arthur's Campaigns

coming to a halt when, while he is crossing the Alps, Arthur hears of a rebellion at home, led by his nephew Mordred. Much of this is clearly fanciful, not least because there appears to have been a significant time gap (circa 40 years) between the end of the Brittany campaign and the Battle of Camlann.

While the Anglo-Saxon Chronicle tells us of various further Germanic migrations to Britain, and of battles allegedly fought at Portsmouth and Netley (near Southampton), the accounts do not appear to be reliable. For example, the Chronicle implies that Portsmouth was named after a Saxon chief called Porta, when it obviously got its name from the Latin word 'portus', meaning port. The description of a long period of peace after the Battle of Mount Badon, which Gildas gives us, seems a more plausible account.

However a massive weather event, possibly the eruption of a volcano, resulted in a vicious cold snap in 535 and 536, and in the 'years of no summer' the crops failed, resulting in a global famine. This in turn caused an outbreak of a plague in 541 – 542, which appears to have started in China, and which became known as 'the Plague of Justinian' because it wiped out a quarter of the population of Constantinople. In one of the Welsh triads, this contagion was recorded as the Yellow Plague.

In Britain, these events appear to have precipitated a civil war between the Celtic western kingdoms and the Belgo-Roman kingdoms of lowlands England. The war culminated in the Battle of Camlann, one of the 'Three Futile Battles of Britain' according to the Annales Cambriae. The battle was reported by Geoffrey of Monmouth, and this is one aspect of his account to which I attach greater credence, the reason being that he tells us that he learned of this story not only from his ancient sources but also from Walter, the Archdeacon of Oxford. Since Walter must have read Geoffrey's book and could hardly have been a conspirator in the publication of a lie, I assume that he did in fact provide Geoffrey with information on which he partly based his work. Moreover the existence of Mordred is confirmed by the Annales Cambriae, the source material for which dates from the mid-10th century, and therefore before Geoffrey's time.

The Annales only mention three Arthurian figures by name, Arthur, Merlin ('Myrddin') and Mordred ('Medraut'). The entry in the Annales for 537 reads: *"The strife of Camlann in which Arthur*

131

and Medraut fell and there was death in Britain and Ireland." If the reference in the Annales to *"death in Britain and Ireland"* describes the Plague of Justinian, which occurred in 541 – 542, the date of Camlann given in the Annales is wrong, and the date offered by Geoffrey of Monmouth, namely 542, is more likely to be right. The Annales do not actually say that Arthur and Mordred were on opposite sides in the battle, but that has been generally assumed ever since. And various theories have been advanced over the years for the location of the battle, including suggested sites in Scotland and Wales. For what it is worth, Geoffrey tells us that it was in Cornwall.

Gildas does not explicitly mention the battle at all, so we might suppose that it took place after he wrote his 'De Excidio'. However Gildas does refer in general terms to 'civil wars', which occurred after the Battle of Mount Badon, and it is possible that Camlann was one of the clashes that he had in mind: *"And yet neither to this day are the cities of our country inhabited as before, but being forsaken and overthrown, still lie desolate; our foreign wars having ceased, but our civil troubles still remaining."*

I have little to add to this, except to say that I think that Camlann may well have been an historical event, and that there may also be some toponymic evidence for Mordred's existence. Modredshale was the Domesday Book name of Moddershall, a borough of Stafford, and I suspect that its name derives from 'Modred's Aula' (Modred's court). Stafford is the county town of Staffordshire (about 40 miles north-west of Atherstone), a location which would suggest that the renegade was the ruler of a north-western kingdom in lowlands England, close to the kingdoms of Wales. We can well imagine a baron from this region, perhaps taking advantage of a period of absence by Arthur in Brittany, attempting to form an alliance with the Welsh to seize power. Ethnically, Staffordshire formed part of the territory of the Cornovii, and it also seems plausible that Mordred might have marched to the south-west to rally the Cornish to his cause, resulting in a battle in their lands. {In the post-Roman era, the ethnic distinctions marked by the Fosse Way may have revived.]

Geoffrey tells us that Mordred was killed and Arthur was wounded in the battle, but in any event, the entry in the Annales Cambriae for 537 is the last historical record that refers to Arthur, so we must assume that he met his end at that time or shortly afterwards. Geoffrey wrote: *"Arthur himself, our renowned King, was mortally wounded and was carried off to the Isle of Avalon, so that his wounds might be attended to….this in the year 542 after our Lord's Incarnation."* Arthur's journey to Avalon apparently involved a sea-crossing, presumably to somewhere within reasonable distance of Cornwall, and although the monks at Glastonbury later claimed that Arthur was buried there, I cannot persuade myself that a voyage across the Somerset Levels would quite answer the description. Perhaps Arthur was trying to reach his estates in Brittany? We will never know.

6.6 The Third Wave

We do know however that there were plenty of other British migrants to the peninsula in the first decades of the 6th century, because Gildas made reference to them and they included many of the early Breton saints. These people came from all over Britain, but in particular from Wales and Cornwall. The process had begun during the second half of the 5th century (St Brieuc was probably one of the first of these people, arriving in the late 440s), but the initial trickle became a flood by the time that Gildas was writing in c.540. This may well prove that the Anglo-Saxon encroachment into Hampshire, reflected in the battles at Portsmouth and Netley recorded in the Anglo-Saxon Chronicle, was a reality, but curiously Gildas saw the period as a time of peace and prosperity. I can only conclude that South Wales was untouched by the conflict, or that Gildas was safely ensconced in southern Brittany, and out of touch with events in Hampshire.

According to Gildas, the many churchmen leaving Britain for Brittany were doing so mainly for financial reasons – they were clerics who had failed to purchase a sufficiently good living in the island: *"And also, if finding resistance, in obtaining their dioceses at home, and some who severely renounce this chaffering of church-livings, they cannot there attain to such a precious pearl, then it doth not so much loath as delight them (after they have carefully sent their messengers beforehand) to cross the seas, and travel over most large countries, that so, in the end, yea even with the sale of their whole substance, they may win and compass such a pomp, and such an incomparable glory, or to speak more truly, such a dirty and base deceit and illusion."* But what is instructive is the omission from his account of the one motive that modern historians most commonly assume for the emigration. The novice priests of Wales may have been going to Brittany for pecuniary advantage, or on a genuine religious mission, but they were not going there for fear of the Anglo-Saxons.

Money, however, cannot have been the only reason for the emigration, and we know that, around the time that Gildas was writing, the plague had become endemic in Britain. It is therefore likely that some fled the country to escape infection. And there was a separate reason why a number of people from south-east Ireland may have sought sanctuary in the peninsula: the Dumnonians who ruled the south-east, under the tribal name of the Dál Messin Corb, were being ousted by the Laigin tribes, and many were forced to flee, perhaps to Brittany.

Whatever the reasons, it appears that there was a very substantial migration which was distinct from the two earlier episodes, the military deployment under Conan Meriadoc and the flight of Belgic Britons from the south-east, apparently caused by the Saxon raid of 441/442.

Some of the early migrants of the third wave would have been established in Brittany by the time of the war against the Franks of the 490s, but I do not think it likely that they were participants. It seems that the pioneers of this wave were mainly men of religion, and that they settled predominantly in the west and north of the peninsula, rather than in the Vannetais where I believe the battles were fought. We know that St Brieuc established his monastery in the town that now bears his name, and another example is the family of St Fragan. Fragan and his wife Gwen arrived in Brittany, probably from Wales and possibly in the middle of the 5th century. According to the second 'Vie de Saint Gwennolé confesseur' (by Clément, c.860) they arrived at the port of 'Brahec' – perhaps Bréhat or Binic. They seem to have fixed themselves at what is now Ploufragan, just to the west of St Brieuc, although they are also associated with other places in Brittany, including a castle at Lesguen (the 'court of Gwen') in Plouguin, Finistère. One of their sons was St Gwenole (or Guénolé), who we have already encountered. St Gwenole was sent to the school at Bréhat run by a St Budoc, who probably came to Brittany from Ireland, via Cornwall.

By the mid 480s, the end of the Roman Empire in Gaul was nigh, and to the inhabitants of the remaining scraps of the Roman province it must have seemed that the world that they knew was collapsing around them. Indeed, this accorded with the Christian teachings of the time, which claimed that the world was coming to an end. In about 485, Budoc sent Gwenole with 11 other pupils from his school westwards, to found a religious sanctuary, and after an abortive attempt to settle on an island in the Rade de Brest, they established a monastery at Landévennec, on the Crozon peninsula, in about 490. Interestingly, the religious rule that they adopted conformed to the Irish rites of Christianity, which were distinct from the Roman version, although it seems that they may have accepted the Roman method of calculating the date of Easter.[77] Gwenole died in 532, and the details of his life as preserved in the collective memory of his abbey, were recorded by an Abbot called Gurdisten and a monk called Clément in the 9th to 12th centuries.

So Gwenole was probably a near contemporary of Arthur, but there is no reason why the two should ever have met. Gwenole was a man of religion, from a family of West Wales, who sought sanctuary from the storms of his lifetime in the furthest reaches of Finistère. Arthur was a Belgic British soldier who fought on the frontlines in the eastern regions of both England and Brittany. Gwenole subscribed to the Irish doctrines of Christianity, whereas Arthur, as a Romanised Briton, presumably adhered to the tenets of the Roman church. In many ways, they typify the differences among the Breton migrants, and highlight the fact that the British in Brittany were far from a homogenous group.

In the following century, many more migrants arrived in Brittany from the western regions of Britain, and the toponymy of the peninsula bears witness to the importance of this immigration. We do not know how many arrived in total, but it must have been many tens of thousands – the earliest data we have on the population of the peninsula dates from 1392, when there were 98,447 'hearths' in Brittany, and allowing say 4 people per household, that would give a total population at that time of about 400,000. Fleuriot suggests

---

77 The community of Landévennec remained true to their monastic code until 818, when the abbey adopted the Benedictine rule, under the influence of Louis the Pious, King of France.

that the population of the peninsula in the 5th century may have been 200,000 – 300,000, but the British component would have been a fraction of that.

6.7 A Footnote on Warfare in Arthur's Day

It is important to dispel any notion of 'knights in armour', when discussing Arthur's military exploits. The battles that he fought would have been predominantly infantry engagements, and the heavy cavalry with which he is associated in legend did not emerge in Europe until the beginning of the 8th century. Cavalry had of course been used since early times, but there is no surviving archaeological evidence of paired stirrups in use in Europe before the late 6th or early 7th centuries. The paired stirrup and the solid saddle tree were essential to the development of heavy cavalry, because without these, a knight did not have a fighting platform sufficiently stable to enable him to wield a lance. These technologies originated in China in the 4th century and were brought to Europe by invaders from the East. In particular, the Arabs brought heavy cavalry to France in their campaign of conquest in the early 8th century. In Arthur's day, mounted soldiers wielded long swords, but they did not carry lances.

Nor would Arthur have worn a full suit of plate metal armour. Chain mail was common, and soldiers wore breastplates and helmets, but their arms and legs were either bare or protected by leather.

Chapter 7
The Aftermath

7.1   The Conquests of 'the Britains'

As the 'Life of St Goeznou' makes clear, Arthur's death paved the way for the Anglo-Saxons to overrun most of modern England. They had not disappeared after the Battle of Mons Badonicus, and indeed their depleted forces were soon reinforced by fresh contingents from the Continent. In 495 The Anglo Saxon Chronicle tells us *"This year came two leaders into Britain, Cerdic and Cynric his son, with five ships, at a place that is called Cerdic's-ore. And they fought against the Welsh the same day."*

Another entry for 501 tells of the arrival of one Porta with his two sons Beda and Mela at Portsmouth, where they slew a Briton of high rank. And we are told that, in 508, Cerdic and Cynric slew a British king whose name was Natanleod and five thousand men, as a result of which the place was called Netley. The details of these events may be unreliable, but it is plausible that the Anglo-Saxon kingdoms of the south-east gradually expanded westwards. And it seems that a new Anglo-Saxon kingdom was soon established in the Upper Thames Valley, perhaps in response to attacks by the British. The Anglo-Saxon Chronicle reports the arrival of the 'West Saxons' in 514, and a victory by Cerdic and Cynric at Charford in Worcestershire in 519, which established the kingdom of Wessex. A battle at 'Cerdic's-ley' (location unknown) followed in 527.

In parallel with the war between the Britons and the Anglo-Saxons, the Anglo-Saxons appear to have been engaged in a struggle with the Jutes. In 530 they took the Isle of Wight, and in 568 they fought against the men of Kent at Wimbledon, slaying two of their Aldermen, Oslake and Cnebba. The Saxons then pursued Æthelbert, the King of Kent, into his home county, and it appears that he subsequently sought to strengthen his position by an alliance with the Franks. From this point on, the conquest of England became more clearly an Anglo-Saxon campaign, and the Danes did not reappear until the end of the 8th century.

As we have seen, the British also appear to have indulged in a civil war in c.442, which must have severely undermined their capacity to resist further Anglo-Saxon expansion. Germanic invaders seem to have been alert to the opportunities presented by civil wars throughout the first millennium, and the Anglo-Saxons began a campaign of conquest in 552 with a victory over the British at Old Sarum. Another battle at 'Beranbury' (presumably Banbury) followed in 556, and Anglo-Saxon hegemony in England was effectively complete after victories at Bedford in 571 and at Dyrham, in Gloucestershire, in 577. The reference to the latter is the first account in the Anglo-Saxon Chronicle to mention the names of the defeated British Kings – Commail, Condida and Farinmail - and we are told that the victory gave the Anglo-Saxons possession of Gloucester, Cirencester and Bath, the major cities of the old Britannia Prima.

Curiously, in this narrative there is no mention of the fall of London, but I think that this must have happened in c.500, as discussed earlier. London existed, as it always has done, as the main port of entry for commerce from the Continent, and the Thames provided its lifeblood. With the Saxons installed at Mucking and the Jutes settled on the Isle of Thanet, from the middle of the 5th century, access to the port was in the hands of the invaders. In times of war between the Britons and the Anglo-Saxons, all trade through the port must have dried up, especially as the obvious ports with which London might have traded were in the hands of the Franks or Saxons on the Continent.

As a result, there probably never was a battle of London. The town would have simply fallen to the Anglo-Saxons when it was abandoned and deserted. The significance of this event was that, once the Anglo-Saxons controlled at least one bridge or ford over the Thames, they were able to link up their kingdoms along the east coast, all the way from Kent to Northumberland. A group of isolated colonies had become a chain of contiguous kingdoms in the space of half a century, and the 'front-line' between the Anglo-Saxons and Britons had moved westwards to the Hampshire downs, the Chilterns and the Nottinghamshire Wolds.

The Aftermath

Most of this history falls outside the lifetime of Arthur. But one aspect of the campaign deserves more attention, namely the relationship with events in Brittany. When Clovis died in 511, he was succeeded by his four sons, and Armorica fell to the share of Childebert I, the King of Paris. Childebert seems to have accepted the settlement reached between his father and the Bretons, and indeed to have encouraged friendly relations with his western neighbours. We read of no conflicts between the Franks and the Bretons during his reign, and he welcomed Welsh saints like St Sampson and St Armel to his court in Paris. However, when Childebert died in 558, his policy of rapprochement with the Bretons seems to have been abruptly reversed by his brother and successor, King Clotaire I. Clotaire was the last surviving of the four sons of Clovis, from whom he had inherited the Kingdom of Soissons (north-eastern France), which bordered on the western limits of Saxony. By the date of Childebert's death in 558, he had accumulated the other three parts of the Kingdom of Clovis, as a result of the deaths of his brothers and nephews (some at his hands).

However, shortly after achieving his ambition of reuniting his father's kingdom, Clotaire faced a revolt by his youngest son Chramn, a dissolute renegade who had conspired against Clotaire with his uncle Childebert. Chramn had married Chalda, daughter of the Count of Orléans, and, having revolted against his father's authority, he took refuge in the cathedral at Tours. The consequence was that the cathedral was burnt down, presumably by Clotaire's men. Chramn was forced to return to his father's court and throw himself on his mercy, and Clotaire forgave him, but put him under surveillance. Then, in 560, Chramn fled to southern Brittany, where he sought an alliance with Count Chanao, one of Childebert's former allies. Chanao was the lord of the Bro Waroch and Cornouaille, and he agreed to give Chramn and his family sanctuary. Clotaire pursued the rebel, and defeated the combined forces of Chramn and Chanao at an unknown location, probably in the Vannetais. Chanao was killed fleeing from the battle, and Chramn also fled towards the ships that he had waiting to evacuate him. But he then returned to collect his wife and daughters, and they were all captured by Clotaire's men. The family was shut in a peasant's hut, where Chramn was strangled and the hut was then set alight.[78]

---
78 Gregory of Tours 'The History of the Franks'

The question that concerns me is why did Chanao decide to fight for Chramn? What did he have to gain, in a war against the King of a united Francia? Why did he not simply hand Chramn back to his father? There is no evidence that Chramn and Chanao were allies prior to these events. I can only assume that Chramn had told Chanao that Clotaire intended to conquer Brittany in any event, and that Chanao would therefore be best advised to take advantage of Chramn's support. Childebert had adopted a policy of rapprochement with the Bretons, but Clotaire was not the conciliatory type, and he may well have intended to add Brittany to his father's empire by conquest.

To some extent he succeeded, because it seems that Nantes and Vannes came under Frankish control after 560. We can also see evidence of a more assertive attitude towards the Bretons in the religious establishment, because the following year, at the Council of Tours, the metropolitan authorities tried to stamp out the appointment of Breton clergymen by their peers. Prior to this, it appears that the Bretons chose their own pastors, without reference to the church authorities.

However Clotaire did not have the chance to consolidate his gains, because he died of a fever on the first anniversary of the killing of Chramn. In accordance with the custom of the Franks, his kingdom was then divided up between his four sons. The Kingdom of Paris fell to the lot of Clotaire's second son Charibert, a reprobate who was eventually excommunicated for his cruelty. He had numerous concubines, but was married to a woman called Ingoberg, by whom he had a daughter called Adelberg. This princess, who was also known as Bertha, married Æthelbert, who was the King of Kent from 558 or 560 to 616. In other words, during the second half of the 6th century, the Frankish kings of Paris, the nominal overlords of Brittany, were closely allied with the Germanic King of Kent, precisely during the period when the Anglo-Saxons overran central England.

When Charibert died of his excesses in 567, his brother Chilperic I inherited his kingdom in Neustria (modern Normandy) and Brittany. But Charibert and Chilperic were not cut from the same cloth as Clotaire, and during their reigns the Bretons effectively recovered their independence, such that by the late 570s the Count of the Vannetais, Waroch II, was militating to recover Vannes. In 578 he seized the city and launched raids into the neighbouring areas of

The Aftermath

the Ille-et-Vilaine, driving the Franks almost to the gates of Rennes. In response, King Chilperic assembled an army of men from Poitou, the Touraine, Anjou, Maine and Bayeux, which included a contingent of Saxons, and fought for three days with Waroch and his men on the Vilaine River. The Saxons in particular suffered heavy losses, but in the end Waroch agreed to formally submit and to pay tribute to Chilperic, on condition that he could rule Vannes 'by order of the king'. He handed over his son as a hostage, but it is doubtful that the tribute was ever paid.

Chilperic was murdered while out hunting in 584, and his kingdom passed to his widow, as regent for his unborn son Clotaire II. The Bretons took full advantage of the resulting power vacuum, and set about freeing themselves from their Frankish overlords. They raided extensively in Anjou, the Maine and the Pays de la Loire, causing the Bishops of Nantes, Angers and Le Mans to send an appeal to King Gontran of Burgundy for assistance (the King of Paris being an infant). Gontran responded, and sent an army to suppress the Bretons, but his intervention annoyed Queen Fredegund, the widow of Chilperic and regent for her young son Clotaire II. Gontran sent an army comprised of two contingents, led by Dukes Beppolen and Ebrachaire, who fell out with each other on the march westwards. Their armies made separate camps, and their campaign degenerated into chaos, made all the more farcical by the intervention of Fredegund, who detested Gontran (her nominal protector) and Beppolen. She dispatched some Saxons under her command to assist the Bretons![79]

Beppolen engaged the Bretons, but Ebrachaire willfully refused to commit his force to the battle, and Beppolen was killed in action. Ebrachaire then succeeded in capturing Vannes, forcing Waroch to formally submit once again, which he did, giving the usual pledges of loyalty. Ebrachaire accepted these, taking hostages as surety, and led his army back to the River Vilaine. But after the main force had crossed the river, Waroch's son Canao attacked the rearguard and captured the army's baggage train (possibly including the hostages and the war booty collected by Ebrachaire's force). Ebrachaire's troops took out their frustrations on all of the villages they passed on their return journey, as far as Tours, and Ebrachaire was banished by Gontran in consequence.

---

79 The Saxons were ordered to cut their hair in the Roman style and to wear Roman clothing, to identify them as Breton allies.

The point in all of this is that the Franks of Neustria were now clearly operating in concert with the Saxons, an alliance that had been cemented by the marriage of Charibert's daughter to the King of Kent. In precisely the period when the Saxons in England were fighting and winning battles at Bedford (571) and Dyrham (577), the Franks were fighting against the Bretons led by Waroch. My conclusion is that the Saxons and Franks had learned a lesson from the events of 497. They realised that if the insular British and the Bretons were taken on separately, they would come to each other's assistance, and the combined force was capable of mounting a formidable resistance. But if they were both challenged at the same time, they could be divided and defeated. Thus the resistance of the British on both sides of the water was eventually overcome, although the Franks did not colonise Brittany in the same way that the Anglo-Saxons took possession of England.

7.2   The Fourth Wave

The history of Brittany in the 7th, 8th and early 9th centuries is obscure, and outside the scope of this book. It appears that the peninsula was very poor, and that its aristocrats gradually became closer to their Frankish counterparts, while always maintaining a staunch independence, at least in fiscal matters. On the death of Charlemagne in 814, a Breton leader called Mormon declared himself to be 'King' of Brittany, provoking an invasion of the western parts of the peninsula by a Frankish force launched from Vannes, which was once again under their control. Mormon was killed in 818, but the Bretons revolted again under Wihomarc in 822, and determined efforts by the Franks failed to dislodge him. A court poet called Ermold the Black accompanied Pippin, the son of Emperor Louis I, who commanded one of the three Frankish forces ('battles') sent into Brittany to suppress the rebels in 824, and he reported a complaint made by Louis at about this time that the Bretons never paid any tribute. However in the 9th century, both Britain and Brittany (along with much of the rest of northern Europe) was under repeated attack from Viking raiders, and they became an increasingly important factor in the struggles between the Franks and the Bretons.

The Aftermath

It is my belief that the ravages of the Vikings had a consequence for Brittany which has not previously been noted, and the evidence for this lies in the toponymy of the Vannetais. We have a particularly valuable resource available for a study of this subject in the charters of the Abbaye Saint-Sauveur de Redon (Redon Abbey), which was founded in 832. The charters were mainly deeds by which benefactors gave property to the Abbot and monks of Redon, and 391 of them, dating from 832 to the early 12th century, have been published (twice). They reveal the names of about 800 places and around 2,000 individuals, of this period. Redon was not the only abbey in Brittany, and nor was it the oldest of them, but it is the abbey with the oldest surviving charters. Unfortunately the contents of the libraries of the older abbeys, such as Landévennec and Dôl, were destroyed by Viking raids in the 9th to 11th centuries, so typically the surviving records from those institutions date from the 11th century onwards.

As an example of what we can learn from the charters, the town which is now called Sixt-sur-Aff was referred to in a charter of 879, as 'Sixti Martiris' (Charter 201).[80] Now, let us pause for a minute. This is a Breton place name in a Latin document written in 879, but 'Sixti Martiris' means exactly what you would think. 'Martiris' is unsurprising, because the Latin word 'martyres' had been adopted from Greek, and was in widespread use all over Europe. But the Latin for 'sixty' is 'sexaginta', and the Welsh word for sixty is 'tri-ugent'. The word 'sixty' derives from the Anglo-Saxon word 'sixtig'.

Another example, although less clearly of the Early Medieval period, is the town which is now called Elven, about 19 kilometres along the old Roman road from Vannes to Ploërmel (now the D775). The town was settled by the British in the 5th or 6th centuries, and its church is dedicated to St Alban. When first recorded in 1427, its name was written as both 'Elven' and 'Eleven', and in Breton the town is called 'An Elven'. The infobretagne website says that its name *"seems to come from the Breton 'Plou' in 'Elf (or Elv) Guen' (the parish of the poplar tree)"*. [My translation.]

I have a better suggestion: 'Elven' or 'Eleven' meant eleven - possibly because it was 11 Roman miles from Vannes. The Breton name An Elven, would then mean 'At the eleven (mile milestone)'. This name is an English number, just as clearly as the number

---

[80] It is also mentioned in other later charters, such as Charter 330 of 1037.

contained in the original name of Sixt-sur-Aff, the only difference being that we cannot trace the name of Elven as far back in time. And the implications of this are clear: these names tell us that by 879, at least part of the population of the Vannetais was English-speaking. This anglophone population may indeed have been the dominant majority, and may explain the sudden drive for Breton independence.

There are of course few literary sources for the Britain of this period, so it is unsurprising that we have no record of a migration of English-speaking Britons to southern Brittany in the 9th century, but we can understand why such a migration might have taken place. Lindisfarne had been sacked by the Vikings in 793, and indeed the '60 martyrs' referred to in the name of Sixt-sur-Aff may have been the unfortunate monks of that abbey. By the 830s, Viking raids on England had become annual events, and from the early 850s the Vikings started to over-winter on islands in the mouths of English rivers, eg on the island of Thanet (in another case of history repeating itself). It is entirely possible that the inhabitants of coastal areas, particularly in the east of England, might have sought refuge on the Continent, and if some of those migrants headed to Brittany, it would have been the fourth wave of emigration from Britain to the peninsula.

These place names are not the only 'English-sounding' names to be found in the charters of Redon, which reveal a Ranloin Picket (Charter 160 of 856), a Villa Burbrii (Charter 26 of 857) and a Gouent (Charter 286, 1062-1080).[81] The word 'picket', meaning a wooden fence, is not recorded in English literature before 1680, but clearly has a much older history. And one of the English-sounding names may provide a clue as to where the migrants came from: there was a place in Brittany in the period 832 to 840 called Camdonpont (Charter 124). Now 'pont' is the Latin for bridge, but could Camdon be related to the British Camden Town, in London? With the Vikings raiding up the river Thames on an annual basis, it certainly seems possible that refugees from north London may have fled across the Channel. But this attribution is uncertain, because Camden Town was called Rugemere in the Domesday Book, and we have no means of knowing how old the name of the British town is. Since the word 'cam' appears repeatedly in place names mentioned in the Arthurian legends, I will return to this subject in Appendix 4.

---

81 Gwent was in the 'land of cal'

The Aftermath

It may be evident that a significant number of English-speaking people moved to the Morbihan in or around the 9th century, but of course that does not prove that they were Anglo-Saxons. We may suppose that many indigenous Britons spoke English by that time, although Bede writing in the early 8th century tells us that the British language was still spoken in his day, and he does not suggest that it was confined to the western extremities.[82] What makes it likely that the migrants were in fact Anglo-Saxons is the same geo-political logic which makes it probable that the refugees of the second wave of Breton migration were Belgic Britons: the areas under most frequent attack from the Vikings were on the eastern seaboard of England, the areas where the Anglo-Saxon settlement was most dense.

If the fourth wave was indeed composed of Anglo-Saxons, they were people to whom Arthur was no hero, and I believe that this explains a mystery that I will return to in Chapter 11. It is likely that the memory of Arthur would have faded from the popular culture of Brittany, especially in the Vannetais where the Anglo-Saxon settlement appears to have been concentrated, over a period of time. I do not suggest that this was a deliberate process of 'sanitisation', because even the Anglo-Saxons seem to have respected Arthur, but rather the process was one of neglect. He was not a hero of Anglo-Saxon folklore – he was not indeed one of them. But in the northern district of Dumnonée, they never forgot him.

---

82 *"At the present time there are in Britain...five languages and four nations – English, British, Irish and Picts. Each of these have their own language: but all are united in the study of God's truth by the fifth – Latin...."*, Bede 'Ecclesiastical History of the English People', Book 1, Chapter 1.

Chapter 8
The Making of the Legends

The story of Arthur remained alive in Wales, and was reflected in poems like the 'Y Goddodin' and the history compiled by Nennius in c.830. And this memory was the fountain which refreshed the pool of legends in Brittany, as the migration of people from Wales and the south-west of England to Brittany continued. The migrations of the third wave continued into the 9th century, as the Anglo-Saxons carried their campaign of conquest into Wales and the West Country. The Mercian Saxons invaded Wales in 798 and again in 816 and 822. The Kingdom of Wessex captured Exeter in 784 and invaded Cornwall the following year. The Cornish suffered a crushing defeat at the Battle of Camelford in 825 and Dumnonia was permanently incorporated into Wessex after the Battle of Hingston Down in 838.

So although Arthur's memory was fading in the English and Gallo-Roman areas of the Bro Waroch, a stream of Welsh-speaking refugees kept it alive in the Bro Sant Brieg, the area around St Brieuc. Then, in the 10th and 11th centuries, the whole of the peninsula was ravaged by Vikings, and even subjected to Viking rule from 919 to 936. During this period, the province was devastated and abandoned by its religious and civil leaders,[83] and most of the literature in the monasteries was destroyed.

Miraculously, the earliest known copy of Nennius survived and was preserved at Chartres[84] (only to be destroyed in World War II). And after the Vikings were expelled from Brittany in 931 by Alain Barbetort ('Alan the Wrybeard'), men of religion returned to rebuild the churches and monasteries. Alain had to cut his way through brambles to enter the derelict cathedral at Nantes[85] but he

---
83 For a full discussion, see Neil Price, 'The Vikings in Brittany' (1989).
84 Chartres MS 98, 9th or 10th century.
85 'Chronicle of Nantes'.

The Making of the Legends

made substantial progress in restoring the religious patrimony of the peninsula before he died.

Alongside the work of physically rebuilding the centres of religion, the traditions of Brittany were gradually restored. But, the Breton aristocracy had been in exile, some in France and some in Britain, where Alain had been a guest at the court of King Athelstan at Malmesbury. So by the time of the restoration, the aristocracy of Brittany was mostly French- or even English-speaking. However, the candle of the Arthurian legends continued to flicker among the Breton-speaking descendants of the Welsh, in northern Brittany.

In 996, Geoffrey I, Duke of Brittany, made an alliance with Richard I of Normandy ('the Fearless'), an alliance that was cemented by a double marriage. Geoffrey married Richard's daughter Hawisse, whose mother Sprota was a Breton, and shortly afterwards, Geoffrey's sister Judith married Richard II, the son of Richard I. Thereafter the Normans and Bretons had a sometimes troubled partnership, with the Bretons in the junior role.

Thus it was that, when William ('the Bastard'), Duke of Normandy, invaded England in 1066, there were several Breton noblemen fighting for his cause. After his victory, William granted lands to his followers, and it is believed that these included the ancestors of Geoffrey of Monmouth. However, only about 8,000 Normans and Bretons actually settled in England and Wales, so it was imperative that William and his followers should win over the people of his new realm as quickly as possible. Revolts were brutally suppressed, and the remaining Anglo-Saxon aristocracy was dispossessed, but force alone could never be sufficient. Even though 95% of all of the land in the conquered kingdom was redistributed, and many Anglo-Saxon nobles fled abroad (a convoy of 235 ships took a large group of them to exile in Constantinople), the Normans had to retain control over a country with a population of not less than 1.25 million (estimates of up to 3 million exist, but an accurate number cannot be calculated).

Geoffrey's family is believed to have originated in La Brussac, near Dôl, and the Breton and Welsh branches of the family remained in close contact until the 12th century. So Geoffrey would have been familiar with Breton folklore, and he hit upon a brilliant solution to the problem faced by the Normans. The Bretons treasured the memory of a Romano-British hero who had fought successfully

The Duke and the Decoy

against the Anglo-Saxons, and if the conquerors could be portrayed as the spiritual heirs of this hero, they could present themselves to the indigenous British as a relief force, that had come to their rescue. The chances of success for this strategy were favoured by the fact that the Anglo-Saxons had long behaved as a conquering elite in England, and had initially treated the 'wealas' with disdain. The laws of King Ine of Wessex (who ruled from 688 to 726) had distinguished six classes of wealas, and made it clear that they were all inferior to the Anglo-Saxons. But of course by the 11th century the Anglo-Saxons had intermarried with the British, and most of the population of the island had some English blood in them, so the strategy would have to be handled carefully.

Accordingly Geoffrey decided to concoct a history of the British kings, which would give prominence to this hero, and he decided to do some more research on him. He obtained some source material from Brittany, as he explains in the Dedication of his book, where he tells us that he based the 'Historia Regum Britanniae' on *"a certain very ancient book written in the British language"* which was *"brought out of Britain[86] by Walter, Archdeacon of Oxford"* who was *"well informed about the history of foreign countries".* This 'source book' has not survived, and so we do not know how ancient it was, or where it was written. In short, we do not know whether the alleged book was significantly more contemporaneous to the events it reported than Geoffrey's 'Historia', and therefore whether it may lend credibility to Geoffrey's version of events. We do not even know for certain whether the book existed at all, but Walter, the Archdeacon of Oxford, was an historical figure who must have read Geoffrey's work, so it is very unlikely that Geoffrey's assertion was a complete lie.

The first question is where was this missing book found? Academics have long debated what *"out of Britain"* means, since Walter obviously lived in Great Britain; but the natural interpretation is that the book was brought out of Brittany in north-western France ('Little Britain'), which throughout most of the latter half of the first millennium was regarded as an extension of Great Britain.

The trail is muddied by the fact that a variant version of the 'Historia' was printed in 1951 by Jacob Hammer, which differs markedly from the other manuscripts. Hammer thought that this

---
86 "ex Britannia advexit" in Latin.

was a copy of the 'Historia' made by someone else, but it has been suggested by Robert Caldwell that this may have been the original version. It does not include the references to Walter, the Archdeacon of Oxford or the references to Geoffrey himself, other than in a brief description of the contents, which may be a fake. So Caldwell's suggestion is that the variant version is the original, and Geoffrey copied it, claiming authorship for himself. This seems very doubtful, for the reason given above: Walter, Archdeacon of Oxford, would have to have been a co-conspirator.

The French historian Arthur De la Borderie (1827 – 1901) claimed that the source was a (now lost) 'Book of the Deeds of King Arthur', written in verse, which is referred to many times in a Chronique des roys et princes de Bretagne armoricane' written in 1505 by Pierre Le Baud. The claims of De la Borderie were generally dismissed in the 19th century, because no evidence of the existence of this lost 'Book of the Deeds of King Arthur' could be found. However, parts of this book were more recently unearthed in note extracts from the original Latin text,[87] notes which were probably made by, or for, Le Baud.

Then, in 1972, Gwénael Le Duc and Claude Sterckx discovered some fragments of the 'Life of St Goeznou' (also a previously lost work), in a 15th century copy of the 'Chronique de St Brieuc',[88] while preparing a new edition of that work.[89] Among these fragments were both a reference to King Arthur and a passage in verse which was identified as a fragment of the 'Book of the Deeds of King Arthur'. The reference to King Arthur, which is contained in the prologue of the 'Life of St Goeznou', was: *"The Saxons, pagans and instruments of the devil, thirsting for blood, never ceased to mistreat the Britons. Their tyranny was then defeated by the king of the Britons, Arthur, who drove most of them out of the island and reduced them to submission. But after numerous victories in Britain and in Gaul, he left this human life: the way was once more open to the Saxons to enter Britain, so that the churches were destroyed and the saints persecuted...."*. Moreover, the 'Life of St Goeznou' also made reference to a 'Historia Britannica', the identity of which is uncertain.

---

87 Found in the Archives of the Ille-et-Vilaine, and long referred to as the 'Vetus collectio manuscripta de rebus Britanniae'.
88 held in the departmental archives of the Ille-et-Vilaine under the reference IF 1003.
89 The first and so far only volume of the book appeared in 1972.

The significance of this is that the preface of the 'Life of St Goeznou' claims that the book was written in 1019, and the implication, therefore, is that the 'Book of the Deeds of King Arthur' predates Geoffrey of Monmouth's 'Historia'. It follows that it is possible that the 'Book of the Deeds of King Arthur' was Geoffrey's missing 'book in the British language'. The only surviving traces of the 'Book of the Deeds of King Arthur' are the quotations from it in French, and the Latin extracts described above, but that does not preclude the possibility that there was an earlier manuscript in the Breton language.

The question of whether the 'Life of St Goeznou' was really written in 1019 or not is controversial, with some critics claiming that the date has been falsified. The Latin notes of the 'Book of the Deeds of King Arthur', seemingly prepared by, or for, Le Baud, are preceded by a text which appears to be a dedication to Duke Arthur II of Brittany (1305 – 1312), and H Guillotel dated the 'Book' to the second half of the 12th century. But other academics, who have studied the contents of the work carefully (eg the place names), claim that it was the versified version of an earlier text. Gwénael Le Duc dated the underlying material to 'the early 10th century', and Leon Fleuriot dated it (in 1980) to the period 954 – 1012. André-Yves Bourgès claimed that the source material for the 'Book of the Deeds of King Arthur' came from the Léon region of western Brittany.[90]

So it appears likely that there was at least one earlier written source of the Arthurian legends, and that Geoffrey of Monmouth copied this material faithfully. In turn, the authors of subsequent texts, like the 'Chronique de St Brieuc', have followed Geoffrey's 'Historia'. But whether or not Geoffrey's source was the 'Book of the Deeds of King Arthur' is less clear. As we have seen, we have no proof that this text was ever written 'in the British language', and both the 'Life of St Goeznou' and the 'Chronique de St Brieuc' mention a 'Historia Brittanica', which could be a separate source, now lost. Indeed, many scholars have assumed this to be a variant name for Geoffrey's 'Historia Regum Britanniae'. The Chronicle was written by an anonymous author in 1394, and Geoffrey's 'Historia Regum Britanniae' was written in c.1136, so this is at least possible, but it is also possible that the 'Historia Brittanica' and the 'Historia Regum

---

90 André-Yves Bourgès, 'La cour ducale de Bretagne et la légende Arthurienne au Bas Moyen-Âge' (2008).

The Making of the Legends

Britanniae' were two different books.[91]

So far as we can tell, the contents of the 'Book of the Deeds of King Arthur' were very similar to those of Geoffrey's 'Historia'. In most cases, when Le Baud cites his sources, he cites both Geoffrey's 'Historia' and the 'Book of the Deeds of Arthur' together. But it may be significant that Le Baud rarely cites the 'Book of the Deeds of Arthur' as a source for events that occurred after the Battle of Bath. There are references to only three such events:

1. when Arthur sends Hoël to fight the Dukes of Aquitaine (p.57);
2. when, during the final battle with the Romans, Hoël, sadly surveying the desolation of his lost companions, places himself among his troops (Geoffrey has Hoël and Gawain rallying their weary troops at this point) (p.60); and
3. when Arthur left Armorica and Gaul in Hoël's care, because he was returning to Britain to deal with Mordred (p.61).

It will be seen that all of these references relate to Hoël, who appears to have been a historical figure, so it may be that the 'Book of the Deeds of Arthur' did not embark on the flights of fancy that overtook Geoffrey in the later parts of his narrative. If this was the case, it would appear that the story in which Merlin transports the stones from Ireland to Stonehenge and most of the subsequent events reported in the 'Historia' were based on other oral traditions or on Geoffrey's imagination.

For this reason, I discount almost entirely Arthur's marriage to Guinevere, the conquest of Europe, Mordred's betrayal of Arthur with Guinevere, the giant of Mont St Michel etc. The only episodes in the later Arthurian legends to which I give much credence are the association of Arthur with Hoël in a campaign on the Continent, for which we have second-hand evidence of a separate source, and the final phase of Arthur's life, when he confronts Mordred in various battles in England. And my reason for attaching weight to the last episodes is that Geoffrey prefaces these passages by saying that he

---

[91] Anne Donnard, 'La Chronique de Saint Brieuc, le Livre des faits d'Arthur et le Librum Vetustissimum de Geoffroi de Monmouth', Proceedings of the 22nd Congress of the International Arthurian Society, Rennes (2008).

found this material not only in his 'British treatise', but *"He learned it, too, from Walter of Oxford, a man most learned in all branches of history."* As with other material for which Geoffrey cites Walter as a source, this is unlikely to be a lie because Walter would undoubtedly have read Geoffrey's book. But of course it is possible, or even likely, that Geoffrey embellished what he learned from Walter.

Whether or not his 'book in the British tongue' existed, from the contents of Geoffrey's 'Historia', it is clear that his source material included, directly or indirectly, the works of Gildas, Bede, the Annales Cambriae and, most extensively, Nennius. If such a book did exist, I therefore think that we can assume that it was itself largely a compilation of earlier material, and written after Nennius (so probably after 830). As we have seen, Gwénael Le Duc and Léon Fleuriot both date the original texts on which the 'Book of the Deeds of King Arthur' were based to the 10th or early 11th centuries, but it is clear that they were written at some point after 830.

It seems that Le Baud accepted Geoffrey's version uncritically for the most part, although he substantially abbreviated the stories. Arthur's campaign against the Romans, which in Geoffrey's 'Historia' takes 20 pages, is described by Le Baud in little more than one. The differences may be explained by Le Baud's editing, or by differences in the two underlying books, or by the introduction of other material from a totally different source. But the only significant point on which Le Baud takes issue with Geoffrey is the date of Arthur's death, which Geoffrey places in 542. Le Baud observes that the Emperor Leo I, against whose army Arthur is said to have fought at Autun, reigned from 458 to 473 (actually 457 – 474, but Le Baud was close enough), and therefore places Arthur's death in 472.

It also appears that Le Baud may have introduced a 'Breton gloss' into the stories, to please his patron Anne, Duchess of Brittany, and his Breton audience. For example, this is Le Baud's account of Arthur's campaign on the Continent (the passages which take 20 pages in Geoffrey's 'Historia'), from a 1638 edition of Le Baud's work, entitled 'Histoire de Bretagne'.

"Après allerent Artur & Hoël à Augftun, & en celuy territoire jouxte le fleuue de Barbe, & y eut bataille entre leurs gens & les Romains, en laquelle après grand occifion defdits Romains, en laquelle fut pris Petreius Senateur, & maints autres de leur partie, que Artur proposa

envoyer en garde à Paris. Les Romains que l'entendirent l'embuscherent par nuiet en la voye pour les resoudre: mais ils furent feconde fois descomfits, & leur fut celle bataille plus dangereuse que la premiere: car le Roy Euander de Surie y fut occis auecques Volterius, & maints autres nobles hommes de leur part. Auffi y moururent de la part d'Artur Vorellus Compte de Maine, & quatre autres nobles & puiffans Barons.

Lucius a donc trifte pour la mort des fiens, douta moult & pensa differer à Artur la bataille & le retraire à Augftun attendant l'aide de l'Empereur Leon qui venoit. Si fe mift à voyè pour entrer en Longres, mais Artur luy fut au deuant qui luy liura la tierce bataille plus griefue que les deux premieres. Et dit Geoffroy, que en celle derniere bataille Artur difpofa les gens de cheval en quatre tourbes, defquelles il commift l'une à Hoël Roy des Bretons Armoricains, & à Gauuain fon neueu. Et dit auffi que comme après long eftrit plufieurs hauts hommes de la partie Artur furent occis, dont leurs forces furent affoiblies, tellement qu'il les conuint reculer iufques à la bataille des Bretons Armoricains, Hoël & Gauuain firent affaut contre les Romains: & affaillirent la compagnie de Lucius: lequel Lucius fe hafta donner fecours aux fiens, & là mourut le Compte de Treguer auec bien deux mil Armoricains. Mais Hoël, felon l'acteur du livre d'Artur, portant triftement la defolation de fes compagnons perdus fe jetta entre les tourbes: lequel Leonenfes, les Corifopitenfes, & les Venetenfes enfuiuirent par grand celerité: Et dit Geffroy, que ces deux Princes Hoël & Gauuain veant l'occision dés leurs furent plus aigres que deuant; & tant firent par leur proeffe & par la force de la bataille d'Artur qui fe joignit à eux, que finablement ils obtindrent victoire: & furent Lucius occis, combien que ce fuft à grand labeur. Car de la part Artur, Kayus & Beduerus furent occis, & furent portez enfeuelis, Kayus à Chinon, & Beduerus à Bayeulx que son ayeul auoit fondee. Adonc commanda Artur que le corps Lucius fuft porté à l'Empereur Leon, & au Senat & leur manda qu'autre tribut ne leur rendrait de Bretagne.

Et l'Efté enfuiuant comme Artur trefpaffoit les Alpes pour aller à Rome contre Leon, luy fut nuncé que Mordret fon neueu, auquel il avoir baillé le gouuernement de l'ifle, s'en eftoit fait Roy & auoir efpoufee Genieure contre le droit de fes premieres nopces. Pour laquelle caufe Artur retira fon pied des Italies & laiffa Hoël fon neueu le Roy de Bretagne Armoricaine auec les Bretons Armoricains es Gaules pour les contenir en obeiffance. Et dit l'acteur du livre des Faits du dit Artur,

The Duke and the Decoy

qu'il commift le pais à Hoël, afin que s'il pouuoit il reformaft les Gaules, & qu'il les gardaft fous le lien de paix amiable; luy remonftrant c'eftoit triftement qu'il luy effoit expedient fe repatrier."

I translate this as follows:

"Afterwards, Arthur and Hoël went to Autun, and in this country by the river Barbe there took place a battle between their people and the Romans, in which after many of the Romans were killed, were captured Senator Petreius and so many others of their party that Arthur proposed to send them under guard to Paris. The Romans hearing of this, set up an ambush in the night on the route to free the captives; but they were beaten a second time, and this battle was more dangerous for them than the first because King Evander of Syria was killed along with Volterius and many other nobles of their party. Also there died there on Arthur's side Vorellus the Count of Maine, and four other noble and powerful barons.

Lucius was therefore saddened by the death of his men, wavered and considered avoiding a further battle with Arthur, and retreating to Autun to await the assistance of the Emperor Leo who was on his way. He took his men to Langres, but Arthur got there before him and gave battle a third time, more bloody than the first two. And, says Geoffrey, at this last battle Arthur deployed his cavalry in four troops, of which one he committed to the command of Hoël the king of the Bretons and Gawain, his nephew. And he also says that after a long struggle several nobles of Arthur's army were killed, so that his forces were gravely weakened and were retreating towards the battle-line of the Armorican Bretons. Hoël and Gawain attacked the Romans who were pursuing the British, and after rallying the fleeing troops, ordered an assault on Lucius's bodyguard. Lucius himself rushed forward to support his men, and the Count of Tréguier was killed with at least two thousand Armoricans. But Hoël, according to the author of the book of Arthur, hearing the sad news of the demise of his companions, threw himself among his troops and was quickly followed by the men of Leon, Cornouaille and the Vannetais. And says Geoffrey these two princes Hoël and Gawain, seeing their dead companions, were more enraged than before, and by their prowess and the force of Arthur who joined them were finally able to obtain the victory. And Lucius was killed, albeit with great effort. On Arthur's side, Kay and Bedevere were killed and were taken for burial, Kay to Chinon and Bedevere to Bayeux, the *town which his grandfather had founded. Then Arthur commanded that the body of Lucius should be taken to the Emperor Leo and the Senate, showing them that no further tribute would be paid by Britain.*

In the following summer when Arthur was crossing the Alps to march on Rome against Leo, he was told that Mordred his nephew, to whom he had entrusted the government of the Isle, had crowned himself king and married Guinevere, contrary to her first marriage. For this reason he withdrew from Italy and left Hoël, his nephew the King of Armorican Britain with his Armorican Bretons, to keep the Gauls in subjection. And says the author of the book of the Deeds of Arthur, he committed the keeping of the peace to Hoël, so that if possible he could reform the Gauls and establish friendly relations with them, telling him that it was sad that it had become expedient for him to return home."

Le Baud's account differs from Geoffrey's mainly in that he identifies Hoël's supporters. It is the men of Léon (in north-west Brittany), Cornouaille (in western Brittany) and the Vannetais (in southern Brittany) who join Hoël in his frenzied attack on the Roman centre, after the death of the Count of Tréguier (a town in northern Brittany). His account therefore has a stronger Breton flavour than Geoffrey's, and we may suspect that this was introduced by Le Baud. As to the general historicity of Le Baud's account, it will be apparent from Chapter 6 that I believe that Arthur travelled to Brittany after the Battle of Mount Badon and defeated the Franks. And from what we can tell, I suspect that the 'Book of the Deeds of King Arthur' did describe a campaign on the Continent, in which Hoël was a leading actor. But it is possible that this account was much less colourful and more condensed than Geoffrey's.

We must also consider the language in which Geoffrey's source book was written. He, of course, claimed to have translated it from 'the British language' into Latin, but some have questioned his knowledge of Welsh.[92] Certainly Geoffrey does not appear to have spent much of his adult life in Monmouthshire. He was a signatory to six charters executed at Oxford between 1129 and 1151, five of which were also signed by Walter, and it appears that he was a teacher and lay canon at St George's College, Oxford. He wrote in Latin, but it is possible that his family had retained a knowledge of Breton.

The oldest surviving text written in Welsh dates from the 8th

---

92 JC Crick, 'Monmouth, Geoffrey of' (2004).

century, and the oldest text written in Breton dates from the end of that century, so it is possible that an ancient text 'in the British language' was available to Geoffrey. But most of the sources on which he relied were written in Latin. Moreover we know that Le Baud was able to read the missing 'Book of the Deeds of Arthur'. He refers to this in French as 'Le livre des faits d'Artur le Preux, autrement nommé le Grand'[93] or simply 'Le livre des faits du Roy Artur', but from the surviving notes extracted from the book, it appears to have been written in Latin.

Nor does it seem likely that Le Baud could read Breton. He was the son of a Pierre Le Baud, a knight from St Oüen in the Maine region, whose wife Jeanne was the illegitimate daughter of a seigneur called Parry from Chateaugiron (in the Ille-et-Vilaine department, an area where Breton was not spoken). He held religious appointments at Vitré and Laval, again in the French-speaking east of Brittany, so there is nothing about his background that suggests he had mastered the Breton language. I therefore conclude that the 'Book of the Deeds of Arthur' was probably written in Latin, albeit that it is possible that Geoffrey had access to earlier source material which may have been written in Breton or Cambro-Latin.

In considering the reliability of Geoffrey's account as a history of Arthur, we must also allow for the political 'spin' which he undoubtedly added to whatever source material he possessed. He was writing in c.1136, 70 years after the Norman Conquest, and it is widely believed that his work had a political motive, as discussed above.

Geoffrey's accounts of the battles of the British with the Anglo-Saxons may even have been consciously designed to echo the relatively recent history of the battles between the Normans and the Anglo-Saxons. For example, his version of the 'Battle of Bath' contains some similarities with the (admittedly incomplete) accounts that we have of the Battle of Hastings. In both cases, the Saxons occupied the higher ground, and the battles continued into the evening, which was unusual for engagements of the Middle Ages: *"Arthur drew up his men in companies and then bravely attacked the Saxons, who as usual were arrayed in wedges. All that day they resisted the Britons bravely, although the latter launched attack after attack. Finally, toward*

---
93 The Book of the Deeds of Arthur the Brave, otherwise known as Arthur the Great'.

sunset, the Saxons occupied a neighbouring hill, on which they proposed to camp. Relying on their vast numbers, they considered that the hill itself offered sufficient protection. However when the next day dawned, Arthur climbed to the top of the peak with his army, losing many men on the way. Naturally enough, the Saxons, rushing down from their high position, could inflict wounds more easily, for the impetus of their descent gave them more speed than the others, who were toiling up. For all that the Britons reached the summit by a superlative effort and immediately engaged the enemy in hand-to-hand conflict. The Saxons stood shoulder to shoulder and strove their utmost to resist.

When the greater part of the day had passed in this way, Arthur went beserk, for he realised that things were still going well for the enemy and that victory for his own side was still not in sight. He drew his sword Caliburn, called upon the name of the Blessed Virgin, and rushed forward at full speed into the thickest ranks of the enemy. Every man whom he struck, calling upon God as he did so, he killed at a single blow. He did not slacken his onslaught until he had dispatched four hundred and seventy men with his sword Caliburn. When the Britons saw this, they poured after him in close formation, dealing death on every side. In this battle fell Colgrin, with his brother Badulf and many thousands of others with them. Cheldric, on the contrary, when he saw the danger threatening his men, immediately turned away in flight with what troops were left to him."

Despite this political spin, I think it very likely that Geoffrey of Monmouth really did have a source book which came from Brittany, based on 9th or 10th century material, and therefore that he did not simply invent the Arthurian legends. And I think that this hypothesis gains credibility from the fact that there is a plausible route of transmission. Geoffrey tells us that Walter, the Archdeacon of Oxford, was *"well-informed about the history of foreign countries",* and that his book was *"brought out of Britain",* so it is commonly thought that Walter collected the book from Brittany. And if a senior cleric of the church in Britain was visiting Brittany in the early 12th century, it is very likely that he would have visited, and probably stayed at, Dôl, which was the most important church and monastery in the north of the peninsula. It was famous as the seat of the Bishop of Dôl, the spiritual heir of St Sampson, who was the first Bishop and one of the founding saints of Brittany.

The Duke and the Decoy

The Bishop of Dôl, between 1107 and 1120, was Baudri de Bourgeuil (1046 – 1130) (his name translates into English as Baldrick, but he was nobody's fool) and I think that he had a significant and hitherto unsung role in the development of the Arthurian legends. He is principally known for his history of the First Crusade and some 256 poems, including material of a homoerotic nature, and material displaying an unhealthy interest in juveniles. But there are a number of pointers to suggest that he was a devotee of the Arthurian legends, and I think it is possible that he knew Walter, the Archdeacon of Oxford.

Certainly, Baudri had a particular friend called Walter, and wrote to him in these terms (possibly in 1110): *"Lately I received a sweet poem from Walter which, since you wrote it, has touched your hand. I received it with the honour that it deserves. And immediately called you to mind with my love. Now my poem returns your visit, and I pray you cherish me with your love. If you wish to take up lodging with me I will divide my heart and breast with you. I will share with you anything of mine that can be divided; if you command it, I will share my very soul".*

Walter, Archdeacon of Oxford, probably lived from c.1075 to 1151. Bishop Kennet's manuscript in the British Museum (Lansdowne, 935) states that Walter was mentioned as Archdeacon of Oxford in 1104 and 1111. He was a witness to the charter of Abington Monastery in 1115 and the charter of Oseney Abbey in 1129. On the basis that he was born in c.1075, he would have been about 32 when Baudri became Archbishop of Dol in 1107 (when Baudri was about 61), and so it is plausible that Baudri and Walter could have formed a friendship during a visit to Brittany by Walter.

This is plausible, but by no means certain. There were many other Walters with whom Baudri may have been in contact, including an Abbot of Redon, who he may well have encountered on church business at Tours. Indeed Charter 309 from the Redon Cartulary (dated 1081-1082), which was executed in the presence of the Archbishop of Tours, was witnessed by *"Baldri, abbas Sancti Petri de Burgolio"*, who was clearly Baudri. There were no signatories to this Charter called Walter, but if Baudri was involved, however peripherally in the business of Redon, it is possible that the Abbot was the object of his affections.

The Making of the Legends

Nevertheless, Baudri visited England in a tour that lasted 2 years, after the Council of Reims in 1119, and around the time that he was suspended from his office in Dôl. Born in c.1046, he was about 75 at the time of his visit, and the journey was very enterprising for one so old, given the transport available at the time. The only place in England that we know he visited was Worcester, since he was so impressed by the pipe-organ in the cathedral of that city that he wrote a poem about it. But plainly it is quite possible that he visited Oxford.

Moreover, it is also possible that Geoffrey would have known of Baudri independently of any relationship between Baudri and Walter, through his family connections with Dôl. There are thus two possible channels of communication by which Geoffrey might have received a book which was in the possession of Baudri.

An identification of Dôl as the source of Geoffrey's book could also help us to narrow down the period in which it was written. As noted above, if Geoffrey's book was referred to in the 'Life of Goeznou', and if that book was written in 1019, Geoffrey's source cannot have been published after that date. But it is also unlikely that the source book entered the library of Dôl before 1014, because that was the year in which the last Viking raid on Brittany took place, during which Olaf Haraldsson pillaged and burned the town of Dôl. While it is possible that old books were subsequently added to the restored library after this event, it seems more likely that the collection would have been rebuilt with recently published works. Geoffrey describes his source book as *"very ancient"*, but even a book published in, say 1015, would have been 120 years old when Geoffrey was writing his Historia, and I think that would adequately answer the description.

Finally, my belief that Baudri was the conduit by which the source material for 'the life of King Arthur' arrived in Britain, is reinforced by my opinion that he was also the source of another significant component of the Arthurian legends. I think he was the man who brought us the legend of the Holy Grail.

Chapter 9
The Grail Quest

The legend of the Holy Grail was first set out in Chrétien de Troyes' last work, 'Perceval, the Story of the Grail'. De Troyes had already made a substantial contribution to the popularity of the Arthurian legends, in particular by introducing us to Lancelot, in 'Lancelot, the Knight of the Cart', which was written between 1177 and 1190. 'Perceval' was written between 1181 and 1190, but left unfinished, prompting four other authors to attempt to complete the account in 'continuations', which leave us with a choice of endings to suit our tastes. So neither Lancelot or the Grail Quest derive from Geoffrey of Monmouth, although I believe that Geoffrey may have been aware of the Grail story.

As we have seen, the trail of source material for Geoffrey's 'Historia' appears to lead back to Brittany, and possibly to Baudri de Bourgeuil. It was this Bishop, in his 'Chronique de Dôl' (the Chronicle of Dôl) written in the early 12th century, who reported a pilgrimage to the Holy Lands that Budoc, the third Bishop of Dôl, had made in the 6th century. He wrote that *"Such was the saintliness of this man, Saint Budoc, that this is attested by the precious gift which he brought back from the sacred City of Jerusalem, that is to say the cup and plate that our Lord used at the last supper which he ate with his disciples."* [94] I think this may well be the basis of the legend that the Holy Grail was brought to Brittany.

St Budoc became the Bishop of Dôl after St Sampson and St Magloire. Magloire is said to have resigned the bishopric of Dôl to set up a monastery on Sark with 62 monks, in c.565, possibly because of a

---

[94] *"Quantae vero sanctitatis fuerit vir iste sanctus Budocus, pretiosa munera quae secum de sancta civitate detulit Jérusalem, scutella scilicet et scutellus quibus Dominus usus est in ultima Coena quam cum discipulis suis fecit testantur."* (Acta Sanctorum Ordinis Sancti Benedicti Saec. I, pages 223-225).

lack of security for his flock at Dôl. This would date Budoc's period of office to the late 6th century, and it might suggest a life span from, say, c.525 to c.590. It is therefore possible that Budoc was born during Arthur's lifetime, but unlikely that he made a pilgrimage to the Holy Lands before Arthur died. It is therefore very unlikely that Arthur ever saw the objects that Budoc brought back with him.

We need not speculate on whether those objects were the real grail and plate. In the Early Middle Ages, many souvenirs were brought back from the Holy Lands, and many more later arrived in France as a result of the crusades. One contemporary example was a splinter from 'the true cross', which the Eastern Emperor Justin II sent to the widow of King Clotaire I, Queen Radegunde, at her monastery in Poitiers in 568. Baudri himself referred to a relic of Christ's blood kept in the Abbey at Fécamp, and there were others of the same ilk at Bruges, Mantua, Reichenau, Westminster and Constantinople.

Nor was the grail of Dôl the only grail – in the Middle Ages there were 'grails' in Palestine, Genoa and Valencia, and many more have emerged since. For our purposes it is sufficient to know that the religious community of Brittany in the 6th century believed that the genuine grail and plate had been brought back to their country, and that these objects were in their custody. This belief would have informed their actions, when there was a further outbreak of hostilities between the Franks and the Bretons towards the end of the century.

The monastery at Dôl had been constructed on a small estate which King Childebert carved out of the See of Alet and gave to St Sampson in c.557 (perhaps in apprehension of his death, which occurred the following year). The land was situated in the Frankish Kingdom of Paris, so St Sampson and his followers were in effect Breton colonists, living in the territory of the Franks.

This must have become very awkward for them when war broke out between the Bretons and Childebert's successor Clotaire, in the context of the rebellion of Chramn (see 7.1), and it would have been still more awkward when Waroch II was ravaging the Nantais in the late 570s (see 7.1). For the Bretons, the consequence of these wars was a long period of life 'beyond the pale'. They were seldom mentioned by Gregory of Tours, who was alive at the time, and only mentioned in disparaging terms by Venantius Fortunatus of Poiters, despite the fact that both prelates lived within 160 miles of the province. Nantes had been served by a Bishop from Aquitaine (Felix) since 549, and Venantius Fortunatus praised him for having *"defeated the British claims",* describing the Bretons as *"ravishing wolves".* When Felix completed a new cathedral in the city, the consecration service was attended by the Frankish Bishops of Angers, Le Mans, Rennes, Poitiers and Angoulême. No priest from Brittany was invited.

In the uncertain conditions which prevailed on the border between the Franks and the Bretons, it is no surprise that Magloire, the Abbot Bishop of the monastery, took 62 of his monks to the island of Sark in 565. Clearly, if the monastery held treasures of any description, let alone the Holy Grail (as they believed it to be), the new Bishop Budoc might well have decided to move the precious objects to a safer location. Indeed, the monastery at Dôl may well have been abandoned completely.

The 'Grail Quest' stories, tell us that the Grail was kept at the Castle of Corbénic, the identity of which has been the subject of much speculation, and I suggest that this may have been the place to which the treasures of Dôl were transferred. From the legends, it was a place that was foreign to the Norman French authors of the legends (or the Franks from whom they may have learned the story), because it is described as being constructed in 'Listenois' (the strange land) or 'Terre Foraine' (the foreign land). Most British commentaries have tried to place Corbénic in Britain, but the French style of the name and the geo-political logic suggest that it was a castle securely within the borders of Little Britain, ie Brittany.

Fortunately, the name itself furnishes us with some valuable clues, if we break it down into its component parts, Cor-ben-ic. There are more than 240 towns in France that have names that start with 'cor' (eg Corseul, Corlay, Corbigny, etc) and it is my observation that they are places associated with hills. There are indeed whole regions with the 'cor' element in their names, which are also associated with ranges of hills, eg the Vercors and the Corbières. So I believe that 'cor' was a Gaulish word meaning 'hill' and that 'corbera' was a word in the same language meaning 'range of hills'.[95]

'Bénic' is the original name of the town on the Côtes d'Armor now called Binic. Its name is also Celtic, meaning 'head of the River Ic'

---

[95] See 'Lisia; Vortigern's Island' for a full analysis.

(pen-ic). So 'Corbénic, in my opinion, meant 'hill at the head of the River Ic'. There are hills to the north and south of Binic, separated by the river valley, and on the cliffs to the south of the town are the remains of a late Roman or Early Medieval castle, known today as the Camp de César or the Camp des Bernains. The castle was constructed on the site of an early Gaulish earthworks, guarding the Roman road leading south to St Brieuc, about 6 miles away. At the beginning of the 6th century, St Brieuc consisted only of a castle, the Castrum de Cesson, and the monastery, which had been founded in c.479 by St Brieuc, a monk from Wales.

Finds from the Camp de César have included Roman coins, bronze swords and Gaulish cartwheels.[96] But more than that is not known at present, because the site has never been studied by archaeologists. Indeed, until very recent years it had been completely overgrown for centuries, having become a nature reserve. The remains of the eastern wall of the castle, including 7 towers, are clearly visible at the site, but the material of the western side of the castle appears to have been pillaged for construction in the town of Binic, possibly including improvements to the harbour in 1816.

Immediately to the south of the castle is the medieval village of Queré, which may also have been constructed from stone quarried from the castle. The name of the village comes from the Latin 'quaerere', meaning to enquire, which is a term generally associated with Roman courts. A magistrate in Rome was a 'quaestor', and in the late Empire the role of the quaestor was expanded to include the supervision of financial affairs. Quaestors who managed the finances of the army became known as 'Quaestores Aerarii'. It is therefore likely that the village of Queré was associated in some way with a court or a treasury, or both, possibly originally in connection with a Roman military garrison (at what may have been a fort of the Armorican Tract).

In February 1824, the remains of buildings were uncovered at the foot of the cliffs below the castle, on the present beach, by the action of the sea. According to reports at the time,[97] more than 200 Roman coins minted by Valentinian and Gratian (Emperors of the 4th

---

96 Christian Querré, 'Binic, Port du Goëlo' (1987).
97 Habasque, 'Notions Historiques sur le littoral des Côtes-du-Nord' (1832).

century) were found at the site. Since Valentinian was the Emperor who sent Count Theodosius to Britain to defeat a coordinated invasion by Picts, Scots and Saxons in 367, and Gratian was the Emperor killed by Magnus Maximus and his British army in 383, it seems likely that the garrison in the late 4th century consisted of British troops, perhaps those commanded by Conan Meriadoc. The construction was interpreted at the time as a Roman bath-house because the foundations showed that the building was rectangular in shape, 80 ft long by 40 ft wide, and divided into small rooms that were served by water channels and a hypocaust.

It seems to me plausible that the monks of Dôl would have moved their treasures to a fortress safely within the boundaries of Brittany in the last decades of the 6th century, and that the castle at Binic would have been a good choice of location. However the traditional view is that Budoc's treasures were deposited at Orléans, based on some further text in the Chronique de Dôl *"which also, with other precious relics removed from the aforesaid [episcopal] see [of Dôl] for fear of the Northmen who were plundering the churches, are kept with honour at the city of Orléans, in the basilica of St Sampson".* This is generally interpreted to mean that Budoc took the relics directly to Orléans after his pilgrimage, but this is not what the text says. And moreover, it seems to me highly improbable. Budoc was a Breton and the monks of Dôl considered their abbey to be the senior church in Brittany – equal in standing to the metropolitan See of Tours (a view not shared in Rome). And there was a distinct gap in time between the life of Budoc and the raids of the 'Northmen'. Budoc lived in the late 6th century, and the Viking raids on France started at the beginning of the 9th century. In the meantime, the risk to the security of the relics came from the Franks, not the Vikings, so why on earth would the Bretons have taken the treasures to Orléans? It seems to me much more probable that any treasures from Dôl would have been secured at a location in Brittany in the late 6th century, and that only later, in the 9th century, would they have been moved away from the peninsula for fear of the Vikings.

How does this history and geography relate to the Arthurian legends? In essence, the 'Grail Quest' tales recount the story of a time when Galahad was involved in a mission to heal a king, or possibly two kings, who were suffering from serious wounds – this monarch, or these monarchs, being called variously the 'Roi Pêcheur' (the Fisher King), the 'Roi Blessé' (the Wounded King), the 'Roi Méhaignié' (the Maimed King), Pelleas or Pellès. The wounded king, or both wounded kings, lived at Corbénic, a castle on the coast, where they spent their time fishing in a river beside the castle. The castle had been constructed in Listenois (the strange land), by King Calafes and two brothers, Alan and Joshua, followers of Joseph of Arimathea. [98] And the legends further tell us that the Holy Grail was kept in the Palace of Adventures, inside the castle.

In Arthur's day, according to some of the 13th century romances, the king at Corbénic was Pellès, who lived there with his daughter Elaine (the mother of Galahad) and his son Eliezer. The castle had, however, been enchanted, which meant that it was very difficult to find. Despite this inconvenience, the castle was visited by various knights, starting with Gawain and including Lancelot. Lancelot was, according to the legend, the son of King Ban of Benoic, the overlord of the whole area.

Pious knights approaching the castle would stop at the 'Castle of Enquiry' to make their confessions before entering the hallowed precincts (according to 'Perlesvaus', one of the continuations of Chrétien de Troyes' 'Perceval').[99] Corbénic, in the legends, has a town and a bridge over the river, which Sir Bromell swears to defend for a year, for his love of Elaine (Sir Thomas Malory, 'Morte d'Artur'). The castle has a seaward gate, which is guarded by two lions and a flaming hand (Lancelot-Grail). And we are told that the castle was eventually destroyed by Charlemagne.

However, generally the visitors did not recognise the Grail for what it was. Gawain in particular was shown the door when his attention became diverted to the beautiful maiden carrying the Grail, rather than the cup itself. One particular story tells us that Lancelot brought the body of Amide (a sister of Percival) to the castle by boat, after seven months of wandering at sea. This tells us that the castle was on the coast (as well as by a river). In his several visits, Lancelot

---

98 Joseph of Arimathea, according to the Gospels, was a Decurion who took Christ's body down from the cross, and placed it in a tomb hewn from rock, which had been prepared for his own interment.
99 'Perlesvaus' is the early 13th century work that introduces Claudas into the legends, and I have little doubt that its anonymous author was familiar with both the history and geography of Brittany.

The Duke and the Decoy

rescued Elaine from a boiling tub, killed a snake and recuperated after a period of insanity. Various magical events happened in the castle, but after Galahad took the Grail to Sarras (a kingdom in Arabia) (from whence it was drawn into heaven), the spell over the castle was broken.

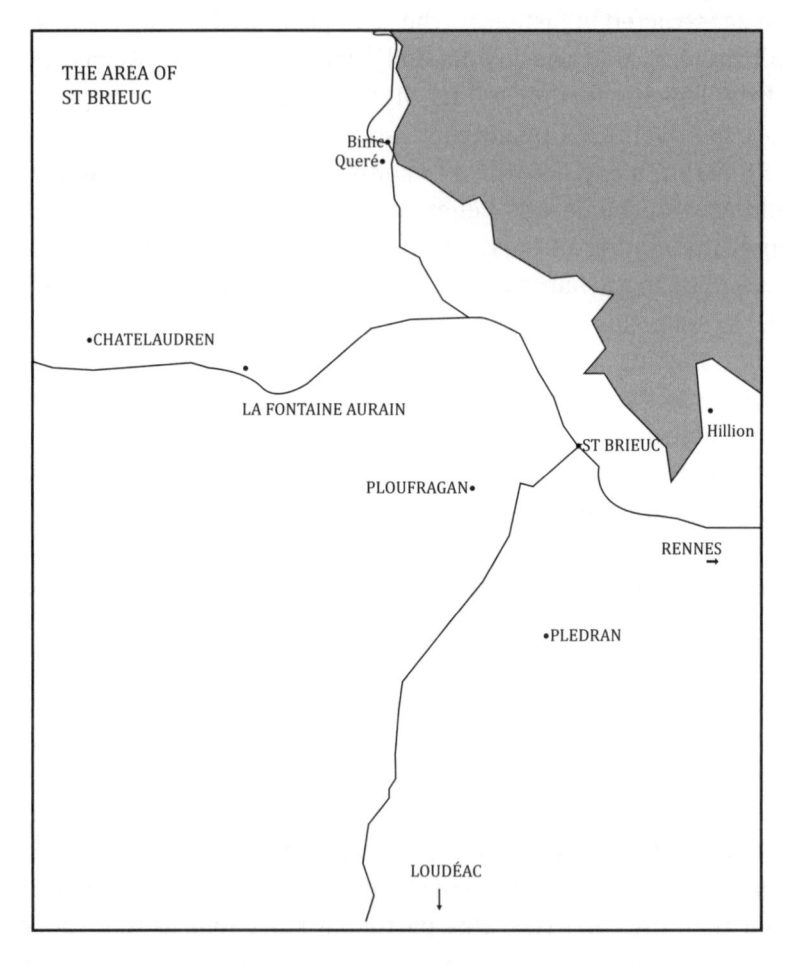

Map: The Area of St Brieuc, showing Binic, Queré, Chatelaudren, La Fontaine Aurain, Ploufragan, St Brieuc, Hillion, Rennes, Pledran, and Loudéac.

St Brieuc is the most southerly point in the English Channel, and sited on the Roman coastal road from Rennes to Brest. The strategic significance of the location is underlined by the Roman fort at Forville in Hillion. The town marks the western boundary of the territory of the Coriosolites and the linguistic boundary between Breton-speaking and Gallo-speaking Brittany, a boundary also illustrated in the Gallo-Roman fort at Péran, near Plédran. Plédran, like Châtelaudren etc, appears to reflect the name of Audren, King of Brittany in the mid-5th century.

The Grail Quest

In another episode involving the castle, Pellès, the King of Corbénic, being aware of prophesies that Lancelot would father a child who would complete the Grail Quest, decided to trick Lancelot into sleeping with his daughter Elaine (knowing that Lancelot loved only Guinevere). Elaine's maidservant told Lancelot that Guinevere was waiting for him five miles away at the Castle of Case. Lancelot duly went to the Castle and climbed into bed with Elaine, believing her to be Guinevere, and thus fathered Galahad.

There are here a number of possible associations of episodes in the legends with the history and physical reality of the site at the Camp de César, including the fact that the castle is on the coast and beside a river. The Roman baths could have been the location of the 'boiling tub' from which Elaine was rescued. The 'Castle of Case' could have been the Castrum de Cesson at St Brieuc. The 'Castle of Enquiry' could have been a building at Queré. Elaine's lover Lancelot was the son of the King of Benoic, which appears to have been the northern part of the border between the Bretons and the Franks (his brother Ban was the King of Gannes, which was presumably Vannes, in the south of the border zone). The main castle in the northern sector appears to have been Châtelaudren, which is 9 miles from Binic – conveniently close for the two lovers. And it is clear from the ruins that the castle at Binic has been destroyed at some point in history, quite possibly by Charlemagne during his campaign against the Bretons in 786 – 811.

It all seems to fit. But really the strongest evidence that the castle on the hill at Binic was the Corbénic of the Arthurian legends is the name itself. Cor-pen-ic is fairly explicit. And in terms of chronology, if my conjecture that the treasures of Dôl were moved to Corbénic at the end of the 6th century is correct, this would explain why none of the legends suggest that Arthur himself found the Grail – he was long dead.

There is one further consideration which reinforces my impression that the Grail Quest legends are associated with the Bay of St Brieuc. In Chapter 8, I set out a possible route by which the Arthurian legends may have been transmitted to Geoffrey of Monmouth, from Brittany, via Dôl. However these legends were clearly based on the early Welsh sources, and they contain a mixture of characters from Welsh and Breton folklore. For example, Merlin,

Gawain, Percival and Guinevere were Welsh, but Lancelot, if he existed, was a Gallo-Roman. Arthur was a Belgo-Roman with Gallo-Roman connections, and the legends are likely to have arisen in an area where all three traditions merged.

It seems to me that eastern Dumnonée would be a very plausible source. The people living in the area of St Brieuc included many from Wales (eg St Fragan and his family) and, since St Brieuc was the first immigrant among the founding saints of Brittany, the members of his community would have been among the few Bretons of Welsh origin who were contemporaries of Arthur.

At the time, the area from St Brieuc to Dôl was a large pagus (administrative district) called Poutrocoët, part of the kingdom of Dumnonée, and what is now St Brieuc was part of the parish of Ploufragan. Poutrocoët later became a diocese, with a Bishop at Alet, and it was only in the 9th century that the Breton Sees of St Brieuc and Dôl were made independent of it. This means that, in the 6th century, Dôl, St Brieuc and Binic were all part of the same administrative district, within the same kingdom, and part of the same diocese. It was a civitas where the Welsh and the Gallo-Romans had co-existed harmoniously since the late 5th century. And it therefore seems to me likely that this area was the crucible from which the legends of Arthur, Lancelot and the Grail Quest emerged.

Chapter 10
Arthurian Britain and Brittany

10.1 Introduction

In the absence of much in the way of literary resources, our best hope of finding evidence of Arthur may well lie in toponymy, the study of place names. Place names seem to be surprisingly durable, and often preserve the memory of an association that has been long lost to history. I have already used such material several times in this book, for example at 6.4, where I discussed the toponymic evidence of a war between the Bretons and the Franks in the late 5th century, and at 7.3 where I showed that toponymy proves that there was an English-speaking population in the Vannetais in the 9th century. I used the possible meaning of the word Corbénic to locate a plausible site for the Grail Castle in Chapter 9, and in Chapter 2, I pointed out that there are few places in Britain that can be reliably connected with Arthur himself, although places containing the names Ather or Athel may have been named after him.

    But in this chapter, I wish firstly to illustrate the possible extent of the 'kingdoms' in Britain and in Brittany that Arthur fought for. I will then go on to consider the toponymic evidence for the existence of Arthur, to be found in the landscape of Brittany. So to begin with, let us consider the territory of the Belgo-Romans in the late 5th century. Although very few places in Britain can be reliably connected with Arthur, we can get a fairly clear idea of the area under his command from the distribution of place names connected with Ambrosius Aurelianus, his predecessor.

10.2 The Kingdom of Ambrosius

The name of Ambrosius may be reflected in a number of English place names. Candidates include Ombersley in Worcestershire, Ambrosden in Oxfordshire, Amberley in Gloucestershire, Ambresbury Banks in Epping Forest (north-east London), Amberley in West Sussex, and Amesbury in Wiltshire. Ombersley was Ambresiege in the Domesday Book, Ambrosden was Ambresdone, Amberley in West Sussex was Ambrelie and Amesbury in Wiltshire was Ambresberie. Amberley in Gloucestershire does not appear in the Domesday Book (which does not prove that it did not exist, but only that it cannot have been of any significance in 1086).

Amesbury in Wiltshire is the parish in which Stonehenge is situated, and Geoffrey of Monmouth wrote that the megalithic monument was erected by Ambrosius as a memorial to the hundreds of British nobles supposedly killed by the Saxons during Hengist's murderous feast at the 'Cloister of Ambrius'. This is clearly nonsense, since the monument was 2,000 years old when Ambrosius was alive, but the association with his name has stuck to some extent. There certainly was a monastery at Amesbury, and Geoffrey tells us that the body of Uther Pendragon (supposedly Arthur's father) was buried at the 'monastery of Ambrius', alongside that of Ambrosius and *"inside the Giants' Ring".* However the monk Ambrius, who allegedly founded the monastery, was apparently unconnected with Ambrosius Aurelianus.

The distribution of the 'Ambrose' places in Britain is interesting, when we consider the likely geopolitical situation of the country in the second half of the 5th century. It seems that the north and east of the territory under British control was defined by Watling Street, certainly by Arthur's time. But the main threat came from the new Saxon kingdom in Sussex, and London was imperiled by a pincer movement of Angles to the north and Saxons to the south.

The Iron Age fort at Ambresbury Banks would have been ideally located to protect London from the north, and Amberley in West Sussex, lies in the shadow of a steep bluff of the South Downs, perfectly situated to guard the south coast. The place names suggest the extent of the area under British control (see map) and within that area, places like Amesbury (Wiltshire) and Ambrosden, near

Arthurian Britain and Brittany

THE KINGDOM OF AMBROSIUS AURELIANUS

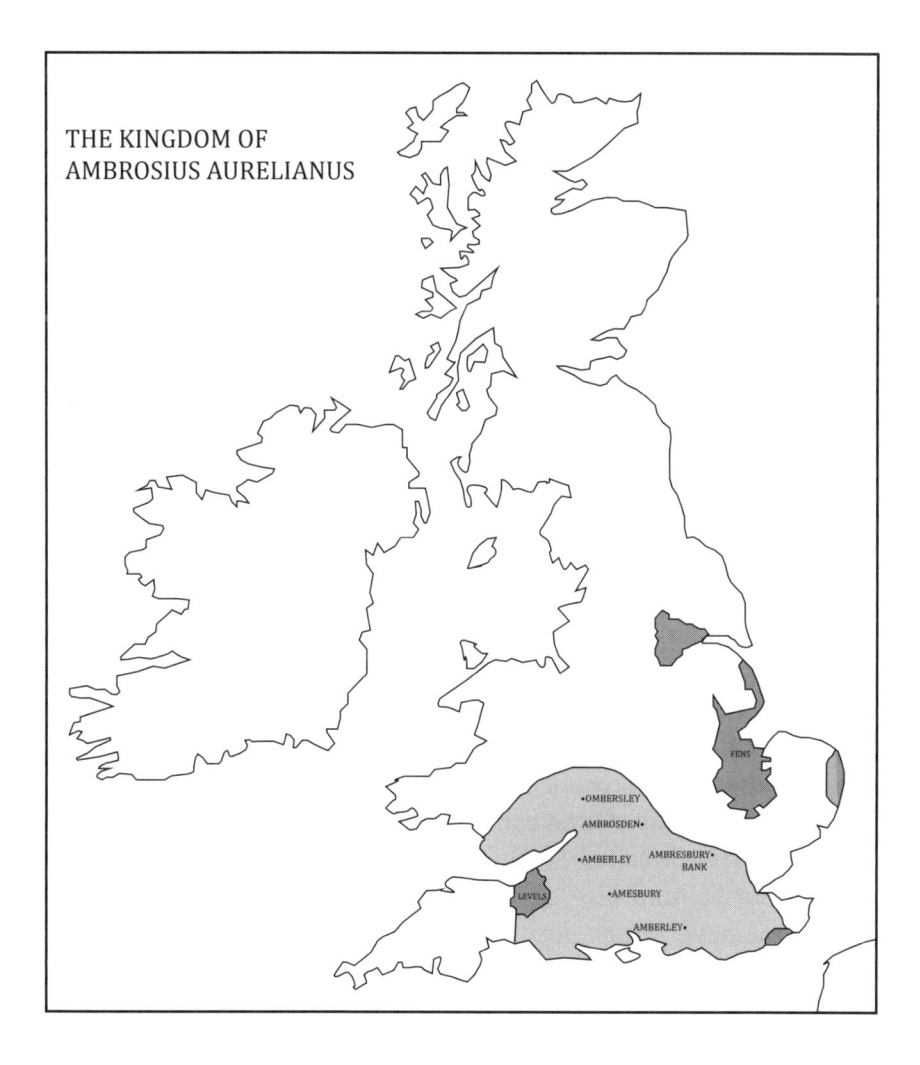

Map showing southern England with locations: OMBERSLEY, AMBROSDEN, AMBERLEY, AMBRESBURY BANK, LEVELS, AMESBURY, AMBERLEY, and FENS.

Judging by the places potentially named after Ambrosius Aurelianus, his kingdom was confined to the south of England. The border may have been largely defined by Watling Street between London and the Midlands. York and much of the north had been abandoned to the Picts, the Anglo-Saxons held the eastern peninsulas and the Scots may have held the north-west of England and northern Wales. However Ambrosius was a hero to Gildas, writing in South Wales, so we can presume that the British still held that region.

the Roman town of Alchester (in north-east Oxfordshire) would have been centrally located as command posts.

Ambresbury Banks in Epping Forest is the site of an Iron Age hillfort, and it is indeed associated in local tradition with Ambrosius.[100] The very substantial fort encloses 11 acres, and was surrounded by ditches 30 ft wide and 10 ft deep.

The association of places with the name 'Ambrose' does not, of course, prove that they were named after this Ambrosius. The name was fairly common in Roman times, being derived from the Greek word for immortal. St Ambrose, Bishop of Milan (c.340 – 397), whose name in Latin was Aurelius Ambrosius, was well-known throughout Christendom, and described by Bede as one of the four Latin 'Fathers of the Church'. He was also mentioned by Nennius, so his fame had spread to Wales. His father, who was also called Ambrosius (d.c.354), was a Roman Prefect of Gaul, and therefore would have governed Britain in the first half of the 4th century. And Sidonius Apollinaris wrote to another Bishop Ambrose (whose identity is uncertain) at some date after 472. However, there is no obvious reason why any of these people should have been associated with military defences in England, so I am inclined to believe that the toponymic connections are indeed with Ambrosius Aurelianus.

Ambrosius may also be commemorated in two places in Brittany. There is a parish called St Ambroise near Carhaix (Finistère), and a chapel of St Ambroise at Saint-Marcel in the Morbihan, both in areas that have strong Arthurian associations. While it is again possible that these are dedicated to the 4th century Bishop of Milan, it is striking that there are only three other parishes or towns in France that carry this name (at Paris, Melun and in the Gard – Saint-Ambroix), and it would therefore be somewhat surprising to find two dedications to this saint in Brittany. Saint-Marcel is the site of a 4th – 5th century cemetery of British emigrants to Brittany, so in my view, the dedications of chapels in Brittany to a St Ambrose are more likely to reflect an insular British influence than an Italian one.

---

100   It is also associated, less convincingly, with a battle fought by Boudicca.

10.3 The Kingdom of Audren

In terms of the British territory in Brittany, the clearest impression can be gained by the location of places named in honour of Audren, the Breton king of the mid-5th century. Although he was probably two generations older than Arthur, it is unlikely that the borders of Brittany changed between 452 (when Audren seems to have made peace with Aegidius) and the early 490s (when the Frankish assaults began). Audren left a substantial toponymic footprint in Brittany, so we can be reasonably confident that he existed, and that he was regarded as something of a national hero. And fortunately, places bearing the name of Audren are not likely to be named after anyone else.

'Audren' is derived from 'alt roen', meaning 'high king', so it is likely to have been used originally for high-status individuals. The name is found in several forms in the Redon charters, eg:

Altroen (Charter 191, 863)
Aldroin (Charter 282, 906)
Aldroeni (Charter 286, 1062-1080)
Audoin (Charter 295, 1081-1083)
Aldroenus (Charter 309, 1081-1082)
Aldroin (Charter 312, 1055)
Aldroen (Charter 364, 1060)

The name of Audren in the Arthurian legends varies similarly, and he appears as Aldroen, Adroenus and Aldroein, but I intend to use Audren throughout for consistency.

So the name was known in the Brittany of the Middle Ages, but it does not seem to have been particularly popular. And it is very helpful that there appear to have been no other Audrens of kingly or ducal status in Breton history, and no other saints of that name either. It was only later that 'Audren', or variations on the theme, became a Christian name (for both sexes) in France. It is therefore very likely that the majority of 'Audren' places in Brittany were named after this specific individual – and there were a lot of them:

Place name	Meaning in English	Location
Châtelaudren	Audren's castle	Côtes d'Armor
Coat Audren	Audren's wood	near Langonnet
Fontaine Auren	Audren's spring	near Plélo
Keraudrain	Audren's village	Férel
Keraudrain	Audren's village	Kergrist
Keraudrain	Audren's village	Plumelin
Keraudren	Audren's village	near Brest
Keraudren	Audren's village	near Camaret
Keredren	Audren's village	near Questembert
Plaudren (Plou Audren)	Audren's parish	Morbihan
Plédran (Plou Audren)	Audren's parish	near St Brieuc
Pré Auren	Audren's meadow	Tregueux
Runaudren	Audren's plot of land	near Lannion
Ville Audrain	Audren's town	near Cadélac

While ordinarily one might not associate relatively modest sites like a hill or a spring with the name of a king, so one might be attempted to assume that such minor place names derived from people with a less exalted status, the proximity of Fontaine Auren and Runaudren to Châtelaudren suggests a regal connection.

The locations of these places are marked on the map below and it will be seen that they all fall within the boundaries of a Brittany that extended to the Rivers Vilaine and Rance. Moreover, they are scattered all over this area, suggesting that Brittany in the middle of the 5th century was united under one ruler. No other Breton 'king' is memorialised to the same extent, and no British king of the period left a comparable mark on the landscape of Britain. As we have seen, by 469 the Bretons were probably capable of putting an army of 12,000 into the field, and I think we can safely conclude that, in the middle of the 5th century, Brittany was politically cohesive, relatively economically sound and increasingly powerful in military terms.

Arthurian Britain and Brittany

THE 'AUDREN' PLACE NAMES IN BRITTANY

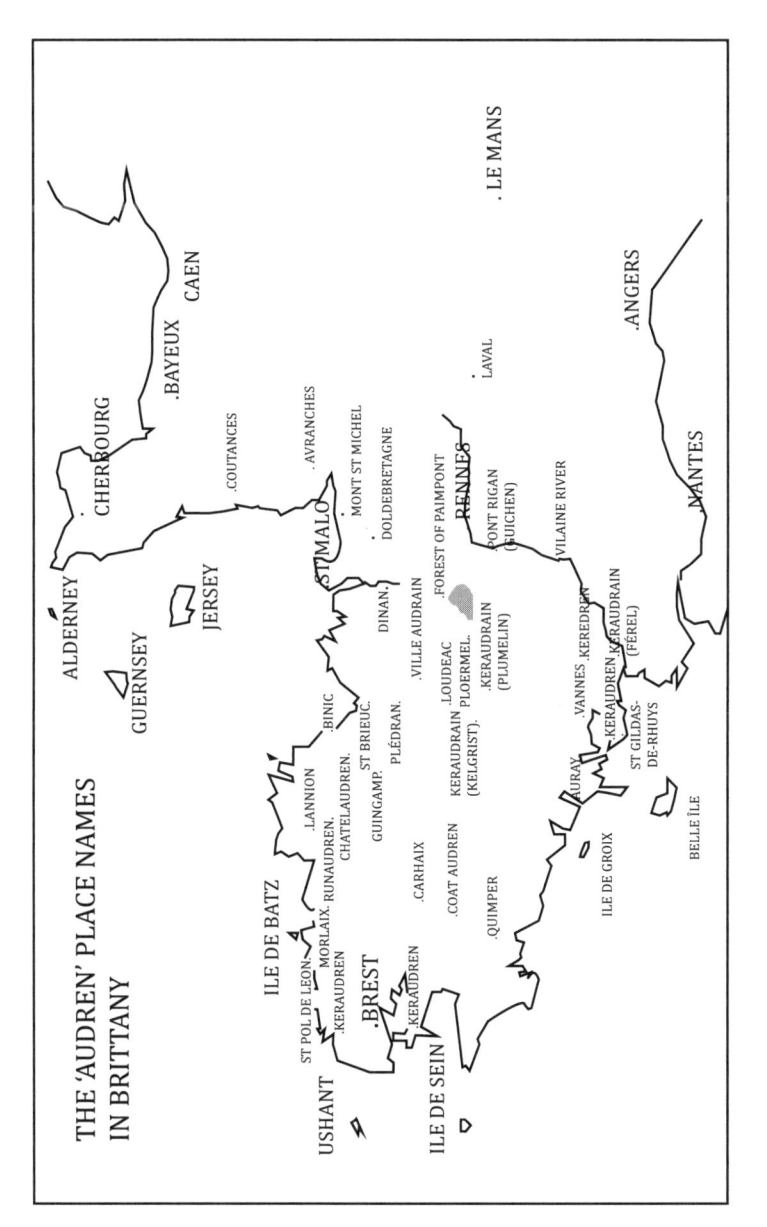

Places in Brittany named after Audren are all found to the west of the Vilaine River, so the 'kingdom' of the Bretons had been reduced to the area of the peninsula by the middle of the 5th century.

175

10.4 Toponymy of Arthur

There are a huge number of places in Britain that claim an association with Arthur, but the waters have become so muddied by the popularity of the Arthurian legends that it is impossible now to say whether any of these claims are valid. I have mentioned the names that reflect 'Ather' or 'Athel', but these are too few in number, and too uncertain in attribution, to enable us to form any view on the extent of Arthur's realm in Britain.

However Brittany may provide a happier hunting ground, because there are certainly several places in the peninsula that are connected to real people with similar names. One difficulty here is that the Bretons of the Early Middle Ages used a large variety of names seemingly based on the word 'arth' meaning a bear, so there are many variations, such as Artur, Arthmael, Armel, or Arzel and it is impossible to tell definitively whether a name incorporating one of these variant forms refers to an Arthur. I have included a list of 'Arthur' type names extracted from the Cartulary of Redon in Appendix 1.

Another difficulty is that there were several Arthurs who were of sufficient importance that places may have been named after them. These issues are explored in more depth in Chapter 11, so for the time being I will content myself with noting the possible 'Arthurian' place names in Brittany, and pointing out some connections with other places which seem to be associated with other Arthurian figures:

Arzal, Morbihan	This town on the Vilaine is near a Ker Anna (Arthur's sister was allegedly called Anna), but the name is taken to mean 'at the salt', in a reference to the salt-pans of the area.
Le Camp d'Artus, Finistère	The 'Kastell-Arzur' in Breton, is a Gaulish oppidum near Huelgoat
Coat Arzur, Lannion	'Arthur's Wood' is close to the port of Le Yaudet.
Ergué-Armel, Quimper	The only possible 'Arthurian' place name in Cornouaille
Grotte D'Artus	(Arthur's Cave), near Camp d'Artus

Arthurian Britain and Brittany

Kerarzur, rue de, in Perros-Guirec	The name of this road suggests the prior existence of a Kerarzur (town of Arthur?) in the Côtes d'Armor
Manoir de Saint-Armel, Bruz, Ille-et-Vilaine	Associated with St Armel les Boschaux
Plouarzel, Finistère	'The parish of Arzel'
Ploemel, near Auray	One of several 'Armel' parishes dotted around the Morbihan
Ploërmel, Morbihan	A town in the north of the Morbihan
Plouharnel, Morbihan	South of Carnac
Port-Arthur, Pluméliau	A place name of uncertain origin, relating to an inland town in the Morbihan
Saint-Armel	A town on the east coast of the Morbihan
Saint Armel en Allineuc	A former chapel on the road from St Brieuc to Loudéac, Côtes d'Armor
Saint Armel les Boschaux	A monastery founded by St Armel in the Ille-et-Vilaine
Saint Armel, Guérande	Almost certainly dedicated to St Armel
Saint Armel en Ploumeur	Near Carnac, Morbihan
Saint–Armelen, Fégréac	On the east side of the Vilaine River
Tombeau d'Arthur Pleumeur	A dolmen on the île Grande, Bodou, Côtes d'Armor
Touche St. Armel, Fégréac	Near Saint-Armelen, and probably connected to the saint of Les Boschaux.

There is also an Arz river in the Vannetais and an île d'Arz in the Morbihan, both of which seem to derive from the word 'arth' meaning bear (ie the île d'Arz probably meant bear island).

I ignore the natural features and the megalithic monuments associated with Arthur, for the same reason that I ignore such places in Britain. And the locations to the east of the Vilaine River are almost certainly connected to St Armel, a 6th-century 'saint' of Breton origin who became a favourite at the court of the Frankish King Childebert I. But the other locations are more interesting. Setting aside Ergué-Armel, all of them are either in the Morbihan (ie the south-east corner of Brittany which became the Bro Waroch and which is sometimes referred to as the Vannetais), or on the Roman roads to the Morbihan from the ports of the north coast of Finistère and the Côtes d'Armor.

It is interesting to note the concentration of Arthurian place names around Carhaix, a city mentioned several times in the legends as a place where Arthur 'had a court'. Here we find Huelgoat, the Camp d'Artus and the forest and chapel of Saint-Ambroise in close proximity to each other. Carhaix was an important Roman town, at the intersection of seven roads, one of which linked L'Aberwrac'h with Loudéac and Rennes. The town was probably the capital of the Osismes and it marked the boundary between the Vannetais, Cornouaille and Dumnonée, so it had always been strategically significant.

In addition to the places listed above, there are also a number of other villages in Brittany, the names of which may include a corruption of 'Arthur'. For example, the impressive 15th century fortress of La Roche Jagu (the rock of Jacut, or James) dominates a bend in the valley of the Trieux River in northern Brittany. It is located in the very ancient parish of Ploëzal. The castle, of which only one side remains, was built on the site of an earlier medieval fortification, and I believe that the history of the site may go back to the Early Middle Ages. I also believe that Ploëzal, may be a corruption of Ploe Arzal, the parish of Arzal. The infobretagne website suggests that the parish was named after 'Saul', an unknown Breton saint, but this is scarcely credible. Others have suggested that 'ëzal' may derive from the Germanic word 'salle', but I find this equally unconvincing.

A little north of Ploëzal is the village of Trédarzec. The 'tre' element comes from the Breton treb, meaning sub-division of a parish, but the infobretagne website suggests that arzec derives from 'tarz', meaning a crevasse. I would have thought that 'treb d'-arzel' was at least as likely.

Another candidate for a place with a name that may be a corruption of Arthur has a strategically interesting location. Limerzel (which is called Lizmerzher in Breton) is situated on a hill just a few miles to the west of the Vilaine River, in the Morbihan, and it is the sort of place where the Bretons might have had a frontier post. The first part of the name is clearly 'lis', meaning a hall or court, but the second part is said to mean 'martyr' – ie the name is supposed to mean 'the court of the martyr'. When a court is named after someone, it is usually named after the person who ruled from it, not after an unnamed dead hero, so I think it possible that the name has been

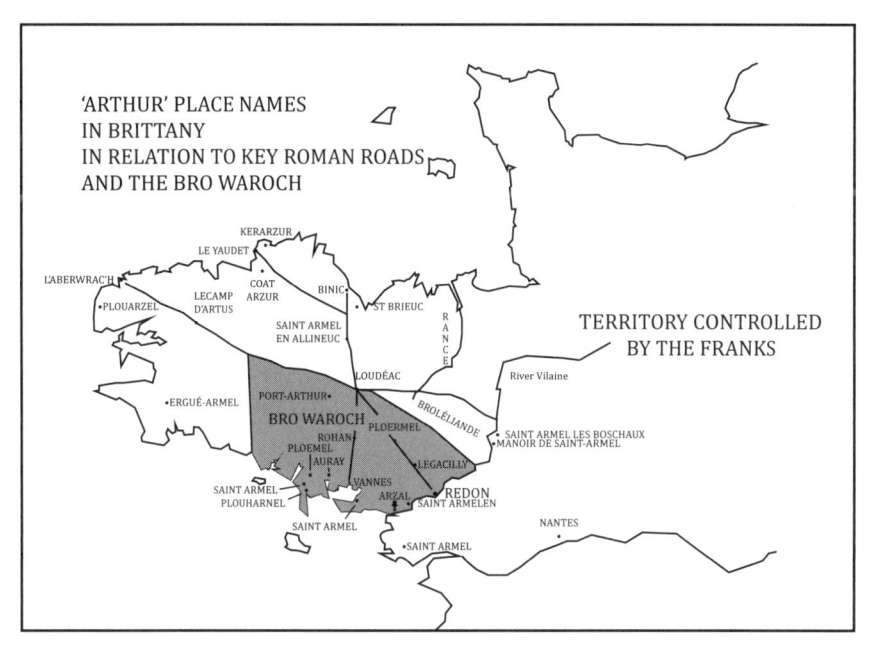

[Map: 'ARTHUR' PLACE NAMES IN BRITTANY IN RELATION TO KEY ROMAN ROADS AND THE BRO WAROCH. Labels include: KERARZUR, LE YAUDET, L'ABERWRAC'H, PLOUARZEL, COAT ARZUR, LECAMP D'ARTUS, BINIC, ST BRIEUC, SAINT ARMEL EN ALLINEUC, RANCE, LOUDÉAC, ERGUÉ-ARMEL, PORT-ARTHUR, BRO WAROCH, ROHAN, PLOEMEL, PLOERMEL, BROLÉLIANDE, AURAY, LEGACILLY, SAINT ARMEL PLOUHARNEL, VANNES, ARZAL, REDON, SAINT ARMELEN, SAINT ARMEL, NANTES, SAINT ARMEL LES BOSCHAUX, MANOIR DE SAINT-ARMEL, River Vilaine, TERRITORY CONTROLLED BY THE FRANKS]

Leaving aside the 'Armel' place names to the east of the Vilaine River, and the part of the town of Quimper known as Ergué-Armel, which first appears in Charter 66 in the Cartulary of Quimper (dated 1244), and which therefore appears to be a later dedication, all the other place names potentially inspired by Arthur are located either:
(a) in what became (during St Armel's lifetime) the Bro Waroch, or
(b) on the Roman roads leading to the Bro Waroch from the three significant Channel ports under Breton control (L'Aberwrac'h, Le Yaudet and Binic/St Brieuc - Plouarzel is a minor port immediately to the south of L'Aberwrac'h).

corrupted, and that the original was 'Arthur's Court'. However, as with all of these more speculative associations, I have not included them on the list of potentially 'Arthurian' places.

It will be seen that a considerable number of the places listed above are explicitly connected with St Armel, the obscure 6th century saint of British origin, who we will be studying in some depth in Chapter 11. The places with this name are broadly located either on the east bank of the Vilaine River, in particular near St Armel les Boschaux where the saint founded a monastery, or in the Morbihan. In some cases, the place itself bears the name of Armel or a corruption of it, but there are other places with different names that have churches dedicated to him.

One of the places which is today associated with St Armel is Ploërmel, a significant town in the Morbihan with an impressive church dedicated to St Armel. The town of Ploërmel first appears in a fragment dated to 834/835, as 'plebs Arthmael' (*"Riwal similiter mactiern in loco nuncupante plebs Arthmael"*), meaning 'the people of Arthmael' (Arthmael means the 'bear prince'). And subsequently it was variously called:

plebe Arthmael	(Charter 24, 859, Charter 204, 858)
Ploiarmel	(Charter 293, 1066-1082)
Armalle	(Charter 369, 1105)
Armaille	(Charter 381, 1141)

Ploërmel may have been associated with St Armel from the 6th century onwards, but the charters do not tell us when this connection arose. However, it cannot have been formed before St Armel's death, in 552 at earliest (or 570 according to one version of his life), and we do not know what the name of the town was before or at that time.

Ancient documents can sometimes reveal place names within personal names, because people are sometimes named after a place. For example, in 1109, the seigneur de Bron (or Brohon), one of the oldest of the great families of Brittany, was called Pleardus de Brohon. His family seat was a castle at La Motte Bron (today called Broons) in what we now take to have been the forest of Brocéliande. 'Pleardus' appears to be a place name, and therefore possible family name, deriving from a 'Plebs Ardus'. In my opinion, this is likely to have been the Plebe Artum, recorded in Charter 313, dated 1100 (of the Redon Charters), but whether that was a corruption of the original name of Ploërmel, or whether it was an entirely different town which has since changed its name or become lost, is impossible to say with certainty. However we know that the name of Ploërmel had evolved in a slightly different direction by 1066 - 1082 (to Ploiarmel), which suggests that Plebs Ardus was another town that cannot now be identified, possibly also in the vicinity of the forest of Paimpont (ie near Broons). At any rate, there are a large number of places in Brittany which are named after an Artus, Arthur or similar.

The important question is whether all of these 'arth' places were named after the same person or a multitude of different people, or indeed after bears. This will be the focus of Chapter 11, but in the meantime I would simply observe that the spelling variations certainly do not rule out the possibility that several of the place names may refer to the same person. In the days before writing became common, names were passed on orally, and it may well be that Ardus, Artum, Arzel and Armel referred to the same person. In particular, the shift from 'th' to 'z' in Breton was quite regular and can be seen in the development of other words.

10.5   Where Would we Expect to Find Places Associated with Arthur?

Turning the question round, so that we are no longer looking for places in Brittany which have names which look as though they might be derived from Arthur, but rather seeking areas where a British military commander may have seen action, our attention is inevitably drawn to the east of the peninsula, where the Bretons must have confronted the Franks. The logic here is exactly the same as that which focuses our interest on the east of England as the probable zone of conflict between the Anglo-Saxons and the Britons, and of course it is ironic from the British point of view that it was very much the same British tribes involved in both conflicts. The fertile river valleys of the region from Loudéac south to Redon have been farmed by man since the Neolithic era, as evidenced by the several stone monuments to be found in the area (eg at St Just), and the archaeological evidence of the cemetery at Saint-Marcel and the tomb at Lomarec confirms that this was an area of early British settlement. The grave goods at Saint-Marcel tell us that it was Britons from Kent and Sussex who had settled in the valleys of the Arz, the Aff and the Oust, and it must have been these people who found themselves in the front-line of the war against Clovis in the 490s.

By this time, any reinforcements coming to the peninsula from the island would probably have had to land on the Côtes d'Armor, because it is quite likely that most of the territory east of the Vilaine and the Rance was under Frankish control. There had been Frankish militia in Rennes since the time of the Notitia Dignitatum (c.420), and it is very likely that Alet was in Frankish territory. So

The Duke and the Decoy

any British reinforcements would have arrived at Binic, Le Yaudet or L'Aberwrac'h, and made their way south and east to the border areas around Rennes and Nantes. It is notable that, whichever of these three ports they may have arrived at, the British would have passed through Loudéac, and I would observe that, on the hills immediately to the north of Loudéac are the villages of Trévé and La Motte, the possible significance of which saw at 6.4.

In other words, the location of 'Arthur' place names in the area west of the Vilaine River is entirely consistent with the pattern we would expect to find, given where any conflict with the Franks must have been fought and given the ports available to a corps of British reinforcements. There are very few 'Arthur' place names in the former territory of the Coriosolites or in Cornouaille, and none that can credibly be associated with 'King' Arthur east of the Vilaine River. I think this distribution is significant. But the curious fact is that many of the places potentially associated with Arthur are expressly identified with St Armel, particularly in the Morbihan, the area where we would expect to find the strongest connections with Arthur. And this requires more detailed consideration.

Chapter 11
The Cult of St Armel

11.1 Introduction

In 7.2, I noted that there is toponymic evidence of a fourth wave of British immigration, particularly focused on the Morbihan district, the area that is most likely to have been the theatre of war in the 490s. These immigrants were in place by the mid-9th century, and they were English-speaking. Indeed they are most likely to have been Anglo-Saxons, and accordingly to have regarded the legends of Arthur with distant respect at best, or indifference at worst. I therefore suggested that Arthur would have faded from local memory at this time, a process that would have been exacerbated by the subsequent devastation and depopulation of the peninsula caused by the Vikings.

When the Vannetais was resettled, after the Vikings had been expelled, it was resettled very largely by immigrants from France, who in all probability would also have been ignorant of, or unenthusiastic about, Arthur. Places that bore names conveying an association with the historical Arthur might very well have been renamed after someone less alien to the new inhabitants. And there was at hand an inoffensive alternative, with practically the same name. It would have been a relatively small step to dedicate the church at Plebs Arthmael to St Armel, and to promote the idea that the town had always carried his name. By the 11th century, 'Plebs' had become 'Plou' and the transformation was complete.

However, in the northern and western parts of Brittany, there is no evidence for a fourth wave of British emigration, and so it is in these areas that the Arthur place names have retained their original form. While I cannot prove that this analysis is correct, it would explain the resulting pattern of 'Arthur' place names in Brittany and the curious enthusiasm for the undistinguished St Armel, so evident in the Morbihan.

11.2 St Armel

Who was St Armel? The literary sources identify three possible 'saints' with the name Arthmael, Armel or Armigali (the Latin version), and the candidates are:
- a Saint Armel, founder of a monastery at Boschaux, near Rennes (d.552 or 570);
- a Saint Armaël, said to have been one of the first Bishops of Dôl, who allegedly succeeded Saint Restoald in 651; and
- a Saint Armel who succeeded Saint Malo as Bishop of Alet, after Saint Colaphin and before Saint Maelmon (6th century).

We clearly need to consider the claims of each of these candidates carefully, but as a preliminary remark, it is worth noting that none of them were beatified by a Pope. Until the late 10th century, saints were 'created' simply by public acclamation, and none of the three are mentioned in the early martyrologies of the Catholic Church. Perhaps more surprising still, Saint Armel is not mentioned in the charters of Redon, even though Redon is only 28 miles from Ploërmel.

Starting with the second in the list, it is almost certain that 'Saint Armaël of Dôl' was not in fact a Bishop. In the 'Episcopal catalogue' of Dôl, which was presented to the Papal court at Rome in the 12th century, it was claimed that a 'Sanctus Armaelus' had been a Bishop of Dôl, and that his body rested at 'Ploasmel' in the diocese of Alet. It was also claimed that many churches in Brittany were named after him.[101] However there is no evidence that such a Bishop of Dôl existed, and by 1502 the diocese had recognised its error, qualifying Armaël simply as a 'confessor'.[102] The interesting point about this apparently fictitious Bishop is that it is suspected that the author of the 12th century 'Episcopal catalogue' may have been Baudri de Bourgeuil, who we encountered as the possible conduit of many of the Arthurian legends, in Chapters 8 and 9. If indeed it was Baudri who promoted the idea of a 'Bishop Armaël of Dôl', and if this story was false, it would cast a shadow over much of the Arthurian legends.

---

101 Dom Morice, 'Mémoires pour servir de preuves à l'histoire écclesiastique et civile de Bretagne, vol 1, 753 (1746).
102 François Duine in 'Annales de Bretagne', vol.20, issue 20-4, pps 431 -471 (1904).

Having considered this point carefully, my view is that the author of the 'Episcopal catalogue' has probably confused Saint Armel of Boschaux with the history of Dôl, and is therefore guilty of no more than an innocent mistake, or perhaps over-enthusiasm.

The third named Armel is very obscure indeed, and since there are no relics of him and he has left no cult, I think we can safely assume that he was not the inspiration behind the names of so many places in Brittany.

However, Saint Armel des Boschaux is a serious possibility, and has been identified by some authors as the real 'King Arthur', living in retirement in Brittany.[103] He was credited by Albert Le Grand as having founded Ploërmel (Morbihan) and Ploarzel (Finistère) among other places, and it is widely assumed that he was the historical figure behind all of the 'Armel' place names in Brittany. We therefore need to consider his candidacy seriously.

In terms of literature, Saint Armel was first mentioned in the 'Lives' of some Welsh saints, but his story was greatly elaborated by Albert Le Grand in 'Les Vies des Saints de la Bretagne Armorique' (1636). Le Grand wrote that he based his account on the 'Breviaire de Léon' (1516) and other manuscripts found in Léon, some of which have not survived. But he has been accused by François Duine (op. cit. infra) of inventing some of the history *("fabriquant avec la sens-gêne le plus délicieux un cadre historique pour la légende Léonnaise"* ('fabricating, in the most care-free way, a historical context for the origin myth of the Léon'). Duine writes that Le Grand invented dates, and confused 'the tyrant Comorre' with King Judwal of Brittany. His account is certainly replete with miracles and dragons, and although such tales were common in medieval hagiographies, they do tend to undermine our confidence in the historicity of the entire work.

According to Le Grand, Armel (*"which in Breton one calls Arzel"*) was born in Glamorgan in 482, and was sent to school at the monastery of Caroncinalis. Deciding on a life in the church, he departed for Brittany and landed at Aber Benniguet in the Pays de Léon in 518. He settled initially at Plouarzel. Being of royal blood, he was well connected and knew King Judwal of Brittany; and in due course he was summoned to the court of King Childebert in Paris. Childebert was delighted with his conversation and counsel,

---

103   See Chris Barber and David Pykitt, 'A Journey to Avalon' (1997).

during the seven years that he spent at court, but eventually St Armel sought permission to retire, in order to escape from the jealousy that his friendship with the King had excited among other courtiers. Permission was several times refused, but eventually St Armel was granted his wish and he took himself to a place 'three leagues from Rennes', which Judwal gave him. There he built an oratory and several monks' cells for his followers. Among many other miracles, he slew a dragon, which was terrorising the area, by lassoing it with his stole (the scarf worn by clergymen) and commanding the dragon to jump into the River Seiche near Rennes – dragons being unable to swim, of course. According to Le Grand, St Armel died in 552 (other accounts say 570). He was reputed to be a great healer, but it is important to note that there is no suggestion that he was a warrior.

Unfortunately, Le Grand was faithfully followed by Père Le Cointe in his 'Annales ecclesiastici Francorum' (1665), Dom Lobineau in his 'Vies des Saints de Bretagne' (1725) and De la Borderie in his 'Histoire de Bretagne' (1896), so his version of the story of St Armel became entrenched. But his account was rejected as unreliable by the Société des Bollandistes in their 'Acta Sanctorum' (1737) (the group did, however, find another source to confirm the existence of St Armel in the 'Bréviaire Malouin') and then it was comprehensively debunked by Abbot François Duine in the 'Annales de Bretagne', 1904, Vol 20, Issue 20-2, at pp 136 – 145.

It is striking that there is no trace of a cult of St Armel in Britain before the 15th century, either in martyrologies or in parish dedications, which seems very odd for a supposedly high-profile British saint. Some academics have tried to identify him with the name of St Erme, a saint celebrated in parts of Cornwall, but Duine rejected this notion. Erme is monosyllabic, and there is no known variant of Armel which has less than two syllables; and Erme appears more likely to be a corruption of Hermes, a saint celebrated in both Cornwall and Brittany, where his name is never confused with that of Armel.

However the cult of Saint Armel later attracted some very influential adherents, particularly during the reign of Henry Tudor (1485 – 1509), who spent a period in exile in Brittany (from 1471 to 1485) (see below). The support of royalty did wonders for the cult, and the monastery of Saint-Armel-des-Boschaux became a destination for many pilgrims, which in turn resulted in the production of quantities of souvenirs. Four badges devoted to Saint Armel have been found in London, dating from the late 15th or early 16th century, and there are two statues of the saint in the funerary chapel of Henry VII at Westminster Abbey.

11.3 Is it Likely that St Armel des Boschaux was the Real Inspiration?

So the question is whether it is likely that this saint left a toponymic footprint of such a size in Brittany. Well, the first point to consider is whether it is probable that he ever even ventured into the Brittany of the 6th century at all – the only place with which he is definitively associated is at Les Boschaux, in Frankish lands to the east of the Vilaine River. In the early 6th century, and after the Treaty of 497, it seems to me that King Childebert set about creating a forerunner of the Breton Marches – a buffer zone along the western edge of his kingdom to protect it against the unruly barbarians. As Procopius said (in c.551) *"the Franks allow them [the Britons] to settle in the part of their land which appears to be more deserted and by this means they say they are winning over the island."*

There was a pattern of the establishment of churches on the east bank of the River Rance by Welsh and Irish saints of this period, and several of them seem to have become loyal subjects of the Franks. St Malo became the Bishop of Alet; an Irish priest called Serf established the church at St Servan, just outside Alet (and he then continued on to Reims in 509); St Suliac (Tysilio to the Welsh) later established a monastery at St Suliac, just upstream from Alet; and of course, in 557 Childebert gave St Sampson some land at Dôl to found that monastery. All of these saints took up residence in Frankish territory, apparently with the blessing of the Frankish King of Paris, and St Armel seems to have been another of the same ilk. We are told that he spent seven years at the court of King Childebert before settling at Les Boschaux, and every circumstance suggests that his sympathies lay on the Frankish side of the border. I think it very likely that most of these Irish and Welsh saints arrived at the port of Alet, and then headed up the ancient 'tin road' to Rennes, entirely on land held by the Franks.

It is possible that they never even visited the land west of the Vilaine, and it is quite likely that the Bretons and Franks were not on good terms, even when they were not at war.

For example, St Melaine, the Gallo-Roman who became Bishop of Rennes in 505 is said to have opposed the British immigration. He attended the Council of Orleans in 511 where he acknowledged Clovis as his sovereign. Together with the (Frankish) Bishops of Tours and Angers, he wrote a letter in c.515 (which survives) to two Breton priests called Lovocat and Catihern, scolding them for using portable altars to celebrate Mass in the cabins of their communicants, and for allowing women to distribute the Eucharist. Quelle horreur!

The dislike was mutual, and by the late 570s, war had broken out between the Franks and the Bretons. When Waroch II, the 'King' of the Bro Waroch in southern Brittany, raided the countryside near Rennes in 579, his advance took him as far as Corps Nuds,[104] and if he had progressed just a few miles further, he would have overrun the monastery of Saint-Armel-des-Boschaux. To me it is unsurprising that St Armel was completely ignored in the country of his birth.

Is it conceivable that St Armel was the 'Arthur' who was celebrated throughout the Brittany peninsula? I don't think so. 'King' Arthur would not have spent seven years at the court of the Frankish King, paying him homage. And even if this particular aspect of the story is ignored, the Bretons of the 6th century would have felt little affection for a British cleric living in Frankish territory to the east of the Vilaine. They would probably have regarded him, at best, with suspicion, or at worst as a Judas.

I therefore need to test the hypothesis that the original inspiration for the names of towns like Ploërmel and Plouarzel was not in fact St Armel, as Le Grand asserts, but someone else – possibly Arthur. And to do this, I must first try to understand how Le Grand could have been so mistaken. He was a native of Morlaix, in western Brittany, whose first language was Breton; and apparently he had access to documents, now lost, in the possession of the religious houses of the peninsula and indeed in the hands of his own family. So at first sight, he had no motive to conceal any trace of the real Arthur, and plenty of evidence to support what he wrote. However there are two

---

104 A Frankish corruption of Cornuz – in my opinion a Gaulish place-name, possibly meaning 'bare hills'.

circumstances which, in my view, explain Le Grand's account. Firstly, I believe that the memory of Arthur had been obscured by the people of the Vannetais themselves, during the 9th century, as discussed previously; and secondly I think that Le Grand was under immense political pressure not to revive the Arthurian legends.

The first point I have covered at 7.2 – it is very likely that any memory of Arthur had been eroded if not erased in the Vannetais by a wave of Anglo-Saxon migrants, and by the subsequent depopulation of the peninsula under the Vikings and the repopulation of the south-east by French-speaking immigrants. But the second point needs explanation.

11.4 The End of Breton Independence

The second factor, which would have weighed heavily on the mind of Albert Le Grand, was the period in which he lived. Le Grand was born in 1599 and died in 1641. In 1491, Anne, the last Duchess of an independent Brittany, had married King Charles VIII of France ('Charles the Affable') and in 1532 the union of France and Brittany was proclaimed, much to the distress of some in Brittany. To publish his book at all, in 1637, Le Grand was required to obtain permission from Julian Joubert, the Vicar-General of the Congregation of Gaul, and this consent was given only on condition that the draft text was approved by Regnaud Le Gendre and J Langlois, both doctors of theology at the Faculty of Paris, as well as by two church officials at Rennes and two at Nantes. The text had to be theologically sound, and I suggest, also politically correct. Le Grand was so concerned *"that some bookshops and printers would not print it"* that he applied to the King of France for his written permission to publish, permission that was granted for a period of 15 years. Why on earth was the publication of a book on the lives of the Breton saints so potentially explosive?

It was a delicate time. A religious revolt took place in 1588, and a revolt of the 'Red Caps' (Bonnets Rouges), caused by an extension of the French Stamp Duty, followed in 1675. Le Grand knew that he would not be allowed to publish anything that might inflame nationalist sentiment, even if he was aware of rumours that St Armel was really just a mask for Arthur. And I think it likely that many influential people were of that opinion, as the following section shows.

11.5 King Henry VII and 'St Armel'

Henry Tudor was a member of the House of Lancaster, with a distant claim to the throne of England. He was born in 1457 to a mother who was 13 and a father who died three months before his birth, in prison. Henry was forced into exile in Brittany in 1471, and spent most of the next 14 years there. However, by 1483 he was the most senior living representative of the House of Lancaster, after a succession of setbacks inflicted on that dynasty by the rival House of York.

Henry, the young Earl of Richmond, was welcomed to Vannes by the Francis II, Duke of Brittany, and given sanctuary at the Château de Suscinio, at Sarzeau on the Rhuys peninsula for a while, before being lodged at the Château de Largoët near Elven, where he resided from 1474 to 1476. He was joined in exile by supporters like John Morton who later became Cardinal Archbishop of Canterbury, and Jasper Tudor, the first Earl of Pembroke, Henry's paternal uncle. During their time in Brittany, Henry and his associates seem to have become devotees of St Armel, the saint who was unknown in Britain, but who had left such a large toponymic footprint in Brittany.

Henry first tried to invade England and usurp the throne of King Richard III in 1483, with support from his host Francis II, but the campaign unraveled and his principal co-conspirator, the Duke of Buckingham, was executed. Richard III attempted to have Henry extradited from Brittany, but Henry fled to France, where he was able to gain support from King Charles VIII ('Charles the Affable').

In 1485, Henry embarked again with a small force of French and Scottish troops and sailed to Pembrokeshire in Wales. Having gathered reinforcements among the Welsh, he moved swiftly to bring King Richard III to battle. For some time it was believed that the Battle of Bosworth Field, which followed, was located near Atherstone in North Warwickshire, because Henry paid compensation to several villages, including Atherstone, for damage to crops at *"our late victorious field"*. But in 2010, Leicestershire County Council announced archaeological finds, which proved that the battle had taken place just to the south of Sutton Cheney in Leicestershire, about 6 miles from Atherstone. It now seems that Henry chose to spend the night before the battle in Atherstone, which he may have regarded as a propitious location. Fighting against a larger force, Henry was victorious and Richard III was killed.[105]

One of the villages to which Henry paid compensation was Merevale, and he also paid for the installation of a stained glass window in the church of this village, in which St Armel is shown in a full suit of armour, in a composition depicting the Tree of Jesse (the genealogy of the biblical Kings of Judah).

The following year (1486), Henry married Elizabeth of York (the sister of the two Princes who were murdered in the Tower of London, presumably by Richard III), and their first son was born, a month prematurely, in Winchester. The boy was christened – wait for it – Arthur; and at the ripe old age of two, it was arranged that Arthur should marry Catherine of Aragon. Unfortunately the prince died at 16, so Henry was eventually succeeded by his second son, Henry VIII, who took not only Arthur's throne but also his wife.

Henry paid an unknown chronicler to make "*a copye of a rolle of diverse kinges*", with the object of proving his descent from King Arthur, and Arthurian themes played a prominent part in the royal pageants of his reign. But he had to exercise discretion in public displays of his enthusiasm, because King Charles VIII, his patron, had long-held ambitions to incorporate Brittany into France. This he achieved in 1491, when he married the Duchess Anne (despite the fact that she had already been married by proxy to the Holy Roman Emperor Maximilian I). Henry mounted several invasions of Brittany in 1492, to try to prevent the absorption of the Duchy into France, but the attempt was hampered by the chaotic politics of Brittany, and he was forced to make peace with Charles VIII at the end of that year. From then until the end of his reign, Henry was an ally of the French king, and received an annual subsidy of 50,000 crowns from France, payments received, at least in part, for abandoning Brittany to its fate.

In 1496, Anne commissioned Pierre Le Baud to write his 'Chronique des roys et princes de Bretagne armoricane', a task which he completed in 1505, the year of his death. Le Baud had already

---

105 The remains of Richard III were recently unearthed under a car park in Leicester.

established a reputation as a Breton historian with his 'Compillation des cronicques et ystoires des Bretons', completed in 1480, and both of his works depended heavily on the 'Book of the Deeds of King Arthur', that we encountered in Chapter 7. It is clear that Le Baud took the opportunity of this second commission to remind Anne of her inheritance of Breton independence, by emphasising the accounts of Arthur's Continental war. But she was by then the Queen of France, and probably sincerely believed that the union with France was both inevitable and in the best interests of Brittany. We can be fairly sure that her husband had given her undertakings to treat the impoverished peninsula with generosity.

Le Baud made only a passing reference to St Armel in his second 'Histoire', in which he suggests no particular distinction for the saint, and certainly no military background: *"Auffi felon l'histoire fainct Armel, en celuy temps Caratinalen un autre homme très-puiffant, coufin de fainct Paul Aurelian, délaiffant fon païs & fes autres richeffes, defquelles il avoit abondance, paffa la mer avecques ledit fainct homme Armel & multitude d'autres qui appliquérent efdites parties de Cornoüailles, où ils demourèrent en une ville appellée en breton Pennohen, qui eft interprété en gaulois Chef de Boeuf; combien que en après ledit Armel habita en un défert ou territoire de Rennes, en un lieu à préfent nommé de luy."*

I translate this as *"Also, according to the history of St Armel, at this time Caratinalen another very powerful man, cousin of St Paul Aurelian, leaving his country and his other riches, of which he had an abundance, passed over the sea with the said St Armel and a multitude of others, who settled in the said part of Cornouailles, where they lived in a town called in Breton Pennohen, which translates into French as Cow's Head; however afterwards the said Armel lived in an uninhabited district near Rennes, in a place at present named after him."*

But then, the unremarkable qualities of the saint are underlined by the fact that he is not mentioned once by Gregory of Tours (538 – 594), in whose diocese Armel constructed his monastery.

However, Henry and his inner circle remained devoted to the cult of St Armel, and two statues of St Armel stand in his funerary chapel at Westminster Abbey. There are about 8 other depictions of St Armel in Britain, dating from this period, including a carving on Cardinal

The Cult of St Armel

Archbishop Morton's cenotaph at Canterbury Cathedral (c.1500) and a figure in the Rebedos at Romsey Abbey, dated to about 1525 – 1530. He is represented in a medieval alabaster at Stoneyhurst College, and another at St Mary's Brookfield in London, which came originally from Wales.[106]

One curious feature of these depictions is that St Armel is always portrayed in full plate armour, often partially hidden under his monk's (or bishop's) robes, which is surprising for a saint with no military history. Generally, a dragon is shown lying at his feet, with a stole around its neck, and St Armel usually carries a book (see front cover).

In the medieval period, the church at Merevale was by no means the only one to be decorated with a 'Tree of Jesse' window, and it is understandable that Henry was so keen on this theme. The tree, which represents the royal lineage from Jesse, father of the Biblical David, stands for royal legitimacy, through an unbroken bloodline. This would have been a sensitive subject to Henry, who was in fact only about 60th in line to the throne. His claim depended on inheritance, at various stages, through the female line and through illegitimate offspring, so he took great care to strengthen his title at every opportunity.

This motif appears in an arch of the chapter house at Westminster Abbey, near Henry VII's chapel. Moreover there is a large stained-glass window above the main entrance to the impressive church at Ploërmel, which also illustrates the Tree of Jesse, and which dates from the period 1511 to 1556. Martin Biddle in 'King Arthur's Round Table, An Archaeological Investigation' (2000) has pointed out that the iconography of these works was appropriate to the new patriotism of the era, *"So talents, nurtured in the language of the church, learnt secular usage. For Jesse substitute Brut; for Abraham read Arthur. Caritas moves into the place of the Virgin. Gog and Magog await, perhaps for the second time, the part of St Christopher. For the Kings of Judah exchange the Kings of Britain."*

If Henry VII could return today, he would no doubt be delighted that the Order of the Bath meets in the Henry VII Lady Chapel at Westminster Abbey, the chapel where his body is interred. The Order

---

[106] Arthur Green 'The Romsey Pained Wooden Rebedos with a Short Account of St Armel' (date unknown).

The Duke and the Decoy

of the Bath is now regarded as the fourth most senior of the British orders of chivalry, but its antiquity is uncertain. It was revived in 1725, at the instigation of John Anstis, the Garter King of Arms, a Cornishman and antiquarian who left thousands of pages of notes on English history. But it goes back at least as far as the reign of Henry VII, because Edward Stafford, Duke of Buckingham (the 7 year-old son of Henry's executed ally), was made a knight of the Bath before Henry's coronation. It is said that the Order gets its name from a bathing ceremony that was part of the process of becoming a knight, but I wonder whether it had anything to do with Geoffrey of Monmouth's 'Battle of Bath Hill'? Certainly, like all the orders of chivalry, the Order of the Bath owes something to the legends of Arthur's Round Table.

The version of Arthur's life that Henry had absorbed was of course the Galfridian one (the story based on Geoffrey of Monmouth's 'Historia'), and no doubt he also read some of the books that amplified the legends, such as Sir Thomas Mallory's 'La Morte Darthur' (c.1470). However, a prominent historian at his court, Polydore Vergil, was skeptical. Indeed, he has been accused of being 'anti-Arthurian', but I think it would be fairer to describe him as 'anti-Galfridian'. Henry died in 1509, and in 1513 Vergil completed a history of England that discounted Geoffrey's 'Historia' almost entirely. He accepted that Arthur was an historical figure, who might have gone on to unite the kingdom if he had lived long enough, but he regarded Monmouth as a fantasist and said that the 'tomb of Arthur' at Glastonbury was an obvious fraud, since it would have pre-dated the foundation of the Abbey.

Vergil's writings provoked a furious response from John Leland (sometimes described as 'The King's Antiquary') who set off on an 'itinerary' around the British Isles to seek out proof of Arthur's existence (between 1535 and 1543). However, the strongest evidence he could find was his identification of Cadbury Castle in Somerset as Arthur's Camelot [See Appendix 4], and the rest is now regarded as unconvincing. The two artefacts on which he relied most heavily were a leaden cross that had allegedly been found in 'Arthur's tomb' at Glastonbury (clearly a fake) and a wax imprint of 'Arthur's seal', supposedly found on a document at Westminster. Neither of these are now extant, but Leland did at least identify the two statues of St Armel in the Henry VII Lady Chapel at Westminster as significant pieces of evidence.

Henry VII died before 'the battle of the books' between Vergil and Leland erupted. But Geoffrey's version of history had been widely disparaged since a time shortly after its publication (eg by William of Newburgh in 1190) and devotees of the legends probably felt that they had to be fairly circumspect in displaying their enthusiasm, even if they were monarchs. This may be another reason why Henry used the device of Armel as a front for Arthur. But whether Henry was aware that the principal historian at his court thought that the vast majority of the literature on Arthur was fiction, is an interesting question. Certainly the two did not publicly quarrel over the issue, but that may be because Vergil did not make his views known during Henry's lifetime.

Vergil was however allowed to publish his views on Galfridian history with impunity during the reign of Henry VIII, and we may suppose that this king associated the name of Arthur more with his father and his late older brother. Arthurian themes ceased to form part of royal pageants after 1522, when it is said that the Round Table in the Great Hall of Winchester was painted. Arthur did not reappear at royal pageants until the reign of Elizabeth I, and it seems that during this interlude the skeptics had prevailed.[107]

But to return to Henry VII, I think it is very clear from the symbolism in the depictions of St Armel that the King (and probably his intimate friends) associated St Armel with Arthur. The pieces of armour glimpsed beneath the monk's robes are sufficient evidence of that, but the deception was multi-layered. Armel was certainly a mask for Arthur, but Arthur, in turn, was a metaphor for Henry, the last English King to win his throne on the field of battle. For him, the expedition from Brittany and the defeat of Richard fulfilled the prophesy that Arthur, 'the once and future king', would return. The (sometimes red) dragon at the feet of St Armel may have symbolised the vanquished forces of the Franks, but it was also the emblem of Cadwalader, the King of Gwynedd, from whom Henry claimed descent. And it was more than that, because it represented the whole of British history, as Sydney Anglo observed in 'The British History in Early Tudor Propaganda': *"There is no doubt that Henry VII made*

---

[107] Martin Riddle, 'King Arthur's Round Table; an Archaeological Investigation" (2000).

much of this dragon symbol from the very beginning of his reign. The red dragon was one of the standards presented at St Pauls after the victory at Bosworth; it figured among the decorations for horse trappers at the coronation; and during those coronation celebrations the king created a new pursuivant named Rougedragon. This proliferation of red dragons, emphasized by the earlier identification of Edward IV with the same symbol, must be regarded as an expression of Henry's British descent, as opposed to his more particular Cadwalader or Welsh descents."

What does this mean for the history of Arthur? It is clear that Henry believed either that St Armel was Arthur, or that he stood for Arthur – he was the decoy referred to in the title of this book. Either way, it follows that Henry believed in Arthur as an historical fact, and associated him with the area of Brittany now called the Morbihan, where Henry had learned the 'secret' of the identity of St Armel. This, of course, does not prove that Henry or his informants were correct: it is possible that Arthur did not exist and that St Armel was the genuine inspiration for the several place names found in the Morbihan that are associated with him. However, as I hope to have demonstrated, the latter proposition is very improbable. And if St Armel was not the true source of these place names, we have to ask who was?

The Bretons with whom Henry had come into contact were 500 years closer to the historical events than we are, and no doubt had sources which are now lost to us. We may never know what evidence they possessed that convinced them that St Armel represented Arthur, but there is no doubt that this is what they believed. If they thought that St Armel was Arthur, I think they were wrong, although I can understand how this opinion might have developed, given the history of the area and the ethnic evolution of its population. If they thought that St Armel was an alter ego for Arthur, I believe they were correct. But whatever may have been the view in Brittany on this issue, Henry VII was certainly happy to continue to use the saint as a decoy, given both the political sensitivities around his relationship with the French monarchy and the anti-Galfridian climate of opinion, evident before and during his lifetime.

If the places in the Morbihan ostensibly named after St Armel are in reality inspired by Arthur, the pattern shows clearly that Arthur was a hero to the population, both there and in the areas through which a British army would have had to have travelled. It then becomes clear that an historical giant has cast a large shadow over the landscape, and this in turn is evidence both for the existence of Arthur, and for the reality of his campaign in Gaul. Perhaps Geoffrey of Monmouth wasn't such a fool after all.

Chapter 12
So What Really Happened?

This is where I have to draw a deep breath, and stick my neck out. I cannot prove conclusively any statement in what follows, but this is my interpretation of the facts as set out in the first eleven Chapters.

I think Arthur was a Belgic Briton, quite possibly descended from the Catuvellauni, and born around 465. He appears to have been a minor noble, possibly with ancestral connections to the 'counts' of Brittany. He seems to have been a career soldier, and it is likely that he served under Ambrosius Aurelianus, although only towards the end of the career of the latter. He succeeded Ambrosius as the commander of the British army in about 490, by acclamation of his fellow officers, at a time when a war between the British and the Anglo-Saxons was finely balanced.

He fought a number of battles with the invaders along a frontier from West Sussex to Lincolnshire, possibly with assistance from units from Brittany. The war culminated in a decisive victory in c.493 at the Battle of Mount Badon, possibly at Arbury Hill in Northamptonshire. The Anglo-Saxon leadership, probably under the overall command of Ælle of Sussex, was decimated at this battle. The capacity of the Germans to wage war was destroyed, to the extent that the surviving immigrants were forced to send to the Continent for replacement commanders and warriors, to secure their survival.

In the meantime, King Clovis of the Franks had cleared the British out of the Loire Valley in 490, and had sent a Saxon force to take Nantes in 491. The Bretons repulsed the Saxons besieging the city, but by 494 or 495, Clovis had returned and was mounting raids into the peninsula. The Bretons sent to Arthur for assistance, and, in repayment of his debt to them, he led a force across the Channel to northern Brittany in c. 495/6. This was probably the only time in the entire era when the British would have been in a secure enough position at home to be able to do this.

So What Really Happened?

Marching south to the Vannetais, where the Frankish raids were taking place, he encountered and defeated a Frankish army, possibly near Loudéac. He chased the remnants of the Frankish army back across the Vilaine. Clovis was now fully engaged in a war with the Visigoths in Aquitaine, and decided to make peace with the Bretons, at least for the time being. In c.497 he agreed to leave the Bretons in possession of the peninsula west of the Vilaine River and of Nantes, in return for their abandonment of any claims to territory further east.

Arthur remained for a period of time in Brittany to secure its borders and restore its damaged defences. Apart from his cousin Hoël, most of the Breton leaders had been killed in the war with Clovis, and so he left senior officers in place to command their forces, possibly including Waroch I (who supposedly gave St Gildas the land on which to build his monastery at Rhuys). Arthur's memory in Brittany was honoured in the names of places in the Morbihan, especially at Ploërmel where he based a command post, and in places where his troops had established camps en route to the war zone of the south-east.

The security position in Britain did not permit him to dally too long on the Continent, so he returned to England and consolidated the security of the kingdom of Ambrosius. To the north and east, the limit of this territory was largely defined by Watling Street (the 'street of the Welsh' to the Anglo-Saxons) and Arthur stationed troops at places like Atherstone to guard the border. He maintained alliances with Cado of Dumnonia, the 'Kings' of western and northern Wales and with Mordred, who ruled the former territory of the Cornovii in what are now Staffordshire and Cheshire.

The situation in Britain was generally settled for 40 years, although the West Saxons were gradually expanding into what are now West Sussex and eastern Hampshire. In the meantime the Franks under Childebert I, the successor to Clovis, maintained friendly relations with the Bretons, so the region was at peace for most of the period. But the whole world was badly affected by a severe weather event in 535 and 536, when the summers were very cold and the crops failed. Famine ensued, and in 541 and 542 the plague of Justinian swept across Europe, killing a significant portion of the population. This particularly weakened the British, as compared to the Anglo-Saxons, because the British had stronger trading links with the Mediterranean, from where the disease came to northern Europe by sea.

Mordred attempted to take advantage of the enfeebled state of the kingdom of Arthur, and the failing health of its elderly ruler, and launched a civil war. He tried to rally the Celtic kingdoms of Wales and Cornwall to his cause, marching down the Fosse Way to join forces with other rebels. But Arthur cornered and defeated him in Cornwall, and Mordred was killed. Arthur himself was wounded in the battle, and since he no longer had the strength to lead his army, he retired to Avalon, the 'island of apples'.

A few decades after his demise, the rulers of Wessex, Kent and Sussex mounted a determined and ultimately successful campaign to conquer Arthur's kingdom, and they succeeded, after victories at Old Sarum, Banbury and Dyrham in Gloucestershire. At about the same time, the British kingdom of Hen Ogledd in the north of England fell to the northern Angles of Deira, and Mordred's former kingdom fell to the Mercians of the Trent Valley. The result was that most of southern Britain became 'English', although the Welsh and Cornish held out for a long time.

Meanwhile the Bretons were engaged in an intermittent struggle with the Franks, in which the Franks won several battles but never quite succeeded in delivering a knock-out blow. Although the Vannetais was occupied by Anglo-Saxons, and the whole peninsula was later ravaged by the Vikings, the memory of Arthur could never quite be extinguished. His shadow was always there, the ultimate totem of Breton independence.

When the Earl of Richmond arrived in the Vannetais as a fourteen year-old in 1471, the young prince charmed the locals, and a savant decided to let him into a secret. The area in which he had taken refuge had once been ruled by Arthur, but he was not to mention it because there were powerful forces that did not want the legends revived. Henry was fascinated, and fell immediately for the romance of the story. He and his companions formed a brotherhood of the initiates, and Henry kept the story of Arthur close to his heart for the rest of his days. He was willing to risk his life to gain his kingdom, but he insisted on staying at Atherstone on the eve of the battle. And once his patron saint had granted him victory, he honoured him at every opportunity, until his end. Two statues of 'Armel' stood guard in his funerary chapel, as he continued his journey into the afterlife.

Appendix 1
The Arthurs of Brittany

There are in France more than 30 places that, loosely, have 'Arthur' names, and although some of these look suspiciously like medieval fakes, the large majority appear to reflect an association with a real person. Arthur and its many variants are unambiguously personal names, and therefore we do not suffer from the problem that we encounter with Hoël ('high'), that the name could simply be an adjective. And although the Bretons have further corrupted the Welsh names, it seem clear to me that 'Armel', 'Arzel', 'Ermel', 'Artus', 'Ardus' etc all derive from either Artur or Arthmael, the names by which Arthur was probably known in Wales.

However, we do still have one problem, and that is that the Arthur we are concerned with was not the only person of that name in the Brittany of the Middle Ages. Arthmael became quite popular in Wales, where it was the name of three historical kings of Glywysing (west Glamorgan) in the 8th to 10th centuries. And as we shall see, it became very popular in Brittany.

As evidence of the popularity of the name in Wales, an 'Arthmail' is referred to in a 10th century charter in the 'Liber Landevensis'. Its use was not confined to royalty in the principality either, because we find, for example an 'Artmali' and an 'Arthmail' on inscribed stones of the 9th and 11th century at Llantwit Manor and Ogmore in Glamorgan. Later on the name was recorded in Wales as Arthuail, Arthvail or Arthuael. So, while there is no suggestion that these individuals inspired the 'Arthur' place names in France, it is very likely that the Welsh migrants to Brittany included some people with similar names, which may now be reflected in Breton toponymy.

In fact, there were clearly a number of 'Arthurs' who have left their mark on the history of Brittany. Later on there were two particularly famous examples, being Arthur I, Duke of Brittany (1187 – 1203) and

The Duke and the Decoy

Arthur II, Duke of Brittany (1261 – 1312), but these individuals were christened a long time after the 'Arthur' places got their names. Plebs Arthmael was recorded in a charter of 834 in the Cartulary of Redon, so it was clearly named after someone who lived before that date.

The charters of Redon demonstrate that there were numerous people with names that were probably derived from Arthur or Arthmael in Brittany in the Middle Ages. Here are some of these references:

Aithlon (Charter 2, 834), Arthieu (Charter 3, 834), Arrthel (Charter 3, 834), Arthmael (Charter 5, 833), Arthuiu (Charter 7, 833), Arthuiu (Charter 10, 833), Arthuiu (Charter 12, 834), Arthuiu (Charter 15, date uncertain), Atoire (Charter 18, 859), Arthuiu (Charter 19, 860), Arthur (Charter 21, 868), Atoire, Arthueu (Charter 29, 832-868), Arthueu (Charter 32, 857-868), Arthwius (Charter 45, date uncertain), Arthuiu (Charter 46, 856-865), Arthnou, Arthwiu (Charter 47, 882 – 899), Arthur (Charter 52, 866), Arthwius (Charter 53, 846), Arthuiu (Charter 58, 838-849), Arthuueu (Charter 63, 863), Arthwolou, Arthueu (Charter 71, 853-864), Arthur (Charter 77, 861-867), Arthuiu (Charter 96, 867), Athoire (Charter 97, date unknown), Arthlon (Charter 99, 866), Arthur (Charter 100, 861-867), Arthwiu (Charter 106, 848/849), Arthueu (Charter 121, 846), Arthuiu (Charter 124, 832-840), Arthanael (Charter 127, 852), Atore (Charter 130, 834), Arthweo (Charter 148, 838/839), Arthwiu (Charter 155, 830), Arthueu (Charter 156, 834), Arthwius (Charter 157, 860), Arthwolou (Charter 161, 850-866), Arthwiu, Arthuiu (Charter 162, 854), Arthuiu (Charter 165, 832-835), Atoere (Charter 176, 836), Arthwiu (Charter 181, 834), Arthwiu (Charter 182, 833), Arthuiu (Charter 183, 845-860), Arthuiu (Charter 184, date unknown), Arthuiu (Charter 185, 865), Arthuiu (domo Arthuiu im Prin) (Charter 186, 867). Arthwolou (Charter 188, 838-848), Arthbiu (Charter 192, 826-840), Arthmael, Autur (Charter 194, 840), Arthwiu (Charter 199, 826-834), Atoere (Charter 202, 858), Arthuiu (Charter 212, 814-821), Arthuiu (Charter 215, 860), Arthur (Charter 235, 878), Arthur (Charter 240, 868), Arthnou (Charter 241, 869), Arthmael (Charter 256, 866), Arthwiu (Charter 261, 874-876), Armail, (Charter 273, 897), Armail (Charter 278, 909), Arthueu (Charter 284, 1051-1060), Armael (Charter 302, 1052), Armel (Charter 336, 1144), Armael (Charter 370, 1112)

As we can see, there were many permutations of these names,

Appendices

and 'arth' was a very popular element in the composition of Breton names.

Appendix 2
Dramatis Personnae

Ambrosius Aurelianus　　　　　　c.430 - 490

Ambrosius is one of the few individuals mentioned by Gildas, as being a commander of the British forces fighting the Saxons, but he does not provide any dates. It appears that he succeeded Vortimer as the commander of the British forces in c.460. The text of Gildas is unclear on the point of whether Ambrosius was the British commander at the Battle of Mount Badon (which I take to have occurred in 493), but if he was, he must have been quite old.

In the 'Chronica Majora', Bede dates Ambrosius' victories to the reign of the Emperor Zeno (474 – 491), which seems consistent with the other information available.

According to Geoffrey of Monmouth, Ambrosius was the second son of Constantine, the younger brother of Audren. I estimate Audren's dates to be c. 400? to c.464? (see below), so if Geoffrey was correct, Constantine's's son might have lived c.430? to c.490? Based primarily on Bede's chronology, I therefore conclude that Ambrosius was the British commander at some period between c.474 and c.491, and at a very rough guess, he may have lived from c. 430 to c.490.

Arthur　　　　　　c.465 – c.542

If Arthur was the British commander at the Battle of Mons Badonicus, as asserted by Nennius, and if, as I believe, the Battle of Mons Badonicus took place in c.493, Arthur must have been of an age in that year. The 'Annales Cambriae' gives the date of the Battle of Camlann, at which Arthur was allegedly mortally wounded, as c.537, and Geoffrey of Monmouth dates it to 542. I therefore suggest dates for his life of c.465 – c.542. For further discussion, see the main text.

Audren   c.420? – c.464?

Audren is significant in the context of the Arthurian legends, because it is said that he sent his younger brother Constantine to England to assist the British in their conflict with the Anglo-Saxons, and that Constantine was Arthur's grandfather. We do not actually need to prove that this was the case to substantiate Arthur, but it is not inconceivable that the Bretons provided the British with support in their struggles against the Anglo-Saxons. As I have suggested, the colony was in some ways the stronger partner in the relationship in the 5th century, and there was a long history of soldiers moving back and forth between the two.

Some Breton legends tell us that Audren had a son called Budic and that his grandson Hoël was a contemporary of Arthur. Others suggest that both Budic and Hoël were sons of Audren,[108] and still others suggest that there were two Budics, father and son, and that Hoël was a son of the younger Budic. But none of this is historically certain, and the details are mostly unimportant for the purposes of establishing the historicity of Arthur. All that we need to bear in mind is that Arthur is said to have been a contemporary of a Hoël, who is said to have been a descendant of Audren.

Bertrand d'Argentré, a respected French historian of the 17th century, suggested that Audren reigned in a period dating, at the extremes, from 412 to 438, but these dates appear much too early to me. Other sources date the construction of Châtelaudren, a major fort said to have been built by Audren, to 447, which would be consistent with Audren succeeding Gradlon in the course of the second Breton revolt against the Romans (339 – 448). But, for the purposes of understanding the Arthurian legends, we do not need to be precise. It seems pretty clear that a Breton king called Audren existed, and that he reigned in the middle of the 5th century.

According to Breton tradition, Audren became king of Brittany in c.446 and died in c.464. He is said to have founded Châtelaudren in c.447. The toponymic evidence for his existence is very strong, but there is no dependable source for his dates. With a high level of uncertainty, I therefore attribute dates of c. 420 – c.464 to his life.

---

[108] For example Nicolas Travers, 'Histoire civile, politique et religieuse de la ville et du Comte de Nantes' (1836).

The Duke and the Decoy

Budic (c. 445? – c. 509?)

According to the Cartulary of Quimperlé, at the siege of Nantes, Count Eusebius was replaced by Budic, who Travers describes as a son of Audren and the brother of Riothamus. This was the Budic who is said to have given shelter to Ambrosius Aurelianus, and who had given him military support on his return to Britain (per Geoffrey of Monmouth). Given that Riothamus fought a battle in Berry 21 years earlier, and seems to have disappeared into Burgundy after the defeat, a sibling relationship between Budic and this general seems to me doubtful, but the filial relationship between Budic and Audren is plausible.

There are numerous published lists of the Breton 'kings' of this period, of which the most definitive is that published by Pierre-Hyacinthe Morice de Beauvois (known as Dom Morice) in 1750.[109] But there are considerable variations between the accounts, and I think they can be treated only as digests of oral traditions of uncertain historicity. The general thrust is that Audren was succeeded by two of his sons, the older son being Erec and the younger being Budic, and that Budic was the father of Hoël.

The first edition of the 'Histoire civile, politique et religiouse' by Travers (1836) was edited by Auguste Savagner, Professor of History at the Royal College of Nantes, who added extensive footnotes to the text, particularly in the section devoted to the siege of Nantes. Savagner wrote *"In 490 at the latest, Budic or Debrock, putative brother of Erech, was summoned from Great Britain, where he had gone, to succeed him. His first exploit was the conquest of the territory occupied by the Alans, called for this reason Alania. He then relieved the town of Nantes, which was besieged by barbarian troops under the command of Marchillon or Chillon. The Franks, always motivated by the desire to extend their domination, launched several campaigns during the reign of Budic, to make themselves masters of Brittany. In the end, having encountered fierce resistance, they negotiated a treaty in 497 with the Bretons, and admitted them to the ranks of their allies."* [My translation] Savagner does not cite any authority for this version of events, but the chronology seems natural. Eusebius was killed in the siege, and Nantes was relieved by Budic. This contradicts Travers,

---
109 'L'Histoire ecclésiastique et civile de Bretagne'.

who tells us that Budic was defending Nantes against the Saxons, but no doubt, after lifting the siege, Budic had to defend the city.

Savagner continues that it is thought that Budic fell victim to Clovis in 509, and that, after his death, the Frisians, led by one Corselde, had invaded Brittany and expelled its leaders. This was probably based on the Chronicle of St Brieuc, which tells us that Brittany was devastated by Frisians and Goths before the arrival of St Sampson (in c.550). Clovis had profited from this war (or may indeed have instigated it) to take control of the region and to install his lieutenants as governors. As evidence, Savagner cites the fact that the Bishops of Rennes, Nantes and Vannes attended the Council of Orléans in 511, and that they there declared themselves to be subjects of Clovis, who they addressed as their seigneur and their master. And he cites Gregory of Tours[110] who wrote *"for from the death of King Clovis [511] onwards the Bretons remained under the domination of the Franks and their rulers were called counts and not kings."*

There is significant toponymic evidence of Budics or Budocs in Brittany, but as we have already seen there were several people of that name in the Early Middle Ages. One was the master of a school on the Île Lavret, in the mid-5th century, where St Gwenole was a student, and another was the third Bishop of Dôl, of the late 6th century, who, in my view, played a significant role in the development of the Arthurian legends. And yet another was a 'Count' of Brittany who appears to have ruled in Cornouaille at about the same time (between 567 and 577). I believe that places in Wales and Devon and Cornwall with 'Budock' names refer to the first of these. Examples of the places which I believe may be named after the Count of Cornouaille are Beuzec-Cap-Sizun ('Budoc Cap Sidun' in 1030), Beuzec-Cap-Caval, Beuzec-Conq and the Forest of Beuzic (according to François Gilles Pierre Barnabé Manet, this forest was the site of the Château Goy la Forêt, the Castle of Joyous Guard – previously the Castle of Dolorous Guard - of the Arthurian legends).[111] It is possible that the Count of Cornouaille and the Bishop of Dôl were one and the same person, but it would then be odd that the connection has not been made in any surviving text.

---

110 'The History of the Franks', Book 4, Chapter 4.
111 François Gilles Pierre Barnabé Manet, 'Histoire de la Petite-Bretagne, ou Bretagne armorique' (1834).

So what evidence is there of a King Budic, who may have ruled Brittany from the late 5th to the early 6th centuries? Our main literary source is Geoffrey of Monmouth, who refers to the king as 'Budicious', but there are relatively few places with names that might be connected to him. Possible examples include Roch Bido ('Roch ar Budo' in Breton), a district in Mur-de-Bretagne, Kerbudin, an area of Colpo in the Morbihan and the similar Kerboudin at Questembert, near Rochefort-en-Terre in the Morbihan. Compared to the abundance of 'Audren' place names, names which may be associated with Hoël and names which may be associated with Arthur, this is a meagre tally. So, I can only conclude that, if he did exist, Budic was not terribly popular.

Geoffrey of Monmouth also tells us that Budic was a son of Audren and the father of Hoël. In Geoffrey's 'Historia', Budic ('Budicius') had custody of Ambrosius Aurelianus and Uther Pendragon, after the murder of their father Constantine, and during the reign of Vortigern. But on my reckoning Budic was younger than Ambrosius, and may well have accompanied Ambrosius back to Britain. Some Breton accounts resolve the problem by saying there were two Budics, and it was Budic I who took Ambrosius under his wing. However, it would be easier to say that Geoffrey was simply wrong, and that Ambrosius took refuge at the court of Audren.

Eusebius, Duke of Vannes   (c.450? to 490)

Eusebeus is a semi-legendary figure, whose life is sometimes used as a reference point for the chronology of events in southern Brittany at the turn of the 6th century. He is sometimes described as 'Count of Nantes and Vannes', but we have no real idea what his rank or position was. He is not to be confused with a Bishop Eusebius of Nantes, who attended a Council of Bishops in 461. That individual had evidently ceased to be Bishop of Nantes by 463, when the office was held by Nonnechius.

Duke Eusebius enters the record in a 'Life of St Melaine' (qv.), which was written before the 10th century, as a man who had visited barbaric punishments on the citizens of Comblessac, for unexplained reasons, in consequence of which he and his daughter Aspasia had been struck down by a serious disease. He repented of his sins, and father and daughter were both miraculously cured by St Melaine, the

Bishop of Rennes. Eusebius gave lands to the Bishop in consequence.

A number of French historians (including Nicolas Travers) tell us that Eusebius died in 490 (possibly on the basis of the Cartulary of Quimperlé), when Eusebius was defending Nantes against the Saxons of Chillon, and that he was succeeded by Budic. This has resulted in considerable controversy, because St Melaine became Bishop of Rennes in 505, but of course it is not essential that St Melaine had been appointed Bishop before he worked his miracles. Aspasia, who is also referred to as St Pompée or Koupaia, is said to have gone on to marry Hoël.

Guinevere   **Fictitious**

Guinevere is a creature of Welsh legends, who appears several times in the Welsh Triads. There is no evidence for her existence.

Hoël   **(c. 475? – c. 520?)**

Hoël appears to have been very popular, although the toponymic evidence for his existence is clouded by ambiguities. There are many place names in Brittany incorporating the word or name Hoël, but unfortunately 'hoël' (or 'hywel' to the Welsh) was an adjective meaning high. Examples of the places are as follows:

Place name	Meaning in English	Location
Canihuel	High (or Hoël's) hill	Côtes d'Armor
Coat Beuz Huel	High (or Hoël's) Elder Wood	Concarneau
Coët Huel	High (or Hoël's) wood	Sarzeau, Morbihan
Crann Huel	High (or Hoël's) grove	Spézet, Finistère
Creach Huel	High (or Hoël's) mount	Plougonven, Finistère
Huelgoat	High (or Hoël's) wood	Finistère
Kerhuel	High (or Hoël's) village	Colpo, Morbihan
Kerne Huel (a lake)	High (or Hoël's) peak	Côtes d'Armor
Kroaz ar C'hoel	High (or Hoël's) cross	Plougras, Côtes d'Armor
Penher Huel	High (or Hoël's) village?	Melgven, Finistère

The Duke and the Decoy

Pors Huel	Huel Port	Kerlouan, Finistère
Saint-Huel	Saint Höel	Langolen
Stang Huel	Huel Lake	Bannalec
Traon Huel	Hoël's hollow	Landunvez
Ty Huel	High (or Hoël's) cottage	Ploudalmezeau, Finistère

While the fact that 'huel' is an adjective meaning 'high' complicates the position, it can be seen that at least some of these appear to relate to a person named Hoël, because they are self-evidently not places at a great altitude, for example Pors Huel, Saint-Huel, Stang Huel and Traon Huel. The Saint Huel in the list was a chapel associated with the church at Langolen, near Coray in Finistère, a church originally dedicated to St Gurtiern (ie Vortigern). Another private chapel dedicated to Saint Uhel (sic) existed until the 15th century, as a dependency of the castle at Tréfaven, near Lorient, where there was also another chapel dedicated to Saint Armel.

However the further complication is that the Hoël associated with Arthur in Geoffrey's 'Historia' was not the only prominent Hoël in Breton history, and therefore, even if the above places were named after a person and not simply a description of the location, they could have been named in honour of someone else. For example there was a Hoël who was a Duke of Brittany (c.1030 – 1084),[112] so even where a place was clearly named after an individual called Hoël, we cannot say that this proves the existence of a late 5th or early 6th century King of that name. While the choice of the Duke's name suggests that 'Hoël' had acquired noble associations by the 11th century, it is of course very possible that places in Brittany were named in his honour. There are not many Hoëls mentioned in the Cartulary of Redon, but Duke Hoël was the Count of Cornouaille before his elevation to the Dukedom, so his associations were with the western peninsula, where we have fewer records. And since he ruled before most of the surviving texts were written, we have no means of telling whether the 'Hoël' places listed above had acquired their names by the the date of his reign.

According to the 'Chronique de St Brieuc', which itself may be based on Geoffrey of Monmouth, Hoël was the son of Budic and

---
112 In the 'Cartulary of Landévennec', he appears as a witness to Charter 25 with the spelling Houuel

the grandson of Audren. The story goes that he was driven out of Brittany by Frisians in 509, and returned after four years of exile in Great Britain to reclaim his throne. The toponymic evidence for Hoël suggests that a Breton King of this name really existed, so I have dated him essentially in relation to Audren.

Lancelot **Probably fictitious**

Lancelot does not appear in the legends until Chrétien de Troyes' work. He earns minor references in 'Erec and Enide', de Troyes' earliest known work, and in 'Cligès', but comes into his own in 'Lancelot, the Knight of the Cart', written in the 12th century. The story of a mysterious knight who appears at a tournament on three consecutive days in different disguises is of very ancient origin, and a feature of the folklore of many countries.

His affair with Arthur's wife, Guinevere, is a central story of the legends, and contributes significantly to the fall of Camelot. Later authors (but not Chrétien) introduce Lancelot into the Grail Quest legend. In the legends he is a son of King Ban of Benoic, which I believe was the area around Binic on the Côtes d'Armor in Brittany (see 'Lisia; Vortigern's Island). Certainly the legends relating to him seem to be firmly rooted in France.

There is little trace of Lancelot in Breton toponymy. One possible reference occurs in the Cartulary of Landévennec (Charter 37), which records that St Guénolé (late 5th and early 6th century) was given some lands in the vicinity of Morlaix, on which his monks later constructed a small monastery in his honour. The monastery was called the Villa Lancolvett, and has since become Locquenole ('lok-gwenole' meaning 'place dedicated to Gwenole'). St Gwenole received this gift for curing someone miraculously after crossing the 'river Coulut' in a westerly direction, and it has been argued that this relates to the monastery at Queffleut. But I would suggest that the river Coulut could be the river referred to as the River of Guyout in the 'Life of St Sampson', which I believe may have been at Guiaudet, the Breton name for Le Yaudet. In that case 'Lancolvett' may have had nothing to do with 'Queffleut', and is possibly connected to Lancelot.

His name may be a distant echo of the title of the Duke of the Armorican Tract ('lan celtoi'), but I doubt that an individual called Lancelot existed.

Melaine, Bishop of Rennes   (c.456 – 530)

St Melaine has been accorded a major role in the war between the Bretons and the Franks, because he is said to have brokered the treaty of 497. He is supposed to have been a Gallo-Roman from the Nantes area, but his sympathies appear to have been with the Franks, and he attended the First Council of Orléans in 511 where he swore fealty to Clovis as his sovereign.

Because of his alleged involvement in ending the war, and the fact that he did not become Bishop of Rennes until 505, some historians have displaced the events at the end of that war to the period 505 – 511 (the year of the death of Clovis). But even if it is true that he played a part in procuring the peace treaty, it is not a foregone conclusion that Melaine was already Bishop of Rennes at the time – the appointment to that See could have been a reward from Clovis for his services. We cannot be certain of the chronology, but if he worked a miracle of healing on Eusebius, and if Eusebius died in 490, we may suppose that Melaine was an active and celebrated figure in the Church in the Pays de la Loire in the 480s. In fact, he is supposed to have lived from c.456 to c.530, so he would have been an adult in that decade, and indeed ten years older than Clovis.

Merlin   late 6th century?

Merlin was possibly mentioned in one manuscript of the Annales Cambriae (probably written in the Cistercian abbey at Neath in the late 13th century), in an entry for the year 573: *"The Battle of Armterid [Arfderydd] between the sons of Elifer and Guendoleu son of Keidau in which battle Gwendoleu fell and Merlin [Myrddin Wyllt] went mad."* The battle appears to have been part of a civil war among the British, because the Welsh triads refer to it as one of the 'Three Futile Battles of the Island of Britain', along with Camlann and the Battle of the Trees. It is thought that the battle may have taken place in Cumbria, and Merlin is said to have fled into the Caledonian Forest after the battle. The cause of Merlin's insanity is said to have been that he killed his nephew, who was fighting for the opposing side.

The legendary Merlin was first mentioned by Geoffrey of

Monmouth, in his 'Prophetiae Merlini', his earliest work, and then in the 'Historia Regum Britanniae'. Geoffrey is also supposed to have been the author of the later 'Vita Merlini', which was written in c. 1150. In these works, Geoffrey combined material from several sources to create 'Merlin Ambrosius', a wizard with prophetic powers, and the eminence grise to Arthur. But even he must have been conscious of the fact that the Myrddin of the Annales Cambriae was allegedly active nearly 40 years after the date (according to Nennius) of the Battle of Camlann (535).

It seems unlikely that Myrddin would ever have met Arthur, being of a different generation and a different ethnic and social background, but it is possible that their lives overlapped in the early 6th century.

Morgan le Fay   **Fictitious**

Morgan is supposed to have been Arthur's half-sister, and a powerful sorceress. In Geoffrey's work, she is one of nine sisters who rule the Island of Apples (Avalon), and Chrétian de Troyes has her carrying Arthur to Avalon, with three other enchantresses, after the Battle of Camlann. Here she is presented as a healer and an ally of Arthur, while in other works (such as the Prose Lancelot and the Post-Vulgate Cycle) she is presented as an adversary of Arthur and the Round Table.

'Le Fée' means 'the fairy' in French, and Morgan was a fairy in both Welsh and Breton tradition. She may also be the Morrigan of Irish folklore, a phantom queen who is a goddess of battle. Pomponius Mela, writing in the 1st century AD, describes the very ancient Celtic tradition of an island ruled by nine sisters:

"In the Brittanic Sea, opposite the coast of the Ossismi [the Osismes of Finisterre], the isle of Sena [Sein] belongs to a Gaulish divinity and is famous for its oracle; whose priestesses, sanctified by their perpetual virginity, are reportedly nine in number. They call the priestesses the 'Galligende' and think that it is because they have been endowed with unique powers; that they can stir up the seas by their magical charms; that they turn into whatever animals they want; that they cure what is incurable among other peoples; that they know and predict the future – but that it is not revealed except to sea-voyagers, and only those travelling to consult them."

As Geoffrey was quite possibly a member of the Breton Baderon family, he could well have been familiar with these traditions, and incorporated them into his imaginative tales. But there has been no suggestion that the Île de Sein was the island of Avalon, so he has mixed together several legends to make a more mysterious composite whole.

Riothamus   c.440? – c. 475?

Jordanes tell us Riothamus brought an army of 12,000 to Berry and fought against King Euric of the Visigoths.[113] The event is confirmed by Gregory of Tours. The 'Essais Historiques sur les Moeurs des Francais', vol 4 (1792) attributes this event to 469. Anthemius reigned from 467 until his death in 472.

Sidonius Apollinaris wrote to Riothamus in c.472 (date suggested by O M Dalton (1915)), which would probably place the letter after the battle.

Nicolas Travers asserts that Riothamus ("Riotime") was a Breton, a son of King Audren and the brother of Budic. He further says that Budic succeeded Eusebius, the Count of Nantes and Vannes, in 490.[114] Jordanes tells us that Riothamus arrived with his army "by way of Ocean", which is sometimes cited as evidence that he was not from Brittany, but it is possible that Jordanes was referring to a voyage up the Loire River.

Moreover, if Audren died in c.464, his son Budic would have been King of Brittany since that date, which makes it unlikely that he would have become Count of Nantes and Vannes in 490. And in turn Budic's son Hoël might have been King of Brittany in c.490.

Several commentators have speculated that Riothamus was Ambrosius Aurelianus, but without any solid evidence.

Vortigern   c.375 - 460

Vortigern is referred to by Gildas as the "proud usurper" at the time when the Saxons were invited into England, by which he probably

---

[113] Jordanes, 'The Origins and Deeds of the Goths' (c.551).
[114] 'Histoire civile, politique et religieuse de la ville et du compté de Nantes', Vol 1, Ch. 13 (1836).

meant 447/449 (as noted above under 'Ambrosius Aurelianus'). Vortigern is referred to by Bede and, extensively, by Nennius. The Anglo-Saxon Chronicle tells us that 'Wurtgern' invited Hengist and Horsa to Britain in 449, and fought against them at Aylesford (in Kent) in 455.

To refine the dates of his life, we need to turn to the history of one of his four sons, Faustus. Nennius wrote *"The Fourth [son] was Faustus, born of an incestuous marriage with his daughter, who was brought up and educated by St Germanus. He built a large monastery on the banks of the river Renis, called after his name, and which remains to this present period."* This Faustus has long been identified with Bishop Faustus of Riez, who was an historical figure, and who is known to have been of British origin.

Faustus of Riez became Abbot of Lerins, a monastery on the islands off Hyères, in 433 or 434. It is therefore assumed that he was born at the end of the 4th century or the beginning of the 5th – in c.410 at latest. And he lived to a ripe old age, probably dying in the period 490 to 493. According to Nennius, Faustus, the incestuous son of Vortigern, was taken under the wing of St Germanus of Auxerre, the warrior bishop who was sent to Britain (possibly twice) to combat the 'heresy' of Pelagianism on the island. St Germanus visited Britain in 429 (and possibly again in 446). [The 'Chronica Gallica'] On the assumptions stated above, Faustus would have then been c.19.

If Vortigern had a son called Faustus by his daughter, we must suppose that he was at least 35 when Faustus was born. So if this Faustus was indeed Faustus of Riez, Vortigern cannot have been born much after 375. This would mean that he was about 54 when St Germanus first came to Britain and about 80 when the Anglo-Saxon Chronicle reports him as fighting Hengist and Horsa at Aylesford.

Certainly, we know that Faustus of Riez was a Briton. Sidonius Apollinaris knew Faustus well (his brother studied under Faustus, and Sidonius visited him at Riez), and he provides us with the curious information that Faustus never cut his hair. At some time after 475, he wrote to Faustus to tell him that he had intercepted Riocatus, a priest and a monk (and thus *"twice a stranger and pilgrim in this world"*), who was taking a book by Faustus back to *"your Britons"*.

Nothing is said of Faustus' father in Sidonius's correspondence, but his mother is said to have been noble and saintly. It is possible that Faustus could have accompanied St Germanus back to Gaul in 429 (being about 19), and with the patronage of the illustrious Bishop of Auxerre, he could have become Abbot of Lerins five years later.

On the basis of this chronology, Vortigern was about 50 in the 420s, when, according to the archaeological evidence, the Angles and Saxons started to settle in the east of England. But he would have been in his 70s in 447/449, if that was when the Saxon war leaders arrived. So it is hardly likely that he would have been an active combatant at the Battle of Crayford in 455, although it is conceivable that he might have been present.

But I do not believe that Vortigern was present at the Battle of Crayford. The presence of an 80 year-old man would have served little purpose, especially as we are led to believe that he was hated and despised by his people. Nennius and the 'Life of St Gurthiern' tell us of several possible ends to his existence, being either an exile or his death by act of God. Nennius says he was either (a) consumed by a fire in his castle at Cair Guorthegirn (which was in a region called Guunessi or Gueneri) or (b) that *"he betook himself to flight; and, that deserted and a wanderer, he sought a place of refuge, till broken hearted, he made an ignominious end",* or (c) the earth opened and swallowed him up. The 'Life of St Gurthiern' says he went by boat from the River Tamar (in Cornwall) to *"a certain island"* and then transferred to another island called Anaurot, where he remained until the end of his days. *"The angel of the Lord committed to him that whole region of Brittany, in order that the whole domain of St Gurthiern served Anaurot, because that city was chosen by God."*[115] If Vortigern went into exile, it would seem probable that this was shortly after the Saxons turned on the British – say c.455 - when he would have been about 80.

What this means is that, if Faustus of Riez was Vortigern's son, the dates suggested above must be fairly accurate, because in terms of practicalities, they could not have been very different. And I think it probable that he was Vortigern's son, by one of his first wives.

---

115 For a full discussion, see 'Lisia; Vortigern's Island'.

Appendix 3
The Land of Cal

The 'cal' place names in England allow us to form an impression of the extent of the territory under Belgic (as opposed to Brythonic Celtic) control. They are found broadly to the south-east of a line extending from the Devon/Somerset border, along the Welsh border to Cheshire, and then eastwards to north Yorkshire. However they are also found in a few places outside these limits. There are several 'cal' place names that may or may not have been associated with a megalithic monument, but where the monument has not survived, or where a connection between the place name and a specific monument is not clear-cut, so I set these aside. Examples include Calstock in Cornwall, Calthorpe in Norfolk and the Derbyshire village of Calver ('Caluoure' in the Domesday Book),[116] may mean 'stone over'. The latter could be a reference to any one of several megaliths nearby, but it is not possible to identify any particular monument with certainty.

There are few 'cal' place names in the extreme south-east of England (Kent, Sussex and Surrey), where the pre-existing Belgic culture was almost entirely displaced by the Anglo-Saxons. One possible survivor is Chaldon, in Surrey, which was called Calvedone in the Domesday Book (possibly 'stone town'). And in another case, we know that the pre-Roman name of Silchester, which was the capital city of the Belgic tribe called the Atribates, was Calleva. This is traditionally translated as 'wooded place', but I suspect that it must have got its name from a standing stone, which has now disappeared. The town is famous as the site where the only Ogham stone in England was found, but this cannot have been the source of its name,

---
116 The Domesday Book was a survey of most of England conducted in 1086 for William I, the Conqueror.

having been carved in the early 5th century. (Ogham stones came from Ireland, where they are called 'gallán'). However, the site of the town on the Roman road from London to Dorchester, via Old Sarum, might suggest the solution, as we shall see shortly.

Another example of a 'bi-cultural' cal is Challacombe, in the north-east of Devon. In the Domesday Book the village was called Celdecome, which means 'stone of the valley' ('cal-de-combe'), deriving its name from the standing stone called the Longstone in the village (the monument is almost 3 metres high, and thus the tallest standing stone in the Exmoor national park). 'Combe' is a Brythonic word meaning 'valley', so the area was clearly in the linguistic boundary zone. A third example of such a hybrid is Callow in Derbyshire, which was called Caldelauue in the Domesday Book. There is a standing stone just to the south of the village, which is wider in its middle section than at the bottom. 'Lau' is a Brythonic word meaning 'hand', so the name appears to mean 'stone shaped like a hand'.

And there are a number of other permutations of names In England involving 'cal', particularly if account is taken of the changes in toponym that have occurred over the last thousand years. An example is Cauldon, a village in Staffordshire where there are Neolithic remains. This was called 'Caldone' in the Domesday Book (possibly meaning 'stone town' or 'stone hill'). But where 'cal' place names appear in Scotland or Ireland, they appear to have a different root, typically the Gaelic word 'cala' meaning a hard beach. Examples are Calgary on the Isle of Mull and Callanish on the Isle of Lewis (where there are in fact standing stones). It has been suggested that the name of the Caledonii, the tribe after whom the Romans named the country Caledonia, may derive from a early Celtic word 'caleto' meaning hard or strong (ie rock-like).

By far the most common of the 'cal' place names are the numerous villages in England called 'caldecote', or some variation of the name, which in my opinion meant 'milestone' (ie cal-de-cote, 'stone at the side').[117] I have identified more than 30 places with these names, and their distribution gives us a very good idea of the borders of Belgic England, or 'the land of cal'.

---

117 see 'Lisia; Vortigern's Island'.

It is notable that one of the 'Caldicot's is in Monmouthsire, in South Wales, and there is also a Calcoed ('stone of the woods') in Flintshire, so the Belgic influence also extended into North Wales. Both of these places are near the border with England. 'Calcoed' is one of a number of hybrid names, in which 'cal' is combined with a Brythonic word to form a compound, indicating an area that was under both Brythonic and Belgic cultural influences.

I have the impression that 'cal-de-cote' was used to describe a milestone of unusual significance, and that it may indeed have been a specific term for a landmark installed every 10 Roman miles. Looking at Watling Street, we can observe that Caldecote, just north of Towcester in Northants, appears to be about 20 Roman miles from the Caldecotte near Fenny Stratford, and that the village half-way between the two is called Stony Stratford.

Similarly Yelvertoft, which was Celvrecot in the Domesday Book, is located to the east of a point on Watling Street which is about 20 Roman miles north of Caldecote in Northants. And Caldecote near Nuneaton is located where the A444 meets the A5, about 40 Roman miles from Caldecote, Northants. On the Roman road from London to Bath (now the A4), we find Calcot in Berkshire, just to the west of Reading, and also Calstone Wellington in Wiltshire, which towns are about 50 Roman miles apart.

Having said that, the measurements cannot be made with pinpoint precision. We do not know exactly where the milestones stood, as none of them have survived, so they could have been anywhere in or near the villages that bear their names. And even if we had the exact locations of the stones, we do not know how accurate the measurements of the original surveyors were. Furthermore, in some cases, as around Fenny Stratford, the road has deviated from its original course. So the evidence is suggestive, rather than conclusive.

To complete the picture, we should simply note that 'cal' names can also be found in north-eastern France, most obviously at Calais. The German philologist Hermann Gröhler suggested in 1906 that Calais derives its name from a pre-Celtic word 'cal', meaning stone, so I am by no means the first person to propose this translation.

In conclusion, the people of the 'land of cal' in England shared

The Duke and the Decoy

a language with the Belgae of north-eastern Gaul. And there is abundant archaeological evidence that they were part of the same trading system. The earliest coin found in Britain is a gold stater of Belgic origin, dating from the middle of the 3rd century BC, which was found at Fenny Stratford in Buckinghamshire. And a large number of coins of a similar period issued by the Belgic Ambiani tribe, who spoke Gaulish, have been found in central southern England.

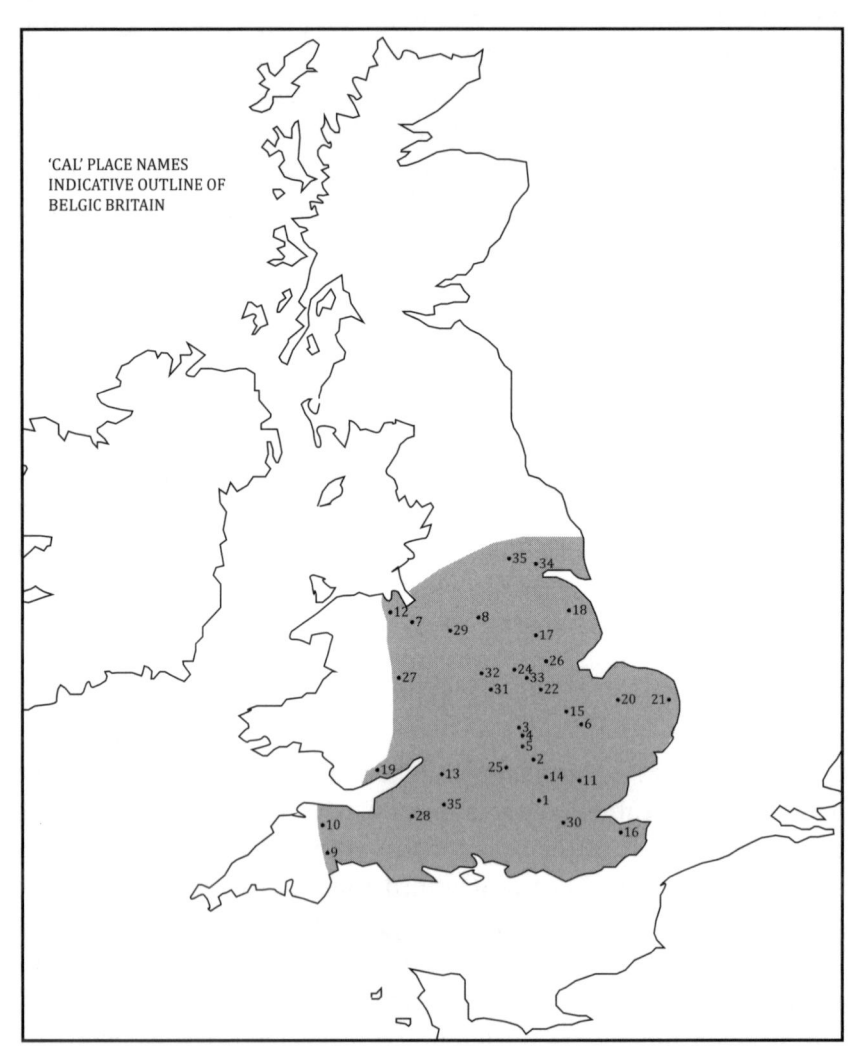

'CAL' PLACE NAMES
INDICATIVE OUTLINE OF
BELGIC BRITAIN

220

Appendices

SOME 'CAL' PLACE NAMES IN ENGLAND

Present name	Name in Domesday Book	County
1 Calcot	Colecote	Berkshire
2 Caldecote		Bedfordshire
3 Caldecote	Caldecote	Buckinghamshire
4 Caldecotte		Buckinghamshire
5 Caldicot		Buckinghamshire
6 Caldecote	Caldecote	Cambridgeshire
7 Caldecott	Caldecote	Cheshire
8 Callow	Caldelauue	Derbyshire
9 Calverleigh		Devon
10 Challacombe	Celdecome	Devon
11 Caldecott	Caldecotan	Essex
12 Calcoed		Flintshire
13 Calcot	Caldecot	Gloucestershire
14 Caldecote	Caldecota	Hertfordshire
15 Caldecote	Caldecote	Huntingdonshire
16 Calcott		Kent
17 Chilcote	Cildecote	Leicestershire
18 Collow	Caldecote	Lincolnshire
19 Caldicot		Monmouthshire
20 Caldecote	Caldachotta	Norfolk
21 Caldecott		Norfolk
22 Caldecott	Caldecote	Northants
23 Chilcotes	Cildecote	Northants
24 Yelvertoft	Celvrecot	Northants
25 Caldecott		Oxfordshire
26 Caldecott	Caldecote	Rutland
27 Calcott		Shropshire
28 Calcott	Caldecote	Somerset
29 Cauldon	Caldone	Staffordshire
30 Chaldon	Calvedone	Surrey
31 Calcutt	Caldecote	Warwickshire
32 Caldecote	Caldecote	Warwickshire
33 Calcutt	Colecote	Wiltshire
34 Calcutt		Yorkshire
35 Coldcotes	Caldecotes	Yorkshire

Appendix 4
The Language of Arthur

Tacitus remarked in c.100 that the British and the Gauls spoke very similar languages, and remarkably, this was still the case in c.800. Both Gregory of Tours (c.538 – 594) and Venantius Fortunatus (c.530 – c.600/609) wrote of the 'Gallica Lingua' in the present indicative, so we know that the Gaulish language had survived on the Continent throughout the Arthurian period. And fortunately, quite a lot of evidence of the language spoken in Brittany in the 9th century has survived in various documents, including the Cartularies of the Breton abbeys. In a very detailed study of the subject by Léon Fleuriot[118] he argued that there was very little difference between the Breton and Gallo languages. He wrote *"one must underline the homogeneity of the language of the 9th century: of all the thousands of words and personal and place names in the Cartularies, there is only one which may, possibly, present the charecteristics of a dialect, hisael barr (mistletoe)."*

This is a somewhat surprising conclusion, because northern France had been ruled by the Franks for more than 300 years by the early 9th century, and we know, from the document known as the 'Oaths of Strasbourg', of 842, that the language of the Franks had a significant Germanic component (up to 15% according to some estimates). If Fleuriot is correct, it means that either (a) that the language of the west of Francia remained essentially the vulgar Latin language called Gallo, with little Frankish influence, or that (b) a similar amount of Germanic influence was visible in the language of the Bretons, possibly as a result of a fourth wave of English-speaking migrants as described in Chapter 7.

If we accept that the language of the Bretons was similar to that of the Gallo-speaking people of northern France, the question then is

---
118 'Dictionnaire des gloses en Vieux Breton' (1964).

whether the language of the Bretons was identical to the language of the Welsh. Clearly all of these languages were closely related, and we know that there had been a very large emigration to Brittany from Wales and Cornwall in the 6th century, so if there were differences between the dialects spoken in lowlands England and in Wales, it is likely that the Breton language would show the influences of both.

Unfortunately, it is now impossible to answer this question with any certainty. As we saw in Chapter 7, there appears to have been an English influence in the language of southern Brittany in the 9th century; and subsequently the peninsula was devastated by the Normans in the 10th century, leaving it almost depopulated. When the area was resettled from the second half of that century onwards, the Breton aristocracy, many returning from exile in France, had become Francophone, and a very substantial French influence was introduced into the Breton language. Today about 20% of the words used by Breton-speakers are of French origin. However, we do have a very complete record of the names of places in Brittany in the 9th century through the Cartulary of Redon, so we have a good idea what the original Breton place names were, before the Vikings destroyed the peninsula.

Having considered the historical background, let us review the evidence that is available to us. Firstly, it must be stated that there is no extant connected text in Old Breton. The language survives only in the form of glosses (marginal notes) in Latin texts and in the names found in some Latin cartularies. We therefore have only a limited knowledge of the vocabulary or grammar of this language, although it is widely assumed that it must have been like Old Welsh or Old Cornish. (Personally I think the similarities may have been exaggerated, as will become clear).

The most contemporary Breton epigraphy consists of two inscriptions on stone, dating from the middle of the 6th century, the first of which we noted at 7.6. Both were written in the capital letters of the Latin alphabet, which were similar to the modern alphabet in use in Europe today. The sarcophagus found at Lomarec, near Auray in southern Brittany, reads "IRHAEMA[chi rho]INRI". This is believed to mean "Here lies the king". If this is correct, the inscription is useful in that it confirms that the Breton word for 'king' was 'ri'. It also suggests that the word for 'here' was 'irha', very similar to the modern English word. 'Ema in' would then mean 'is within' or 'lies in'.

223

The Duke and the Decoy

The second inscription, on a granite monument found at Gomené in the Côtes d'Armor, roughly on the route between Rennes and Carhaix, and on the route between St Brieuc and Ploërmel, reads "CED PARTH SO". The meaning of this is unknown, but it is thought that the monument may have been a boundary stone, perhaps marking the boundary between the Vannetais and Dumnonée.

The earliest literary sources date from the 9th century, and comprise various documents, mainly created in the Breton abbeys. The most important of these are the charters in the Cartulary of Redon, which we have aleady encountered. But another interesting example of a manuscript of the 9th century is the 'Leiden Leechbook', or more technically, the 'Vossianus Latinus folio 96A', in the collection of the University of Leiden. This is a medical compilation written in the 9th or 10th century, mostly in Latin, but employing the vocabulary of 9th century Breton in about one-third of the text.

The Leiden Leechbook contains recipes for herbal remedies, and hence the vocabulary preserved is essentially botanical. But the text tells us that the following words had the following meanings:

aball	apple
barr	branch (or bough)
caes	seek
colaenn	holly
dar	oak
guern	alder
hisael-barr	mistletoe
penn	head
scau	elderberry
spern	thorn

Further evidence that the Bretons were interested in science is provided by a gloss in the manuscript 10.290 (9th century) in the Bibliotheque Nationale in Paris, which contains the Breton word 'doguonimereticaith'. The meaning of the first part of this is uncertain, but the last part means 'arithmetic'.

The second main literary source is the Cartulary of Redon. As explained at 7.2, this contains copies of many of the charters by which land was given to the Abbey, and 391 of these dating from the early

9th to the early 12th century have been published (sadly an unknown number have been lost). The charters are particularly interesting, because they provide us with the names of about 2,100 people and 800 places in Brittany, from the Early and High Middle Ages. Redon is in the south-east of Brittany, and so a considerable number of these names related to people or places in the Morbihan, Ille-et-Vilaine and the lower Loire, but the charters reflect donations of property from almost all parts of Brittany. Since the south-east of the peninsula appears to have been particularly attractive to the British emigrants of the second wave, this is especially interesting to students of the Arthurian period.

Redon was not the only monastery to maintain such a cartulary, but tragically most of the early records of monasteries such as the ones at Landavennec and Dôl have been destroyed, probably by the Vikings. The Cartulary of Quimperlé is of much later date, because the abbey was only founded in 1026, and the records were first compiled in 1127. So Redon, is by far the most contemporaneous and complete of these sources (although here too the Abbey was eventually sacked by the Vikings). The charters were of course written in Latin, but they reproduce the personal names of the parties to the charters, including a large number of witnesses, and the names and descriptions of the estates that were being transferred. The question is, whether these names shed any light on the events of the Arthurian period, and that is what we shall now discover.

When studying the names of people and places in Brittany in the Early Middle Ages, we have to make due allowance for variations in spellings. At the time, very few people wrote, so when attending the signing of a charter, the parties and witnesses, noble as they may have been, would have given their names to a scribe, who would have chosen spellings as he saw fit and written the names down. The parties and witnesses would then have made their marks. The result is that orthography was vague, to say the least, and no great significance can be attached to spelling variations.

Breton personal names were themselves very diverse, because people generally had only one name at this time, so it was necessary to employ a wide variety of names to avoid misidentifications. While a number of simple names were used, some of which are recognisable to us today, most names were compounds of several words, and seem very foreign. The names quoted in the remainder of this section are extracted from Charters in the Cartulary of Redon, and references to Charter numbers and dates are references to those Charters.

Among the simple names in use we find people called Ewen (Charter 5, 833), Woron (Warren) (Charter 6, 833), Cristian (Charter 6, 833, Charter 7, 833) Johan (Charter 9, 833/834), Louui (Charter 13, 837), Alan (Charter 21, 868), Jacob (Charter 22, 854), Simeon (Charter 28, 858), Abraham (Charter 29, 832-868, Charter 32, 857-868), Alberto (Charter 33, 847), Gregari (Charter 49, 866), Tomas (Charter 63, 863) and Alexander (Charter 63, 863). Other names are known variants of familiar names, eg Jagu which was the form of James then in use (Charter 9, 844/834), and some names are familiar to us as surnames, eg Benitoe (Charter 8, 833) and Rioch (Charter 281, 904). Some names were derived from Latin, such as Fracan (Charter 5, 833), which comes from 'fracanus' meaning strawberry, Benedic (Charter 27, 832-868), and Felix (Charter 30, 859).

Female names appear in fewer Charters, and often seem strange (eg a Cleroc in Charter 28 of 858), but some at least resemble names with which we are familiar, eg a Telia in Charter 41 of 845 and a Judita in Charter 53 of 846.

More often the names were created by adding together two or more words in the Breton language. We can also see this process in the few names of the insular Britons that survive to us, for example those of the three British Kings who were killed at the battle of Dyrham, namely Commail, Condida and Farinmail. The compound names for men were often of a war-like nature, and the permutations were almost endless. Some examples of the words used as building blocks were as follows:

1. '-car' ('kin'), which always appeared as a suffix: eg in Guethencar ('warrior-kin') (Charter 2, 833), Gurhugar (Charter 4, 834), Kewirgar, Haelocar, Lowencar (Charter 8, 833), Comaltcar (Charter 9, 833/834), Riantcar (Charter 12, 834) etc.
2. 'Cat' ('battle'), is found as a prefix in many names, for example: Catworet (Charter 4, 834) Cathoiarn (Charter 8, 833), Catwobri (Charter 9, 833/834), Catweten (Charter 19, 860). Catwallon (Charter 26, 857), Catlowen (Charter 53,

846), Catnimet (Charter 56, 865/866), Catwodu (Charter 58, 838-849), Catworct (Charter 99, 866) and Catmonoc (Charter 109, 869) etc.
3. 'Hael', meaning 'generous' or 'prince' is found in such names as: Hailgugur (Charter 2, 834) Haelwobri (Charter 9, 833/834) (Charter 11, 834), Haelmoeni (Charter 11, 834), Haelvili (Charter 11, 834), Meranhael (Charter 16, 833), Haelowen (Charter 36, 858), Haelhowen (Charter 37, 858) etc.
4. 'Hoiarn' ('iron') could appear as a prefix, as in Hoiarnweten (Charter 97, date unknown), but was more often a suffix, eg in: Loieshoiarn (Charter 2, 834) Cathoiarn, Rishoiarn, Euhoiarn, Winhoiarn (all Charter 8, 833), Merthinhoiarn (Charter 34, 826), Hirdhoiarn (Charter 56, 865/866), Finithoiarn (Charter 63, 863) etc.
5. 'Loies-' meant 'hunt', and is found in: Loieshoiarn (Charter 2, 834), Loiesoc (Charte 11, 834), Loieswallon (Charter 26, 857) Loiesweten (Charter 30, 859), Loiesbritou (Charter 44, 858-865) etc
6. 'Ri' meant 'king'. We have already encountered a Riothamus and we will meet a Riocatus in Appendix 1 (in a letter written by Sidonius Apollinaris). But the Charters contain a number of other 'ri-' prefix names, such as Riskipoe (Charter 2, 834), Riwalt (Charter 5, 833, Charter 6, 833), Riawal (Charter 8, 833), Rishoiarn (Charter 8, 833), Rihowen (Charter 31, 832-868), Rithoiarn (Charter 32, 857-868) Rihowen (Charter 12, 834) etc.
7. 'Roen' meant 'royal', or 'lineage of a king', as seen in Roenhoiam (Charter 5, 833, Charter 6, 833), Roencomal (Charter 7, 833), Roenhoiarn (Charter 34, 826), Roenwallon (Charter 72, c.859) etc

Of course the most important component of Breton names, from the perspective of this book, was the word 'arth', meaning 'bear', and we considered the huge variety of names incorporating this element in Appendix 1

Another component which particularly interests me is the word 'wallon', which meant 'valorous'. This appears on its own as a name in

The Duke and the Decoy

Charter 4 of 834 and again in Charter 58 of 838-849. But it was also a common suffix, and in the latter charter we encounter a Roiantwallon . Elsewhere we meet a Dumnowallon (Charter 97, date unknown), a Judwallon (Charter 110, 859-864), and a Catwallonus (Charter 158 of 866). Moreover, in Charter 284, we learn that there was an 11th century Abbot in Brittany called Catwallon, who had a name shared by Cadwallon ap Cadfan, a King of Gwynned from c.625 to 634.

'Catwallon' meant 'battle valorous', and it seems similar to the name of the Belgic tribe of England called the Catuvellauni, who we have already met, and who were mentioned by the Roman geographer Ptolemy in the 2nd century. The curiosity is that there was a tribe in what is now Belgium called the Catalauni, who appear to have been the ancestors of the people of Belgium who are now called the Walloons (Wallons in French). According to French etymologists, this name derives from the very ancient Germanic word 'wahl' which was applied by the Germans to all the peoples of Roman Gaul (and which was the ancestor of the Anglo-Saxon word 'wealah', meaning foreigner, which became 'welsh'). As we have seen, this explanation differs from the one accepted in Britain, and this is used as an argument that the two tribes were unrelated. But the similarities are so striking that it is hard to resist the conclusion that the names of the two tribes shared a common root, and that one or other of the etymological explanations for their names must be wrong. On this occasion, I am inclined to favour the British interpretation.

'Ri' was the word for king, and 'rigan' was the word for queen. The ancient name of Pont Réen, south-west of Rennes on the road from Rennes to Redon, was Pont Rigan (Queen's Bridge') (although, amusingly, some French etymologists believe that 'rigan' was a Breton word for a type of frog!).

'Uuin' meant 'pure', 'blessed' or 'holy', and it is interesting to speculate whether this may explain the names of some British places that commence with 'win'. For example Wincanton might have been the 'Holy Canton', Windsor (uuin-soer – 'soer'' is visible in the ancient (pre-12th century) name of Shoreditch) might have been the Holy Stream and Windermere (win-dur-mere) might have been the 'holy water lake'. In my view it is also possible that Winchester was the 'Holy City', before the Anglo-Saxons arrived, and that they merely

Appendices

corrupted its name to Uintancaester – in which case the original name outlived their regime.

The dialect of the Belgic British, who made up most of the first and second waves of British emigration, reflected a Germanic influence which was absent from the dialects of the Welsh and Cornish speakers who made up the third wave. This Germanic component may have been reinforced in Brittany, both by the fourth wave of English-speaking migrants, and through the influence of the Franks. We know that there were a number of Franks living in Brittany in the 9th century, because in Charter 124 of 832-840, we read that the document was witnessed by *"XIII Franci"* (13 Franks), who are then named. There are also a large number of parties to other charters who appear to have Germanic names, eg: Edelfrit (Charter 13, 837), Altfrid (who was a machtiern, or baron) (Charter 20, 852), possibly the same Alfret Machtiern (Charter 21, 868), Otto (Charter 27, 832-868), and most of the signatories on Charters 41 of 845, 42 of 850, 43 of 833, 59 of 849, 211 of 837/838 and 217 of 845-850.

I set out below a short dictionary of words in Old Breton, so that readers can form their own impression of the language. My view is that, from what we can tell, Old Breton had a recognisably 'English' flavour. That is not to say that, if we could travel back 1,600 years in time, we would be able to understand Arthur and his contemporaries – I imagine that we would struggle to make out one word in ten - but I do believe, as I argued in 'Lisia', that the influence of Belgic has been understated.

Nor is it to deny that Belgic British, Brythonic Celtic and Gallo all had much in common – they may well have shared more than 80% of their vocabulary. But to claim that they were identical surpasses the available evidence. I have been particularly amused by the struggles of the Breton philoligists to understand the marginal note 'crap', found in a Latin text. Clearly this most English of words predates the vitreous china products of Sir Thomas Crapper (1836 – 1910), and it is well known that it goes back as far as Middle English. But in my view the Breton gloss shows that it predates the Anglo-Saxons, and that it is Belgic in origin.

Here are some other English words translated into Old Breton:

English	Old Breton
alder	guern
all	hol
angry	angruit
apple	aball
are/is	bit
branch (or bough)	barr
black	dub
blue	glas
brave	deurr
butter	emmeni
candle	cannuill
caution (canny)	cannat
copper	emid
cradle	cauell
denude	dino
door	dor
elated	eli
elderberry	scau
father	hen
fifteen	tripimp
finger	bis
fire	tan/ur
five	pimp
fork	gablau
front (line of battle)	van
grandson/desendant	uir
great	maur
head	penn
holly	colaenn
house	teg
in	hin/in
land (piece of)	tir
long (higher)	hir
man	gur

me	mi
mistletoe	hisael-barr
more	immor/moi
mother	mam
name	anu
niece	nith
not	ni
oak	dar
of	di
old	hen
other	han
part	parth
pay	tal
ran	plot of land
sail	huil
seat	estid
seek	caes
strict	distrit
the	der
thirty	trimuceint
thorn	spern
three	tri/dri/tier
to	do
troop/dragoon	drogn
two	dou/diu (m/f)
victory/profit	bud
wall	aul
well (feeling)	guell
wine	guin
wool	gulan
writing	graph
you	ti
your	dit

Given the historical background it would be very surprising if there were no Germanic influence in the languages of the northern Gauls and the Belgic British. In Gaul this affected the language that developed to become what is now referred to as 'La langue d'oïl', after

231

the pronunciation of the word 'oui' (yes) in the region north of the Loire. And it would also be very surprising if the Germanic influence in Gaul and Britain was not very similar. After all, the Franks and the Belgae came from exactly the same area of eastern Gaul. So there may have even been more in common between Gallo and Belgic British than there was between those languages and Brythonic Welsh, notwithstanding that all three languages were very closely related.

The place names in the Cartulary of Redon inevitably reflect the language of property, so we can read that a community was called a 'plebs', a subdivision of a parish was a 'treb' (often abbreviated to 'tre'), a court or manor-house was either a 'lis' (Breton) or an 'aula' (Latin), a large house was typically called a 'villa' (Latin), a general word for house was 'teg', and a plot of building land was called a 'ran'. So a plot of land with a house on it was called a 'tegran'. A field was a 'camp' and an area enclosed by a ditch or a hedge was a 'garth'. 'Din' was a fort (or 'castel' in Latin) and 'dinan' was a small fort. 'Laedti' meant dairy, 'enes' meant island etc.

Features of the land, including a ditch ('fosse') might be mentioned, or that it might be described as fronting on to a particular road ('via'), or that it was on a hill ('bron').

The name of a site would sometimes contain adjectives, so for example, 'ard' and 'hir' both meant elevated, while 'cain' meant beautiful. Thus a Ranarhuual (Charter 113, 848) was a plot belonging to a Huual, and a Camphincoet (Charter 117, 843) was a field in the wood.

From the point of view of a student of Arthurian history, we can note that there was an Avaellon, in an area called Chaer, which was given to Redon with other properties including an island in the Morbihan called Enes Manac (the Île-aux-Moines, or island of monks) (Charter 70, 851-856). Elsewhere, there was a Villa Bothavalon, at Karnun (Charter 368, 1101), so the name Avalon was certainly not unknown in Brittany.

The names of places also sometimes give clues as the origins of their owners, and we saw in Chapter 7.2 that there was a place called Camdonpont in Brittany in the 840s, which may be related to Camden Town in London. Camden was called Rugemere in the Domesday Book, but perhaps there was a Camdon nearby which has since been adopted as the name of the whole area. If so, what would 'Camdon' mean? Well, 'don' is relatively easy – it meant hill or perhaps fortified hill. It is visible in many British place names, including that of London. But what did 'cam' mean? This is particularly important to a student of Arthurian history, because the syllable appears as the first part of two places of immense significance in the legends, Camelot and Camlann.

Camelot is of course said to have been the name of Arthur's principal court, and Camlann is the location of his final battle. The two names may be superficially similar, but I suspect that they come from different languages: 'lann' is Brythonic and 'lot' is either Belgic or at least pre-Celtic. 'Camlann' is commonly supposed to be a place by a river called 'cam', of which there are two in 'the land of cal' – one flowing through Cambridge and one in Somerset. The name of the Cam in Cambridge probably derives from a Continental Celtic or pre-Celtic word 'cambo', which meant bend or curve (the Roman name of Kempten in Bavaria, a fortress on a river bend, was Cambodunum).

The name of the river 'Cam' in Somerset may derive either from the same source, or from the similar Cornish word 'Kammel' meaning crooked. But 'lann' is a Brythonic word meaning court, country, or region. The name of Camlann is spelt 'Cambala' or 'Camblan' in some of the source manuscripts, and since 'blan' and 'bala' both seem to have been Brythonic words referring to a river flowing from a lake, it seems probable that Camlann was located in or near a lake in Wales or the West Country. Geoffrey of Monmouth tells us that it was in Cornwall.

In Britain, Camelot has often been identified as Cadbury Castle in Somerset, an Iron Age and Bronze Age hillfort on the southern edge of the Somerset Levels. The suggested association was first published by John Leland in 1532, allegedly reporting a long-standing local tradition, and it received significant endorsement after the 1960s excavation of the site by Leslie Alcock, which revealed a substantial redevelopment of the fort in the period from 470 until some time after 580. The work carried out in this period included the construction of a hall, 20 metres by 10 metres, and a gatehouse, which added to the already impressive earthbank, timber and stone wall defences. Cadbury Castle was the largest fortification in the Britain of the Arthurian period, and it was clearly used as a defence against the Anglo-Saxons.

Cadbury is close to the villages of West Camel and Queen Camel, and supporters of the idea that Cadbury Castle was Camelot draw heavily on this geographic association. While it seems unlikely that there was any fighting at Cadbury Castle during Arthur's lifetime, the legends do not actually suggest that there was a battle at Camelot, so the possibility that Cadbury Castle was Camelot cannot be discounted on these grounds. Nevertheless it seems that Cadbury Castle may have been in the possession of the Kings of Dumnonia, and this may be a more substantial argument against the identification.

The name 'Cadbury' is generally taken to be a composite word 'cat bury' meaning 'battle fort', but there is also a theory that it derives from the name of a Dumnonian King called Cado (c. 483 – 537), who appears in Geoffrey of Monmouth's 'Historia' as Cador, Earl of Cornwall. On balance I prefer the latter interpretation, but in either case, there is no obvious etymological relationship with 'Camelot'. If it were not for the names of the nearby villages and the river Cam, there would be nothing to tie the castle to Camelot, and the connection seems rather flimsy.

The name 'Camelot' first appears in Chrétien de Troyes' 'Lancelot, le Chevalier de la Charrette' ('Lancelot, the Knight of the Cart') where it is spelt 'Camaalot', and I think that this spelling may give us a clue as to the etymology of the name. As spelt by Chrétien de Troyes, it appears to be a compound made up of 'cama-a-lot', in which 'lot' may be a Continental Celtic or Belgic word for lake or fen (equivalent to the Gaelic word lough). It does not appear to be Brythonic.

There are numerous place names in France that contain the 'cam' prefix, and they are not all located at river bends. Examples are Cambrai in the Nord Department (Camaracum to the Romans), Chambray, Eure (Cammeragus), Chambry, Aisne (Chameriacum), Chamery, Marne (Camerai in the 11th century), Chemeyrat, Corrèze (Chamairacum) Chémeré, Loire-Atlantique (Camariacus), Camaret-sur-Mer, Brittany and Camaret-sur-Aigues, in the Vaucluse. This abundance of similar names suggests that there was a Continental Celtic or pre-Celtic word, which sounded something like 'camara', the meaning of which is uncertain. It does not seem to be Brythonic, because 'cama' in Welsh means 'step', which seems to be completely unrelated,

In Latin the word 'camera' means 'chamber', as does 'câmara' in Portuguese, while in Spanish the word 'cama' means bed. And 'Kamara' is the name of villages in Greece, Crete, Salonica and Estonia. The general impression is that this lost word, 'camara', must have meant something like 'house', and that it was largely displaced in the Roman era by 'villa'. In which case 'Camaalot' may have meant something like 'villa by the fen (or lough)', probably a place in 'the land of cal'. Lowlands England was penetrated by a number of loughs, especially along the east coast but also in Somerset, so it is easily possible to imagine that Camelot was located by one of these inlets or fens. Cadbury, Glastonbury or Atherstone could all be candidates.

On the basis that 'cam' meant villa, 'Camden' would mean 'villa on the hill' or 'villa of the fort', and we can well imagine that such a structure could have existed in or near what is now Regent's Park. The British would then have brought the name with them from the south-east of England to Brittany.

We also saw in Chapter 7 that the names of two places in Brittany appear to contain English words for numbers. But I have to add a note of caution that it is not certain that similar words were not in use among the Belgic British, before the Anglo-Saxons arrived. In particular I would refer to the Antonine Itinerary, which dates in its origins from the 3rd century. This refers to some islands called 'Sicdelis', in the sea between Britain and Gaul, which I take to be the Sept Îles. If I am correct, 'Sicdelis' probably meant 'Six Isles', and the name strongly suggests that the Old Breton word for six was six. [119] It would also suggest that the Old Breton word for 'island' was very close to 'isle', in contrast to the modern Breton word 'enes', which derives from the Welsh 'ynys'. Again, it appears that the dialect of the Belgic British may have been significantly closer to modern English than the dialects of the Celtic west.

Many of the 'British' place names in Brittany appear to be connected with lowlands England, but the influence of the Welsh is also clearly visible in the Breton landscape. For example, there are four rivers in Brittany called 'avon', the Welsh word for river, but there are more than thirty names that reflect the word 'ster' or 'staer'.[120]

---

[119] Whether there are six or seven islands is a matter of definition: at what point on the scale of size does a rock that is permanently above water become an island? But in my view there are only 6 of them.

[120] eg Stergaule, in Charter 334 (date unknown).

And I believe that 'staer' was either a Belgic British word for river, possibly derived from a low-Latin 'esterium'.[121] The Anglo-Saxon word 'staer' meant story or starling, and seems to be unrelated.

In lowlands England there are rivers called 'Stour' in Suffolk, Kent, Dorset and Worcestershire, and near Exeter there is a town called Starcross, which is situated at the lowest ferry crossing-point on the river Exe. In an article published in 'English Language and Linguistics', Volume 10, Issue 1 (2006), Richard Coates described the etymology of the word 'stour' as 'disputed', and argued that 'stour' was a term from the classificatory system imposed on rivers in England during the Anglo-Saxon period. This may be true, but the cognate word 'staer' or 'ster' used in Brittany is obviously not of Anglo-Saxon origin, and I suggest that 'stour' must have been in use in England before the Anglo-Saxons arrived. In Kent, the word may even have been pronounced the same way as it is in Brittany: was Broadstairs really named after a flight of steps constructed in the 14th century, as the standard texts suggest? Or was it the name of the historically important anchorage in the Wantsum Channel, where the four River Stours flow into the sea (an anchorage that separated the island of Thanet from the mainland)?

There are a number of other names in the charters that attest to the popularity in the Early Middle Ages of names found in the legends. The only significance of this is that these names were inscribed at the Cartulary of Redon more than 300 years before Geoffrey of Monmouth wrote his 'Historia', so their existence proves that Geoffrey was at least using names which would have been recognisable to his reading public.

In particular, the name of Merthin was quite common in the Brittany of the 9th century, as found for example in Merthinhoairn ('Iron Merthin') (Charter 133, 826), and so presumably 'merthin' had a meaning – some say it meant 'sea fort'. There are also mentions of one or more Modrots, in Charter 104 of c.859 and in Charter 132, which was written before 867.

In the Arthurian legends, the most famous of Arthur's swords is called Excalibur (when referred to by Chrétien de Troyes) or Caliburn (according to Geoffrey of Monmouth). Arthur is in fact identified with

---

121 See the article by Gildas Bernier in the 'Annales de Bretagne', (1969) vol 76, Issue 76-4, pp 649 – 657.

several swords, so for example Excalibur might or might not be the one that he pulled from a stone to prove that he was the rightful king of Britain (according to Robert de Boron's 'Merlin'). My observation is that the name of Excalibur may be a compound word including the element 'cal', and that 'ex-cal-y-burn' could mean 'out of the stone of the stream'. The curiosity of this interpretation is that the name draws on three languages, Latin, Belgic (or Continental Celtic) and Brythonic, which either tells us that the solution is implausible or that the language of Roman Britain was a mélange of all three languages. I prefer the latter interpretation. But what is clear is that the name did not come from Wales, where the sword was known as Cadelfwich.

The translation that I have suggested, however, clearly did not occur to the authors of the Arthurian legends, because the 'Estoire de Merlin' (c.1230s), in the Vulgate Cycle, tells us that the sword's name meant 'cuts through iron and steel and wood', while Sir Thomas Malory, who based much of his book 'Le Morte d'Arthur' on the Vulgate Cycle, thought it meant simply 'cuts steel'. I find this quite comforting: the name of Arthur's sword may be pure fiction, but the facts that (a) the name can be given a Romano-British meaning, (b) that this meaning is consistent with the legends, and (c) that the anonymous author of the Vulgate Cycle was clearly unaware of this, could indicate that the name was not his invention.

SELECT BIBLIOGRAPHY

Historical Sources (pre-20th century)

Anglo-Saxon Chronicles, The	trans. Michael Swanton (2002)
Argentré, Bernard d'	L'histoire de la Bretagne (1588)
Bede	Ecclesiastical History of the English People (Penguin Classics)
Cartulaire de Landévennec	edition de la Borderie (1888)
Cartulaire de Quimper	edition Peyron (1909)
Cartulaire de Quimperlé	edition L Maître and P de Berthou (1904)
Cartulaire de Redon	edition A de Courson (1863)
Chronique de St Brieuc	edition Gw. Leduc and Cl. Sterckx (1973)
Clark Hall, JR	A Concise Anglo-Saxon Dictionary, 1894
Gildas	De Excidio Britanniae, tr. Giles (1838)
Geoffrey of Monmouth	The History of the Kings of Britain (Penguin Classics)
Gregory of Tours	The History of the Franks (Penguin Classics)
Le Baud, Pierre	Chronique des roys et princes de Bretagne armoricane' (1505), last published 1911
La Borderie, Arthur de	Histoire de Bretagne (1896 – 1899) (7 vol.)
Le Grand, Albert	Vie des saints de la Bretagne armorique (edition of Quimper, Salaun and Rennes (1901))

Liber Landevensis	edition G J Evans and J Rhys (1893)
Lobineau, Dom Guy-Alexis	Histoire de Bretagne (1707)
Morice, Dom Hyacinthe	Mémoires pour servir de preuves à l'histoire ecclésiastique et civile de la Bretagne (1742 – 1746) (3 vol.)
Nennius	Historia Brittonum, Fordham University (online) Irish version: CELT (The Corpus of Electronic Texts) online
Procopius	History of the Wars, ed. Henry Dewing (1914-40) (7 vol.)
Sidonius Apollinaris	Poems and Letters, ed. WB Anderson (1965)
Travers, Nicolas.	'Histoire civile, politique et religieuse de la ville et du comté de Nantes' (1836) (available online)
Vie de Gwénolé, La	see Cartulaire de Landévennec (supra)
Vie de Saint Samson, La	R Fawtier (1912)
Vie ancienne de St Samson, La	ed Pierre Flobert (1997)

Selected Bibliography

Contemporary Literature

Alcock, Leslie	Arthur's Britain: History and Archaeology AD 367 – 634 (1971)
Ashe, Geoffrey	The Discovery of King Arthur (2005)
Bromwich, Rachel	Trioedd Ynys Prydein, 2nd ed. (1978)
Carley, James	Polydore Vergil and John Leland on King Arthur: the Battle of the Books, in Kennedy, ED, King Arthur a Casebook (1996)
Chadwick, H M	Studies in Early British History (1954)
Chadwick, N K, et al	Celt and Saxon, Studies in the Early British Border (1963)
Chadwick, N K	Early Brittany (1969)
Chambers, E K	Arthur of Britain (1964)
Collins, Roger	Early Medieval Europe 300 – 1000 (3rd ed. 2010)
Cunliffe, Barry; Koch, John et al	Celtic from the West (2012)
Davies, Wendy et al	Inscriptions of Early Medieval Brittany (2000)
Deegan, Alison Foard, Glenn	Mapping Ancient Landscapes in Northamptonshire, (2008)
Duine, F	Inventaire Liturgique de l'hagiographie bretonne (1922)
Fleming, Robin	Britain after Rome (2010)
Fleuriot, Léon	Les Origines de la Bretagne (1980)
Giot, Pierre-Roland Guignon, Philippe Merdrignac, Bernard	The British Settlement of Brittany, (2003)
Merdrignac, Bernard	D'une Bretagne à l'autre (2012)
Oppenheimer, Stephen	The Origins of the British: a genetic detective story, (2006)

Querré, Christian	Binic, Port du Goëlo (1987)
Riddle, John M	A History of the Middle Ages, 300 – 1500, (2008)
Smith, Julia M H	Europe after Rome, (2005)
Sykes, Brian	Blood of the Isles: exploring the genetic roots of our tribal history, (2006)
Venning, Timothy	The Anglo-Saxon Kings, (2011)
Williams, Hugh	Two Lives of Gildas by a monk of Ruys and Caradoc of Llancarfan (1990)

INDEX OF PLACE NAMES

Abbaretz	36	Autun	125, 128, 152
Aber Benniguet	185	Avallon	77, 128, 232
Abingdon	41, 42	Avalon, Isle of (Apples)	
Adrianople	16		133, 200
Alchester	172	Aylesford	62, 63
Alet	7, 19, 38, 100, 161, 168, 184, 187	Badden Byrig	120
		Badon, Mount	115, 117, 119, 120, 121, 123, 124, 125, 127, 137, 155, 198
Amberley, Gloucestershire	170		
Amberley, West Sussex	170	Banbury/Beranbury	138, 200
Amboise	94	Bannalec	130
Ambresbury Banks	170, 172	Bannavem Taburniae	48
Ambrosden	170		
Amesbury	170	Basingstoke	10
Amiens	22, 72, 98	Bath	138
Anaurot	54	Bavay	73
Angers	76	Bayeux	82, 84, 141
Arbury Hill	118, 120, 198	Bedford	122, 138, 142
Arles	24, 25, 31, 36, 73	Bennaventa	48
		Bénouville	98
Arras	22	Bath	27, 119
Arzal	176	Billingsgate	122
Ashburnham	86	Binic	129, 134, 162, 163, 164, 167, 168, 181
Athelney	108		
Atherstone, Warwicshire	107, 132, 190, 191, 199, 200	Blois	34, 92
		Bordeaux	18, 82, 94
Atherstone, Somerset	107	Borough Hill	120
Auray	5, 54, 101, 176	Boulogne	11, 24, 33, 62, 82

243

Bourges	37, 77, 78, 81, 125, 126	Coat Audren	174
Bourg-de-Déols	78, 91	Colchester	10, 43, 117
Brain-dur-Vilaine	96	Cologne	73
Brancaster	33	Concarneau	130
Bréhat, île de	134	Constantinople	38, 131, 147, 161
Brest	40	Corbénic	162, 163, 165, 167, 169
Breteuil	24		
Bretoneux	24	Corbières	162
Bretteville	24	Corbigny	162
Bretzenheim	24	Corlay	162
Broons	180	Corps Nuds	188
Bruges	42, 161	Corseul	5, 162
		Crayford	62
Cadbury Castle	194, 233, 234		
Caerleon	10, 20, 117	Dôl	143, 147, 157, 159, 160, 161, 162, 164, 167, 168, 184, 185, 187
Calleva Atrebatum	10		
Calverton	116		
Cambrai	72		
Cambridge	107		
Camden Town	144	Dorchester-on-Thames	41, 42
Camelford	146		
Camlann	80, 131, 132	Dover	4, 11
Camp d'Artus	176	Dumbarton	49
Camp de Bernains	163	Durham	107
Camp de César	163, 167	Duston	120
Carcassone	129	Dyrham	122, 138, 142, 200
Carhaix	7, 50, 130, 172, 177		
Carlisle	117	Eliseg, Pillar of	47
Carmarthen	54	Elven	99, 143, 144, 190
Castrum de Cesson	163, 167		
Châlons	39	Ergué-Armel	176, 177
Channel Islands	7	Exeter	4, 7, 10, 146
Charford	137		
Chartres	146		
Châtelaudren	167, 174	Fécamp	161
Cherbourg	19	Fontaine Auren	174
Chester	10, 18, 19, 20, 99, 117	Genoa	161
Cirencester	15, 27, 138	Glastonbury	104, 133, 194
Cleatham	45	Gloucester	27, 48, 138
Clermont Ferrand	128	Great Ormes Head	1
Coat Arzur	176	Groix, Île de	54, 55

Index of Place Names

Grotte D'Artus	176		118, 122, 138, 170, 187
Guer	100	Longthorpe	117
Guernsey	54, 61	Long Wittenham	41
Guidcruic	30	Loudéac	130, 177, 181, 199
Guingamp	101	Lovedon Hill	45
Hillion	7	Lundenwic	122
Hingston Down	146	Lyon	17
Huelgoat	176		
		Mainz	22
Irchester	59	Malmesbury	147
		Man, Isle of	3
Jersey	7	Mantua	161
Jerusalem	87, 160	Marsas	82
		Merevale	191, 193
Keraudrain	174	Moddershall/Modredshale	132
Keraudren	174	Mold	30
Kerarzur	176	Mons Badonicus see Badon, Mount	
Kerbors	130	Mons Lactarius	129
Keredren	174	Morlaix	188
Kettering	59	Mucking	45, 118, 138
L'Aberwrac'h	7, 128, 177, 181	Nantes	5, 35, 36, 37, 38, 40, 91, 92, 93, 94, 95, 111, 126, 129, 140, 146, 162, 181, 199
La Bouëxiere	101		
La Brussac	147		
La Motte	130, 181		
Landévennec	135, 143		
Le Croisic	82		
Le Donjon de Vez	91		
Le Mans	76, 91		
Le Mont St Michel	7, 125, 151	Nanterre	33
Le Roche Jagu	177	Netley	131, 133, 137
Lesguen	134	Northampton	59
Le Yaudet	7, 19, 181	Norwich	45
Limerzel	179		
Lincoln	4, 10, 15, 43, 45, 118	Ombersley	170
		Orkney Islands	58
Lindisfarne	144	Orléans	15, 34, 74, 75, 92, 93, 164
Llandudno	1		
Lomarec	101, 181	Oxford	155, 159
London	4, 10, 15, 25, 33, 41, 42, 43, 51, 62, 107,	Paris	75, 76, 90, 139, 154

245

Penshurst	86	Ringlemere	61
Peterborough	117	Rome	4, 23, 36, 37, 41, 82, 89, 104, 164
Pevensey	85, 117		
Plaudren	174		
Plebs Arthmael	179	Runaudren	174
Plédran	174	Ruthin	104
Plésidy	101		
Plobannalec-Lesconil	130	Saint-Armel	176, 177
		Saint-Armel-des-Boschaux	176, 179, 184, 186, 188
Ploemel	176		
Ploërmel	52, 98, 99, 100, 143, 176, 179, 180, 185, 188, 193, 199	Saint-Armelen	177
		Saint-Marcel	51, 52, 98, 99, 100, 172, 181
Ploëzal	177, 178	St Ambroise	172
Plouarzel	176, 185, 188	St Brides	122
Ploufragan	128, 134, 168	St Brieuc	5, 7, 128, 129, 134, 146, 163, 167, 168
Plouguin	134		
Plouharnel	176		
Poitiers	161	St Herpes	98
Pont-de-Buis	98, 99	St Johns, Clerkenwell	123
Ponthieu	82, 84		
Port-Arthur	176	St Just	181
Portsmouth	131, 133	St Malo	5
Poutrocoët	168	St Renan	36
Pré Auren	174	St Servan	7, 187
		St Suliac	187
Queré	163	Saintes	93
Quimperlé	81	Sark	160, 162
		Sarras, Kingdom of	166
Ravenna	22, 38, 39, 63	Sarum (Old)	122, 138, 200
Redon1	9, 52, 96, 143, 181	Sarzeau	190
		Saussy	125
Reichenau	161	Silchester	10
Reims	22, 159, 187	Sixt-sur-Aff	143, 144
Rennes	5, 35, 36, 96, 101, 141, 177, 181, 186, 187, 188, 182	Soissons	72, 73, 74, 89, 90, 111
		Solsbury Hill	2
		Southampton	131
Réville	98	Spong Hill	45
Ribemont-sur-Ancre	2	Stafford	132
		Staines	41
Richborough	4, 11, 19, 20, 42, 62	Stamford	59
		Stonehenge	105, 170

Index of Place Names

Street	104	Westminster	161
Sutton Cheney	191	West Stow	45
		Wight, Isle of	33, 58, 137
Teutoburg Forest	97	Wimbledon	137
Thanet, Isle of	57, 58, 63, 138, 144	Winchester	10, 31, 41, 195
		Worcester	159
Thennes	98		
Thorney Island	41	York	9, 10, 15, 18, 28, 42, 43, 117
Tolbiac	96		
Tombelaine	125		
Tombeau d'Arthur	177		
Topsham	33		
Touche-St Armel	177		
Tournai	22, 72, 73, 87, 88, 89		
Tours	15, 19, 34, 37, 41, 75, 76, 91, 92, 93, 139, 140, 141, 164		
Towcester	59		
Town Creep	86		
Trèbes	126, 129		
Trédarzec	179		
Trévé/Treves	130, 181		
Trier	12, 22, 36, 73		
Troyes	75		
Uttoxeter	4		
Valencia	161		
Vannes	5, 19, 35, 36, 41, 99, 129, 130, 140, 141, 142, 143, 191		
Venta Belgarum	10		
Vercors	162		
Ville Audrain	174		
Vorgium	7, 50		
Vouillé	93		
Vron	82, 84		
Wall	107		
Water Newton	59		
West Heslerton	45		

INDEX OF PEOPLE

Adelberg, Queen of Kent	140	Anstis, John, Garter King of Arms	193
Aegidius	73, 74, 75, 90, 173	Anthemius, Western Emperor	76, 77, 78
Aelfric, Bishop of Hereford	120	Apollinaris	24
Ælle	85, 86, 112, 118, 121, 198	Aramont, legendary King of Brittany	81, 126
		Arbogast	20, 22
Æsc	62, 64, 67, 79	Arcadius, Eastern Emperor	20
Æthelbert, King of Kent	137, 140	Ardaric, King of the Gepids	63
Aëtius, Flavius	31, 32, 37, 38, 39, 40, 55, 72, 73, 93	Armel, St	139, 177, 179, 180, 182, Ch 11, 200
Alain Barbetort	146	Arthur	5, 66, 80, 81, 90, 101, Ch 5, Ch 6, 139, 145, 146, 149, 151, 152, 153, 154, 155, 156, 165, 168, 169, 173, 175, 181, 182, 183, 185, 188, 189, 194, 195, 196, 197, 198, 199, 200, 204
Alaric, King of the Visigoths	23		
Alban, St	99, 143		
Alun of Dyfed	102		
Ambrose, St, Bishop of Milan	172		
Ambrosius Aurelianus	40, 41, 48, 55, 64, 65, 66, 67, 68, 69, 70, 79, 80, 81, 86, 111, 112, 117, 118, 123, 169, 170, 198, 204		
		Arthur I, Duke of Brittany	201
Ambrosius, Prefect of Gaul	172	Arthur II, Duke of Brittany	150, 202
Amr	109	Arthur Tudor, Prince	191
Andragathius	17	Arthmael	106, 107, 175
Anne, Duchess of Brittany	152, 189, 191, 192	Artur	107, 175
		Arzel	175

Index of People

Arvandus, Praetorian Prefect of Gaul 76, 77, 78
Athelstan, King of England 147
Attila the Hun 38, 39, 40, 56, 63, 72
Audren, King of the Bretons 37, 38, 66, 67, 68, 81, 102, 108, 173, 205
Augustine of Canterbury, St 113
Augustine of Hippo, St 113
Aurelius Conanus 69, 70
Avitus, Western Emperor 74
Avitus, Bishop of Vienne 89

Ban 126, 130, 165
Baudri de Bourgeuil, Bishop of Dôl 157, 158, 159, 160, 161, 184
Beda 137
Bedevere 154
Belisarius, Count 128
Beppolen, Duke 141
Bors (or Bohort) 126, 130
Boudicca, Queen of the Iceni 4, 120
Brieuc, St 38, 112, 134, 163, 168
Britu 47
Bromell 165
Brutus 1
Brychan, King of Brycheiniog 113
Budic, King of Brittany 66, 67, 81, 93, 112, 206
Budoc, St, of Bréhat 134, 135
Budoc, St, of Dôl 160, 161, 162, 164

Cado, King of Dumnonia 234
Cadoc, St 113
Cadreith 102
Cadwalader, King of Gwynedd 195, 196
Caesar, Julius 2, 4, 7
Calpornius 48
Canao 141
Caracalla, Emperor 9
Caradoc of Llancarfan 104
Cas 102
Castus, Lucius Artorius 9
Catherine of Aragon 191
Catigern 63, 67
Catihern 188
Celestine, Pope 30, 31
Cerdic 121, 122, 137
Ceretic 46
Chanao, Count of Vannes 139, 140
Charibert I, King of Paris 140, 142
Charlemagne, Holy Roman Emperor 142, 165, 167
Charles VIII, King of France 189, 190, 191
Childebert I, King of Paris 139, 161, 177, 185, 187, 199
Childeric I, King of the Franks 73, 75, 76, 83, 84, 86, 88, 89, 90
Chilperic I, King of Paris 140, 141
Chillon, or Marcel Chillon 93, 112
Chramn 139, 140, 161
Cissa 85
Claudas 125

249

Clotaire I, King of the Franks 139, 140, 161
Clotaire II, King of the Franks 141
Clotilde, Queen of the Franks 94
Clovis, King of the Franks 88, 89, 90, 91, 92, 93, 94, 95, 96, 97, 111, 126, 139, 181, 188, 198, 199
Cbebba 137
Coel Hen 46
Commail 138
Conan Meriadoc see Meriadoc, Conan
Condida 138
Constans 24
Constantine the Great 12, 121
Constantine III 24, 25, 46, 110
Constantine, brother of Audren 66, 68, 108
Constantius III 25
Cyman 85
Cyngen ap Cadell, King of Powys 47
Cynric 121, 122, 137

Diocletian. Eastern Emperor 12

Ebrachaire, Duke 141
Edmund I, King of England 120
Edward IV, King of England 196
Elaine 165, 167
Eliezer 165
Elizabeth I, Queen of England 195
Elizabeth of York 191
Eochar 37, 38

Erme, St 186
Ermold the Black 95, 142
Eudoxius 37
Euric, King of the Visigoths 74, 75, 76, 77, 78, 91
Eusebius, Count 93, 208
Exuperantius of Poitiers 35, 36

Farinmail 138
Faustus, Bishop of Riez 4, 7, 67, 111, 215
Felix, Bishop of Nantes 162
'Fisher King', the 165
Fragan, St 127, 128, 134, 168
Francis II, Duke of Brittany 190
Fredegund, Queen of Paris 141
Frederic, Prince of the Visigoths 75

Galahad 164, 165, 166, 167
Gawain 151, 165, 168
Geiseric, King of the Vandals 73
Genevieve, St 75
Geoffrey I, Duke of Brittany 147
Germanus, St 28, 29, 30, 31, 33, 37, 38, 47, 51, 54, 55, 75, 94, 113, 215
Gerontius 24, 25
Goar 37
Goeznou, St 124, 130, 137, 149, 150
Gontran, King of Burgundy 141

Index of People

Gradlon, King of Brittany 37, 112
Gratian, Western Emperor 16, 17, 163, 164
Gratian 24, 110
Guénolé, St see Gwenole
Guinevere, Queen 151, 167, 168, 209
Guitolinus or Guithelinus, Archbishop of London 68
Gurthierni, St 47, 54
Gwen, St 134
Gwenole, St 112, 127, 128, 134, 135
Gwladys 113
Gwynllyw, St 112, 113

Haraldsson, Olaf 159
Hawisse 147
Hengist 47, 58, 62, 64, 67, 79
Henry (Tudor) VII, King of England 186, 187, 180, 190 - 197
Henry VIII, King of England 119, 191, 195
Hoël, King of Brittany 81, 96, 109, 125, 130, 151, 153, 154, 155, 205, 209
Honoria 39
Honorius, Western Emperor 20, 24, 25
Horsa 58, 62, 63
Huail ap Caw 104

Ine, King of Wessex 148

Jerome, St 22
Joseph of Arimathea 165
Judith 147

Judwal, King of Brittany 185, 186
Julian ("the Apostate"), Emperor 42
Justin II, Eastern Emperor 161
Justinian, Eastern Emperor 95

Kay 154

Lancelot 126, 130, 160, 165, 167, 168, 211
Leo, Eastern Emperor 76, 90, 152
Léon, Bishop of Bourges
Libius Severus, Western Emperor 76
Litorius 37
Louis the Pious, King of the Franks 95, 142
Lovocat 188
Luomadus 3, 4, 92
Lupus, St 28, 29

Magloire, St 160, 162
Magnus Maximus see Maximus, Magnus
Majorian, Western Emperor 74
Majorian 37
Malo, St 184, 187
Mansuetas, Bishop of Brittany 41
Marcus 24, 110
Martin of Tours, St 15
Maxen Wledic see Magnus Maximus
Maximilian I, Holy Roman Emperor 191

251

Maximus, Magnus, Western Emperor	16, 17, 18, 19, 20, 24, 53, 164	Paul, Count	76
		Paul Aurelian, St	69
		Paulinus of Nola	18
		Pelagius	28
Mela	137	Pellès	165, 167
Melaine, St, Bishop of Rennes	93, 95, 96, 188, 212	Percival	165, 168
		Pippin I, of Aquitaine	95, 142
Meriadoc, Conan, King of Brittany 'King' of Brittany	17, 34, 37, 69, 112, 134, 164	Pleardus de Brohon	180
		Porta	131, 137
		Potitus	48
		Radagaisus	22
Merlin	70, 105, 131, 151, 167, 212	Radegunde, Queen of the Franks	161
Merovech, King of the Franks	72	Radimius, St, Bishop of Rennes	81
Mordred	109, 113, 131, 132, 151, 199, 200	Ragnachar, King of Cambrai	90
		Remigius, Bishop of Reims	88, 89, 90
Morgan le Fay	213	Richard I, Duke of Normandy	147
Morgause	109		
Mormon, 'King' of the Bretons	142	Richard II, Duke of Normandy	147
Morton, John, Archbishop of Canterbury	190, 192	Richard III, King of England	190, 195
		Ricimer, Magister Militum	74, 75, 76
Namatius	83	Riocatus	111, 215
Napoleon	88	Riothamus	68, 76, 77, 78, 79, 80, 111, 112, 214
Natanleod	137		
Nepos, Julius, Western Emperor	89, 101	Romulus Augustus, Western Emperor	89
Odo	34	Rufinus	20
Odoacre (Adovacrius)	83	Rutilius Claudius Namatianus	35
Odoacre ((Odovacrius)	63, 83, 84, 89		
Orcades	109	Salomon I, 'King' of Brittany	37
Oslake	137	Salvian	35
Padern, St	113	Sampson, St	69, 139, 157, 160, 161, 187
Palladius	35		
Pascent	66, 67		
Patrick, St	30, 46, 48		

Index of People

Seidi	101	Vortigern, King of the British	
Serf, St	187		40, 41, 46, 47, 48, 49, 50, 51, 53, 54, 55, 56, 57, 59, 61, 62, 63, 64, 65, 66, 67, 68, 69, 70, 214
Severus Alexander, Emperor	10		
Severus, Septimius, Emperor	9		
Bishop of Clermont		Vortimer	50, 55, 61, 62, 63, 64, 65, 66, 67, 68, 112, 123
Sigismer, Frankish Prince	86, 88		
Stafford, Edward, Duke of Buckingham	194	Vortipore	50
Stilicho	20, 22, 23, 47, 72	Walter, Archdeacon of Oxford	131, 148, 149, 152, 157, 158, 159
Suliac, St	187		
Syagrius, 'King of Soissons'	75, 76, 79, 89, 90, 91, 92, 95, 97, 126, 127	Waroch I, King of Vannes	101, 199
		Waroch II, Count of Vannes	8, 140, 141, 142, 162, 188
Theodoric the Great, King of the Ostrogoths	96	Wihomarc	142
Theodoric I, King of the Visigoths	39	William I, the Bastard/the Conqueror, Duke of Normandy and King of England	108, 147
Theodosius I, Eastern Emperor	16, 20, 46	Winnoch	87
Theodosius, Count	16, 164	Wlenking	85
Tibatto	37		
Tudor, Jasper, Earl of Pembroke	190	Zeno, Eastern Emperor	64, 66, 89, 101
Uther Pendragon	81, 108, 125, 126, 170		
Valens, Eastern Emperor	16		
Valentinian I, Western Emperor	163, 164		
Valentinian III, Western Emperor	39, 46		
Victorinus, Vicar of Britain	23, 24		